Where The Water Kept Rising

A College Athletic Director's Fight to Save a New Orleans Sports Institution

Thanks for helping our city!

Jim Miller

By James W. Miller

New Orleans, Louisiana
August 29, 2005

Arthur Hardy Enterprises INC

To my wife Jean, whose patience, spirit and strength helped us endure our trials. You are the best person I have ever known.

ISBN 978-093089238-8

Printed in the United States

Published by
Arthur Hardy Enterprises, Inc.
230 Devon Drive
Mandeville, LA 70448
arthurhardypublishing.com

Book design: David Johnson

Acknowledgements

An author can't get to the point of authoring without having some help along the way. Therefore, at the risk of inadvertently leaving somebody out, I wanted to acknowledge a number of individuals whose contributions resulted in this book.

My brother-in-law Gary Solomon, a University of New Orleans graduate, didn't have much interest in athletics, but tried in many ways to help me and our program survive and prosper. Sun Belt Commissioner Wright Waters always was a supportive presence, whether over the phone or during one of our enlightening lunches at Commander's Palace. My friend of 32 years, Bob Leffler, was a comforting voice and donated much time and effort to help our program in his role heading up the premier collegiate sports promotions agency in the country. Bob also was the first to say my experiences would make a helluva book. Former Athletic Director Ron Maestri was an inspiration to anyone who valued Privateer athletics. He told me the athletic director's job would be frustrating, but his warning was couched in a love for the program second only to that for his family.

I owe a special debt of gratitude to Sara Rooney who told me the tragic story of her godparents, Margarita and Manuel Romero, who refused to leave their beloved home in Lakeview as Katrina approached.

From the university community: Professor Rick Barton, former Provost, author and head of the creative writing program, provided insight into the inner workings of the UNO administration, and his line-by-line review of a first draft produced reams of single-spaced notes on how I could improve our story. Dr. Robert Dupont always provided wise counsel and friendship, while Dr. Scott Whittenburg allowed me to vent while trying to teach me to shift my weight on the downswing and follow through. UNO Foundation president Pat Gibbs provided advice on finances, filtered through good humor and the same jokes retold. The effervescent Dr. Dennis McSeveney's outspoken defense of UNO's basketball team once required a police escort to rescue our small group of supporters after a close loss at Louisiana Lafayette. Dr. Russ Trahan, dean of the College of Engineering, and Dr. Jim Meza, dean of the College of Education, became fast friends who supported our efforts in the good times and bad. Librarian Sybil Boudreaux gave us many hours of her time and dedication during our NCAA self-study process and throughout the year as head of our Athletic Council. Dan and Donna Harper were always first in line to help our student-athletes get the proper academic support they needed.

Supporters who put their money where their mouth was include Gabe Corchiani, a great Privateer point guard in his day who became our biggest benefactor along with his business partner John Georges. New Orleans attorney Rob Couhig was the driving force behind construction of the University Tennis Center, and became a close friend as did Dominick Musso, who donated much time and money to endow the baseball hitting facility. Mike Sapera, whom I enlisted for the Privateer Athletic Foundation board, supported our program financially and with his presence at nearly every event while I was athletic director. Mike was ably supported by men like Hugh Hamilton and Chris Keene whose efforts to raise money for our program was often like trying to raise the Titanic. UNO was plagued over the years with sparse attendance at games, but nobody can blame the small core of avid fans such as Glenn Scorsone, Richard Muller and others. And the baseball rat pack of Will Peneguy, Bob and Norma Sternhell and Ray Stephens helped make an afternoon at the ballpark more than entertaining.

Outside the UNO family, I want to thank my ex-officio editors, Jeffrey Marx and John Schulian. Jeff is known to the public as a Pulitzer Prize winning reporter, but to me will always be the electric haired 14-year-old who followed me around the Baltimore Colts training camp begging me to read his prose. Jeff helped me channel my emotions into rational descriptions of what it meant to lead from behind. John Schulian, who was one of the best sports columnists in the country before heading off to Hollywood, provided valuable criticism on the numerous drafts I shipped to him.

Although their exploits and deeds are included in the book, I would be remiss if I did not acknowledge the coaches and staff members over the years who toiled against the odds during my tenure.

Last, but certainly far from least, I want to thank Jeremie Davis, the young basketball player who rode out Katrina, then came back to lead the team in scoring only to become engulfed in the storm's aftermath. His willingness to talk candidly about a hard life gave our story a sensitivity and dimension of soul that it could not have had otherwise. During our interviews, both in person and over the phone, he was candid and forthright, even if it meant casting himself in a negative light. May he find happiness.

James W. Miller
New Orleans
March 2012

Contents

The Storm Approaches...

The bridge on Lakeshore Drive, clearly visible the night before, had disappeared by the time Jeremie Davis woke up. In fact, the water had risen so high during the night that no evidence existed of the concrete span, the roadway or the London Avenue drainage canal. They all were now under Lake Pontchartrain.

The rising wind increased the rain's staccato rap against the window, sounding like a hundred north Louisiana woodpeckers. Davis wished he was back there now, at home in the piney woods of Arcadia instead of sitting in a lakeside apartment at the University of New Orleans waiting for a hurricane to hit.

He had slept little with the drumbeat of wind and rain pelting the windows so he got out of bed at 6:30 A.M. and reached for the remote. Davis was transfixed, staring at the Weather Channel like a cornered rat peering into the eye of a cobra. He feared the danger he knew was drawing near, yet hoped it would somehow miss him when it struck.

On the screen, a storm-chasing meteorologist held his microphone with two hands as he was whipped by the gale. He reported the hurricane had made landfall 30 minutes earlier at Buras, Louisiana, which is about 70 miles from New Orleans. The report that it was now a Category 3 storm with sustained winds of 125 miles per hour was a lot better than the last thing Davis had heard. When he went to bed, the storm boasted sustained winds of 175 miles an hour with gusts to 215. This was good news. Maybe it would lose even more steam before it hit New Orleans.

The tumult outside Davis's window argued otherwise. Waves were splashing over the top of the canal and spilling into an adjacent parking lot. He looked to the right and saw a row of newly planted 20-foot palm trees along Lakeshore Drive fall one-by-one, uprooted by the roiling water. He'd been told the view from his apartment on the lake was the best in the city, but now it was much too close to the action.

Davis passed up a chance to leave Saturday when all students were told to evacuate campus. A friend offered him a ride out, but he couldn't leave his roommate, Wayne Williams, who chose to stay along with his girlfriend and infant son. Williams had no car and no place to take Sheena and Wayne Jr., who had arrived from Orlando Friday night. "Don't worry, we'll ride it out," Williams boasted when Davis pleaded with him to leave. Wayne had not seemed concerned, perhaps because he was from Florida and had been through hurricanes before. He was stubborn and probably deserved to be left, Davis thought, but it wouldn't be right to leave them. So he stayed.

Davis was questioning that decision now as the storm worsened, while Wayne and his family slept in the next room. The wind blew harder and pushed the lake higher with each gust. What if it comes over the levee that separated the Privateer Place housing complex from the lake, he thought? What if the storm's relentless pounding weakens the levee and it crumbles altogether?

Davis had passed up a second chance to leave, on Sunday. The university scheduled buses to transport any students who did not have transportation to a shelter in Baton Rouge. However, Williams insisted on staying so they made no effort to wake up in time for the 9 A.M. departure. When they finally awoke, everybody was gone. They were alone, which increased their anxiety. They spent the rest of the day calling family members and watching the Weather Channel for storm updates.

Late Sunday, the television reported that thousands of residents who either could not or would not leave began trekking to the Louisiana Superdome, which Mayor Ray Nagin had designated a "refuge of last resort." The mayor had ordered a mandatory evacuation of the city, but he had underestimated both his constituents' desire to stay in their homes and their ability to leave if they wanted to.

Williams, Sheena and Wayne Jr. all were up now, awakened by the ruthless wind and horizontal rain. Waves began splashing over the 15-foot earthen levee that separated the housing complex from the lake. Davis saw shingles on the adjacent building start to shred and tear away. A small piece of wood or a can became a lethal projectile that crashed through the window of a nearby apartment.

Sheena was terrified and began crying. Her fear was contagious, and the baby started screaming.

Their anxiety increased when the television's screen went blank. The electricity had gone out. They were alone in the dark with no lifeline to the outside world. They tried to use their cell phones, but heard only the busy signal of interrupted service. They could hear little else over the roar of a nightmare raging outside.

They huddled in the living room, praying that the levee behind them would hold and the wind would not blow the building apart. If the levee broke, the lake's fury would topple their building like a box of kindling. The force of the wind continued to increase, and Davis heard strange explosions like wood and metal breaking apart in the distance. Soon, their worst fears appeared to be realized as water began to seep under the door.

Why didn't we leave when we had the chance? We're all gonna die! I'll never see my momma or brothers again. We'll be washed into the lake, our bodies never found.

Davis had only met Williams a few weeks earlier, and you aren't supposed to die surrounded by people you don't know. But teammates stick together, don't they?

He knew only that this wasn't what he'd bargained for when he agreed to come to New Orleans. The honey-tongued recruiter talked about playing time and conference championships and an apartment on the lake and an education. He said Davis could put the University of New Orleans basketball back on the map.

He didn't say nothin' about dying in no hurricane!

Part I

Disruption

CHAPTER
1

N ew Orleans is a city where you can sit on your second-story balcony near the Mississippi River and look up to see the smokestacks of the boats going by. The bottom of the bowl upon which much of the city is situated sits 14 feet below sea level.

That tidbit of local lore was well known to the University of New Orleans administrators attending an emergency meeting on Saturday, August 27, 2005. The subject was a rapidly growing hurricane in the Gulf of Mexico that had failed to turn northward into the Florida panhandle, as predicted, and was headed straight for New Orleans.

Overnight it had developed into a Category 5 storm, the most severe category on the Saffir-Simpson Hurricane Scale. The practical definition of a Category 5 hurricane was winds of at least 155 miles per hour and an anticipated storm surge of 18 feet or more. In one word, "catastrophic."

Chancellor Timothy P. Ryan, the university's chief executive officer, began to update his vice chancellors and me, the director of intercollegiate athletics, on the storm's threat and plans to evacuate the campus. The meeting was sparsely attended with less than a handful of people, and more out of duty than expectation of the worst. After all, we had been through false alarms before.

Ryan, an economist, had been chancellor less than two years after a distinguished decade as dean of the College of Business Administration. His graying crew cut and athletic build more resembled a Marine drill sergeant than an educator in his early 50s. His casual wardrobe of preference was a pastel golf shirt, tan slacks and socks that would shame a decent rainbow. The New Orleans native and UNO graduate was well liked around campus and respected in the community.

Ryan told those present the news was not good. The storm, named "Katrina," had formed near Bermuda and attracted little attention as it meandered across Florida as a modest Category 1 storm. But when it hit the warm waters of the Gulf of Mexico, its intensity increased at an uncanny rate. The campus, and the entire region, appeared in great danger. After a brief discussion, Ryan ordered his lieutenants to implement the evacuation plan.

I left the meeting to provide an update of the situation to my coaches, our student-athletes and our staff. Our first duty was to assure that our students would be safe. Unfortunately, we did not have a comprehensive disaster plan that could guarantee it or even state the responsibilities of each staff member in case of a cataclysmic event. Until then, there was no need for one. The last hurricane that had flooded New Orleans was Betsy in 1965, four decades earlier, and that had prompted improvements in the levee system to prevent future disasters.

The Flood Control Act of 1965 was enacted by Congress on October 27, 1965, and gave the United States Army Corps of Engineers responsibility to design and construct numerous flood control projects around Lake Pontchartrain and the New Orleans region. With the federal government taking responsibility for flood protection away from the patronage-dependent local levee boards, residents assumed an added sense of security.

That is, if anyone even thought about it. The fact that nobody living in New Orleans under the age of 50 had experienced a major hurricane created a perilous denial. The old-timers who had been flooded out of their homes by Betsy when they were young remembered and cautioned their children and grandchildren. Never trust a storm, they said, but they were ignored.

Peace breeds prosperity, but also complacency. It hadn't happened in 40 years. Why should this one be any different? Wasting time preparing for something so unlikely made as much sense as carrying a snakebite kit to church.

We were one week into the fall semester that Saturday morning and were conducting physical examinations for our student-athletes at Lakefront Arena. Most of the coaches strolled about, making certain their student-athletes proceeded from station to station in this necessary, but tedious requirement. A handful of medical professionals were present to examine our nearly 200 athletes, so lines were long while patience was short. My news that the chancellor had ordered an immediate evacuation of the campus was not met with apprehension, but as a welcome relief to more blood tests, electrocardiograms and urine samples.

I met with the coaches individually to make sure each had a plan to keep their students safe. Amy Champion, our women's basketball coach, would take her entire team to a hunting camp in north Mississippi owned by her father, Bill Champion, a former football player at Ole Miss. Monte Towe, the men's basketball coach, had made arrangements to send most of his student-athletes to Rice University in Houston where beds would be made available. Other coaches instructed their out-of-town students to buddy up with local students and evacuate with their families. For students with no transportation, the university would provide buses to transport them to a safe area away from the storm's path.

We told our students to take three days of clothing with them. They should not need more than that. Hurricanes usually go around the city or blow out before they get to New Orleans, which is actually 90 miles from the mouth of the Mississippi River. We all saw the preparation and evacuation process as little more than a temporary inconvenience. Satisfied with their preparations, I wished them a safe journey and told them I'd see them in a couple of days.

None of us were aware of an alarmingly predictive story that had appeared in the Houston *Chronicle* a few years earlier, three months after the terrorist attacks on the World Trade Center. The story said the "deadliest" of all disaster scenarios facing the country would be a direct hit of a massive hurricane on New Orleans.

It was a nice day, with the late August humidity at a tolerable level. On my way home, I stopped at the driving range in City Park and worked on my putting and chipping. Although approaching 60, I kept myself active, running and lifting weights four or five days a week. Golf was more a vehicle to reduce stress than to stay in shape. After about 45 minutes, when I decided my golf game wasn't going to get any better, I went home to receive my instructions.

My wife Jean reminds the old guys of Gina Lollobrigida, the striking brunette actress of the 1960s. Beneath the movie-star looks, she is a caring and loving partner and parent who is never without a plan. Jean has three sisters and a vibrant 79-year-old mother, Gloria, from whom all major family decisions flowed. It's a running joke among the four brothers-in-law — and even one former brother-in-law — that when we married into the Newman family, we never had to make another decision. Jean and sisters Patricia, Martha and "Little" Gloria would caucus with mother Gloria, and when they would break the huddle the boys would receive their orders.

The sisters decided we would evacuate early on Sunday morning for, in the grand party vernacular of New Orleans, our "evacu-cation." Martha's husband, Gary Solomon, had two sisters who lived in Baton Rouge, about 80 miles northwest of New Orleans. One used her connections to secure rooms at a hotel, so at least we would have lodging until this nuisance passed.

I had grown up in Kentucky, where the most serious natural disaster outside of a UK basketball loss was the occasional snow or ice storm. I was not sensitive to the havoc a hurricane could produce. But Jean had childhood recollections of Betsy, and her mother's brothers and sisters in Gulfport, Mississippi, related horrific stories of Camille's devastating visit in 1969. I particularly recalled the one about the relative who refused to evacuate and rode out the storm in a rowboat. They said he was never the same after that.

Still, I took the news of evacuation with skepticism. I had no reason to think this storm would be any worse than those I had experienced since moving to New Orleans in 1986. I encouraged Jean to have a cocktail and join me in front of the television to watch the progress on the Weather Channel.

We packed light for our trip. I threw three pairs of walking shorts, three golf shirts, four pairs of underwear and my running shoes, shorts and socks into a small suitcase. Jean said her sisters were moving valuables from the first floor to the second floors of their houses, just in case. My only significant precaution was to pick up some books and papers from the floor of my first-floor home office and place them on my desk. Just in case a window blew out and rain dampened the floor. I did put my laptop and some files in my briefcase to take with me.

My older daughter, Lindsay, then 25, was visiting that week from her home in Washington, D.C. She helped Jean pack up our daughter Layne, who was almost 11, and our son Charles Connor, who was 9. To the kids, this was a great unexpected adventure to be savored, like the snow day vacations they enjoyed when we lived in Chicago. But this was even better, because we were going to bring Elmo, our 3-year-old beagle. We filled a container with a week's worth of dog food and pulled Elmo's small travel kennel from a shelf in the garage. I locked my one-year-old Mercedes in the garage to discourage potential looters, and we loaded our Chevrolet minivan for the next day's trip.

We awoke about 6 A.M. to discover that most of New Orleans had chosen the same departure strategy. A "contra flow" evacuation plan was in effect whereby all lanes of all highways led out of New Orleans. The plan effectively doubled the potential volume of traffic, but even that was not sufficient to keep the lines moving faster than frozen molasses. We headed west toward Baton Rouge on Interstate 10, but after two hours we were still in suburban Metairie, having traveled only about three miles. I decided to turn north on Causeway Boulevard, cross Lake Pontchartrain and hit Interstate 12 north of the lake.

Since we had not planned to go that way, I did not research the route, and I was not familiar with the restrictions of the contra flow plan. When we arrived at Interstate 12 north of Mandeville, we discovered westbound I-12 was closed between Hammond and Baton Rouge, and traffic was being diverted onto I-55 toward Jackson, Mississippi.

State police had blocked all the exits in Louisiana, probably to guard against smart guys like me who would circumvent their finely tuned system. They would not even allow us to exit at Kentwood, which upset Layne because it was the hometown of her primo chanteuse, Britney Spears. We drove 36 miles up I-55 before we could exit at the first Mississippi interchange, Highway 584 at Osyka.

We snaked back along side roads through miles of pine forests and open fields. Small crossroads communities featured rusted trailers and shanties with flowers growing out of old truck tires turned into yard ornaments. These people of Easleyville, Chipola and Ethel did not seem overly concerned about the threat we were fleeing or that it could, in fact, threaten them. They tended to their normal Sunday activities of services at the local Baptist church or fishing in a farm pond.

About 12 hours after we left home, we pulled into Baton Rouge. We found our way to the hotel and checked in with three exhausted adults, two tired children and a very impatient beagle pup.

The television reports early Monday said Katrina was tracking further east and might miss New Orleans entirely. That was welcome news. The wind outside our hotel started blowing fiercely about 9 A.M. and the electricity went out an hour later. We went out to the car to check the radio reports, but news was scant. Reporters from the local stations and networks such as CNN and the Weather Channel who had stayed in town were restricted to safe locations. They were not allowed to venture out into the city to see the effects of the storm. No news was good news in a sense, but it only delayed the inevitable.

Monday afternoon, our families convened at the house of Gary Solomon's sister, Gladys Brown, whose house had not lost power. Gary, president of Crescent Bank & Trust and a community leader in New Orleans, had access to police reports, which began to paint a picture of impending doom. The most frightening was an unconfirmed report that a levee somewhere in New Orleans had been, in the vernacular that would become frighteningly familiar, "breached." Did that mean a levee was leaking or it had failed totally? We did not know.

What we did learn was the location of the levee in question. It was along the 17th Street canal, less than a mile from our house in the Lakeview section. We still did not know if the entire levee failed or only on one side? If the latter, was it the west side that would flood Metairie or the east side which would pour water into our neighborhood?

Nothing personal, Metairie, but self-preservation is a tremendous motivator.

Unfortunately for us, a stretch of the 17th Street canal levee wall two city blocks long had collapsed on the New Orleans side. That meant Lakeview was inundated with 10 to 12 feet of toxic drool, and our house was sitting right in the middle of it.

Our worst fears were confirmed when the first video came out of New Orleans. It was sobering. A fly-over revealed a solid sheet of water that extended Lake Pontchartrain into many neighborhoods, including our own of Lakeview. The Southern Yacht Club, a focal point of the prominent West End neighborhood, was on fire and burning out of control. The top floors of condominiums at the yacht basin were visible, but the one- and two-story restaurants that dotted the fringes of the harbor were … gone!

The continuing images revealed an apocalyptic Venice where water filled the streets and rooftops were barely visible in many areas. One interstate highway ran straight into the water, cutting off an overpass upon which hundreds of people congregated, apparently chased from their homes. The video panned downtown, where the fabric roof of the Louisiana Superdome looked as though it had been ripped off with a paring knife. The gruesome scenes came rapidly, one after another, in the manner of a futuristic sci-fi disaster movie, *Mad Max beyond Superdome.*

As I watched, I had the feeling I was hovering above, seeing it but not a part of it. I was watching a movie where a disaster strikes poor, unsuspecting people who do not know what they've lost or what prospects they have for the future. But it wasn't the movie of the week. It was reality, and it was happening to us. The illusion that a tragedy can't happen to me was suddenly replaced with a sobering sense of dread.

We are trained as children that our parents can make everything better, so I persuaded Jean that we should drive to Kentucky to stay with my father, at least until we knew more about the long-term status of New Orleans. On Tuesday morning, we loaded up the van again and the six of us — Jean, the kids and Elmo — left the hotel and set off for Louisville. It turned out to be one of my Top Ten worst decisions of all time. Driving north, we quickly discovered our route took us right up Katrina's tailpipe. We were driving into a wasteland of massive power outages, closed gas stations and a freshly flattened landscape. It was becoming less and less likely we would get to Kentucky, so we decided to stop in Jackson, Mississippi, where Jean had a cousin. However, another setback soon made Jackson appear as distant as the moon.

We stopped at a rest area to use the facilities, but when I tried to restart my car, the battery was dead. Fortunately, the rest area was being used as a staging ground for emergency vehicles, and one of the workers let me jump my battery off his truck. We were on the road again, but without a radio and air conditioning so we could preserve what little battery life was left.

About 50 miles from Jackson, Jean tried to call her cousin, but the phones were dead. Our gas tank was nearing empty, and I had visions of us stranded on the side of the road with no gas, a dead battery and no way to summon help. Fortunately, we found a hotel on the outskirts of Jackson that appeared to be open. I walked inside the darkened lobby, and the clerk said they had no electricity but did have one room left. Under the circumstances — it looked like a five-star hotel — we took it. I expected a disaster discount, but the front desk charged us full rate, even without air conditioning or lights.

At least we had a place to gather our senses and assess the situation. I had to get a new battery for the car, which was dead again the moment I turned it off, and we had to get Lindsay back to Washington. My enthusiasm for driving further north was gone since we did not know how far the desolation existed. We determined that our best course was to rejoin Jean's family in Baton Rouge and take our chances together.

After a hot night with little sleep, we finally got through to Jean's cousin, who met us at the hotel. I jumped my dead battery off her car, and she directed me to a nearby Chevy dealership. I saw no lights, but I was relieved to see a handful of workers standing in the service bay. I told them my tale, and the manager said he would be happy to install a new battery. However, when I asked him how much I owed him, he shook his head. He said the owner of the dealership had lost his brother the day before when a tree fell on him during the storm. "You all've been through enough," he said.

He directed me to a gas station that was open, where I took my spot behind a long line of cars and soon refilled the tank. I drove back to the hotel, picked up Jean and the kids and took Lindsay to the Jackson airport. The only departing flight was to Miami, but at least she could get to D.C. from there and return to a normal life. The rest of us had a full tank of gas and a new battery, but were driving back into an unknown future.

CHAPTER
2

For the first time since the winds and rains came, Jeremie Davis thought they might get through it. The wind died down about 11 A.M. as the eye passed over New Orleans, and he and roommate Wayne Williams went outside to survey the damage. They looked for a campus police officer or anybody who could help them, but the stone silence was an eerie counterpoint to the deluge they had endured for the past several hours. They did not see another soul, convincing them they were the only people left in New Orleans. They were unaware of the chaos elsewhere in the city.

The effects of the storm on the campus, however, were obvious. Trees were down all over, and branches, trash cans and other loose debris littered every parking lot and lawn. Davis and Williams looked south, past the campus's boundary at Leon C. Simon Boulevard, and saw water pooling in the streets and around the houses. The level had risen to the windows on the nearer houses, and further down the street, where the elevation began to recede toward the middle of the topographical bowl in which the city sits, the water was lapping at the eves of many roofs.

The rising water was the result of a violent 20-foot storm surge that had caused three levees to break in the morning hours, flooding most of the city. Fortunately, most of the campus remained dry, thanks to its location on the lake at the top of the bowl.

The rain and wind soon picked up again, and Davis and Williams returned to the relative safety of their apartment. They were unharmed, but they had nowhere else to go. The electricity was out, and air conditioning and the television were dead. They still had some sandwiches and potato chips, but with the refrigerator also out the food and baby formula would not last long.

They spent the next two days and nights in the apartment, sweltering in the 90-degree heat. Davis slept sparingly, his dozing interrupted by the baby's frequent crying and by the uncertainty of their situation. *What if nobody knew we were here?* Jeremie had talked to one of the coaches Sunday, but he already was in Mississippi and couldn't come back into town for them. Davis wondered how long they would be missed and would help be sent to find them?

Davis did not even know Williams's story. All he knew was that when the players reported for workouts a few weeks earlier, he found out Williams was a shooter. That was the same thing Davis was recruited for. When workouts began, he and Williams found themselves at the "2" guard position, behind incumbent starter James Parlow and a couple of white guys. Davis thought he was recruited to be the man, but when he arrived he found out there were several shooters and still only one ball.

That did not matter so much now. Basketball seemed a long-time ago.

D avis saw the first helicopters on Tuesday, but they were off in the distance and could not be signaled. On Wednesday morning, he heard the faint *whuppa-whuppa-whuppa* of the rotors outside as they came closer, like a flock of seagulls to a landfill.

Finally, they've come to save us.

He shouted to Wayne and Sheena that they were going to be rescued. The first helicopter was setting down about 300 yards away in the parking lot near Kirschman Hall, which housed the college of business. Davis started running toward the helicopter, hoping to get the crew's attention. About halfway between the apartment and the helicopter, he stopped.

The helicopter crew paid no attention to the man running toward them, but instead dropped off six or eight people onto the asphalt parking lot. Just as quickly, the bird lifted off, banked left and flew south, toward downtown. Davis soon would learn the relatively dry university grounds made an attractive drop-off point for those rescued from more perilous spots such as the Superdome and the New Orleans Convention Center.

Davis, Williams, Sheena and Wayne Jr. were not about to be rescued. They merely became four more refugees in a growing list of thousands who must be saved.

When the helicopters finished their touch-and-go's in the parking lot, more than 2,000 refugees had been dropped onto the UNO campus. They were without food, water or toilet facilities, which led to looting. It wasn't long before Davis saw several men breaking into Kirschman Hall and several adjacent buildings. Most were looking for food and water. Some were looking for a violent outlet to their frustration and panic. When a group of them started moving toward the apartments at Privateer Place, Davis ran back to warn the others to lock themselves in.

There they sat, throughout the day and into the night. They could not sleep, hearing the occasional sound of broken glass or a door being kicked in by looters. They had endured the terror of a hurricane only to be threatened by irrational and panicked refugees whose base instincts put survival above any other human impulse. Sheena was convinced she would be murdered by a hungry mob looking for food or water. She spent much of the night clutching Wayne Jr. and weeping in fear.

On Thursday morning, the helicopters came back. Davis went out to find out what was happening, while Williams and his family remained locked in the apartment as a precaution. This time, U.S. Navy helicopters clearly were loading people instead of dropping more off. Davis went back to get Williams, Sheena and Wayne Jr., and they joined the crowd of the terrified, the hungry and the angry. They were all survivors, jostling on who would be the first to get out.

The helicopters were assigned to Helicopter Sea Combat Squadron Two Eight

(HSC-28), which flew the MH-60S Seahawk variant, based out of Norfolk, Virginia. They had embarked aboard the amphibious assault ship *USS Bataan*, which had been dispatched by the Defense Department to participate in humanitarian assistance operations led by the Federal Emergency Management Agency (FEMA). The *Bataan* was the Maritime Disaster Relief Coordinator vessel for the Navy's role in the relief efforts. Davis and Williams did not care about the origin or the pedigree of the rescue vehicles, only that they would ferry them to a place of refuge.

Williams, Sheena and the baby were taken to the front of the line and loaded aboard the next chopper. The passenger load was six for each vehicle, so Davis waited for space on another helicopter. He was confident they would be taken to an air-conditioned shelter where they could get a shower, some hot food and the baby could get formula and clean diapers.

As he boarded and his helicopter took off, a crew member handed him a water bottle and gave him an MRE military meal package. Davis couldn't at first recognize the substance contained in the pouch, but it did not matter. It was his first food in two days, and he ate greedily, while absorbing the view below. The entire city seemed to be sitting in the middle of a lake. One rooftop had a makeshift "HELP" fashioned out of what appeared to be bed sheets or towels. People were going through the streets in boats where a few days before cars traveled freely. Those same cars now sat partially submerged, their roofs breaking through the smooth water that covered everything. Near one car, submerged to its roof, a body floated in the water.

Davis was surprised when his helicopter descended and landed, not at an obvious place of refuge, but onto an overpass to Interstate-10. The lower end of the on-ramps were submerged, but the ramp snaked up onto the overpass to create a dry area at the top. One passenger seated near Davis questioned why they were being dropped on an overpass. A crew member tried to calm the man by telling him that buses would be along shortly to take them to a shelter.

The helicopter crews were instructed only to find dry land on which to deposit the refugees. The assumption was that others would finish the mission. Nobody realized that the number of people needing help far exceeded any governmental preparation or ability to provide the necessary assistance. Whatever system was supposed to be in place failed miserably. Buses that were supposedly ordered on Monday would not be dispatched until Wednesday, with an expected arrival time of late Thursday.

So many people were on the overpass; Davis thought it must be all the people who were left in the city. As far as he could see, hundreds sat or stood or walked around. Most were black, all were homeless and many were angry that such a tragedy could happen in the United States of America. Elderly people were lying on the concrete, some attended by others and some alone. One family of eight adults and children surrounded the lifeless body of an elderly woman. Young children were running around or leaning against the concrete barrier, their forlorn faces looking like pictures that could have been taken in Somalia or Uganda after a plague. The odor of feces and unwashed bodies was unbearable.

Davis spotted Williams and his family, and the four were together again. They had no protection from the wilting heat nor a bed to buffer the hard concrete. The refugees far outnumbered the few cots the Navy had dropped on the overpass. When one person would get up from a cot and go away from the crowd to relieve themselves, another would grab the cot, and fights would break out over the precious bedding.

The baby cried constantly at the discomfort and hunger from the diminishing food and water supplies. As darkness fell, they moved away from the group to get away from the odor and to reduce the chance they would be killed in their sleep. They were fearful of attack by the more animated refugees, whose derangement and desperation were aggravated by their circumstances.

Davis hadn't slept at all when the buses started arriving in the morning darkness of 4 A.M. Friday. After the first bus arrived, others came at 30-minute intervals to take 40 or 50 refugees at a time off the overpass. Davis feared they were being taken to yet another makeshift drop-off point, but their rescuers assured them they would be taken to safety. Some of the buses were going to Houston where a massive refugee center had been set up at the Astrodome. Wayne, Sheena and Wayne Jr. got on a bus to Houston, while Davis boarded a bus he learned later was headed for Dallas.

He stepped onto the bus, and the driver handed him a water bottle. Davis slumped down in a back seat and took his first cool drink since the helicopter. Some of the passengers opened windows to relieve the pervasive stench, but Davis simply sat there holding the sweaty water bottle with both hands. After sitting on the concrete ramp, the bus seat felt like a feather pillow. He leaned his head back and thought about what he had seen and what he had endured. He vowed he would never fear hell because it couldn't be worse than what he had been through. He did not yet know his misery was comparable to that suffered by an estimated 35,000 refugees who took shelter in the Louisiana Superdome and the city's Ernest N. Morial Convention Center.

The bus rolled down the ramp and headed west on Interstate 10, past the suburbs of Metairie and Kenner and onto the Bonnet Carre Spillway over the southern edge of Lake Pontchartrain. Davis dozed as the air circulating through the windows refreshed him. He decided he would go back to his hometown of Arcadia, and then decide what to do next. The city boosters called Arcadia "Heart of the Louisiana Piney Woods Country," but Davis knew that only once in its history had Arcadia drawn national attention. In 1934, bank robbers Bonnie Parker and Clyde Barrow were ambushed by lawmen just southwest of town on Louisiana State Highway 154. Their bodies were taken to Arcadia where they were embalmed at the old Conger Funeral Home.

That was a dubious distinction at best, but Arcadia was home, and once there Davis would contact the other schools that had recruited him. Somebody would want him,

Davis thought, and he could transfer far away from this bad memory. Wherever he wound up, he knew he would never go back to New Orleans.

The bus turned north at Lafayette on Interstate 49, and after six hours on the road stopped for fuel in Natchitoches, Louisiana. Davis knew he was little more than an hour from Arcadia, and when the bus pulled away he was still at the station. His cell phone was working again, so Davis called a friend who attended Northwestern State University in Natchitoches and asked if she would pick him up.

His next call was to his mother Barbara. He had not spoken to her since Sunday. When she answered, she heard a voice like that of a ghost calling from another world. Her son assured her he was alive and well, although he withheld the details of the past few days. They did not matter so much anymore. Jeremie Davis was going home.

CHAPTER
3

We reconvened at Jim and Gladys Brown's house in Baton Rouge, which had become Disaster Central. Jim is a former Louisiana state insurance commissioner who had been accused of malfeasance by the FBI and had spent nearly a year in a federal prison. I always was convinced the charges were false, because Jim might have been the most scrupulous public official I ever had known, When I was an executive with the New Orleans Saints, Jim would sometimes call for tickets. In every instance, he made certain he was not receiving special privileges unavailable to others. Unlike most public officials, he always insisted on paying for the tickets. I knew Jim as a solid guy whose generosity was welcomed and appreciated during the evacuation.

Rumors were circulating that New Orleans might be closed down for months, which meant we would be in Baton Rouge for the foreseeable future. When or even *if* the University of New Orleans would resume normal operations was unknown. UNO, which was part of the LSU System, probably would be shifting operations to Baton Rouge for the time being, so a temporary relocation there made sense.

I was having no luck trying to get in touch with Chancellor Tim Ryan, my coaches or staff by telephone. Telephone service was out for anyone with a 504 area code, and my cell phone did not have text messaging capability. E-mails were getting through, but the university servers were down, which meant all university e-mail addresses were useless.

I finally reached Ryan, who had evacuated to Athens, Georgia, where his daughter was a student at the University of Georgia. Ryan confirmed UNO offices would be set up at the LSU System Office in Baton Rouge and all available personnel should report for duty there as soon as possible. He would be back in town by the weekend.

I recalled the first time I had spoken with Ryan about the possibility of coming to UNO, but not as athletic director. When I decided to end a 20-year career in the National Football League in 2001, I considered teaching. Teaching appealed to me because it would allow me to impart the experience I had gained in professional sports while allowing me the time to return to my first love, which was writing.

I met Ryan in 1993 when the Saints commissioned him to conduct an economic impact study on the importance of the Saints to the city. We used his favorable study to bolster our efforts to sweeten our lease at the Superdome. He was a friend of Jean's family, particularly sister Martha and her husband Gary Solomon. As a young faculty member, Ryan had stepped in to tutor Martha after a severe Crohn's attack hit her just before final exams. Without Ryan's intervention, Martha would not have graduated on time, and might have dropped out of school altogether. Gary's and Martha's relationship with Ryan had strengthened over the years.

When I decided to leave the NFL I called Ryan, then dean of the business school at the University of New Orleans, to see if any opportunity existed. Ryan welcomed the idea to bring real-world experience to the classroom, but it wasn't a simple process. He said the ways of college finances required that I find somebody to endow a chair so I would, in effect, have to pay for myself. The prospect of teaching at the University of New Orleans was attractive, so I set about to identify a benefactor to endow the chair.

I called my old boss, Tom Benson, owner of the New Orleans Saints, and pitched the idea to him. The Tom Benson chair for Sports Management Studies at the University of New Orleans had a nice ring to it, and he initially showed some interest. Benson and I had maintained a cordial relationship even after he had dismissed me as the team's executive vice president in 1996.

Benson and I first spoke about the endowed chair in November 2001 during my final season as an executive with the Chicago Bears. I told him I would be coming to New Orleans in December to scout the Super Bowl site on behalf of the Bears, which were one of the contending teams. He told me to contact him again as the trip grew closer, and we would sit down and discuss it. Based on Benson's response, I felt confident something positive would happen. I began making notes and filling binders full of material that would provide resource material for lectures.

What I did not count on was the Saints' year-end swoon. The team lost its last four games by a combined score of 160-52. As I knew from working for Benson 10 years, losing put him in a bad mood. I called him to set up the meeting, but a secretary called me back and left a voicemail. Benson no longer had any interest in endowing a chair at the University of New Orleans.

That message put me as close to panic as I ever have been. I had made the decision to leave the NFL and to return to New Orleans to enhance our quality of life, but we still needed to pay the bills. I did not have a Plan B.

I told Jean about the voicemail, and she took it as she took every bit of uncertainty that has faced us throughout our marriage. "It's in God's hands, and we should not worry about it." My wife was much more spiritual and trusting than I, but at that point I did not have a better idea.

Now, four years later, sitting in someone else's house in Baton Rouge with no home, our possessions lost, a family uprooted and in doubt about the immediate future, the perceived uncertainty of those days seemed trivial.

Jean and I assumed our house was sitting under water, damaged beyond repair. With our house went our possessions and such irreplaceable items as the baby pictures and the tapes of our children's early years. The immediate effects of the storm were obvious, but the uncertainty of what lay beneath the disruption was suffocating. The children were asking questions we could not answer about their school and their friends and where we were going to live. All we knew for certain was things would never be the same again.

I was not the only one in the household who suffered a professional interruption. A year earlier, Jean had left the Hornets and with her friend, Melissa Swarr, had opened "Pizazz," a women's active wear shop in Lakeview. The shop had become a gathering place for Lakeview's working moms and was even beginning to turn the corner financially. Now, the shop was under water and with it about $70,000 of uninsured merchandise.

While the rest of the family members were glued to the television in the Browns' den, I walked into the kitchen and poured myself a Makers Mark and water. As I savored the first sip, I thought of the Randy Newman tape titled "Rednecks" that I had bought years before and was now under water in my first-floor home office. That tape contained a song about the 1927 Mississippi River flood that devastated parts of Mississippi and Louisiana. Most haunting were the lyrics:

Lou-eeesiana. Lou-eeesiana.

They're trying to wash us away.

They're trying to wash us away.

At that moment, we had no idea when, or if, we ever would return to New Orleans. And, if we could return, what would be left to return to?

We had returned to New Orleans before, when the questions were different and we defined disaster as bad things that happen to somebody else.

CHAPTER
4

Ｗe pointed the car south toward New Orleans. In the rear-view mirror was the National Football League. It was May 15, 2002, and I was leaving my last NFL posting, with the Chicago Bears, and heading into life as a civilian.

I did not really recall what civilians did, because I had spent the past 20 years in the protected, pampered world of the NFL. I was *The Evening Sun* beat writer covering the Baltimore Colts in 1981 when assistant general manager Ernie Accorsi recommended me to Commissioner Pete Rozelle and his staff. The NFL was preparing for a difficult labor negotiations with the NFL Players Association and needed someone who had credibility with the writers.

I spent five years in the League's labor relations' office in New York, then moved to the Saints, the Buffalo Bills and finally the Bears. It was a great ride with the most efficient and best-managed sports organization in the world. I had been chief contracts negotiator and salary cap manager for my three clubs, but I was ready for a change. The money was getting bigger, the agents were getting younger and slicker, and the pressure to win was overwhelming. As far as the press and the fans are concerned, every league year ends with one team of geniuses and 31 teams of idiots.

My contract with the Bears had expired, and Jean and I decided it was time to go home. We sent the moving van on the way and packed up our leased SUV to start the drive back to New Orleans with a stopover to see my parents and brother in Louisville.

I had met Jean while working with the Saints, and I had shanghaied her to Buffalo and then to Chicago for five years. Living that close to the North Pole was culture shock for a New Orleans girl who never had owned a winter coat. Jean's introduction to northern weather came during our first summer in Buffalo. It was a mystery to both of us why the municipal workers were going around our neighborhood tying 20-foot red poles to the fire hydrants. An amused neighbor explained that when the snow drifted to heights of 20 feet or so, the firefighters needed to know where the fire hydrants were located in case of a fire. *When, not if,* the snow drifted 20 feet, he said!

Chicago had much more to offer as a city, but during our first winter there we experienced a 30-day stretch when the temperature did not rise above zero. It could not have been much colder if the NFL had expanded to Siberia. The weather was a good reason I promised Jean that someday we would return to New Orleans. However, we were influenced greatly by Jean's close-knit family and decided our two children should grow up close to their six cousins.

Family is important, but it does not pay the bills, and I was reluctant to return without a safety net. Being unemployed at age 54 was not the way I wanted to end a respectable career.

I tabled the idea of teaching after Tom Benson changed his mind on endowing my academic chair. I understood Benson and did not hold any resentment for his decision. I spent nearly 10 years with the Saints, defying the slogan among NFL employees that the iconic initials really mean "Not For Long." While I worked for him, Benson never interfered in football matters, and he always supported recommendations to improve the team.

Benson helped me find another job in the NFL, calling Bills' owner Ralph Wilson on my behalf. After I started work as Vice President of Administration for the Bills in 1997, Benson pulled me aside at an NFL owners meeting to make an unusual confession. "I just want you to know that I fired the wrong guy," he said. I appreciated the gesture, assuming he meant Coach Jim Mora, who had resigned during the 1996 season, five months after I was fired. I wish Benson would have come to his epiphany earlier, but I was in Buffalo trying to understand an aging owner with a faulty memory and a temperament that swung wildly if he missed his daily medication.

Wilson required that his head coach, general manager and chief administrative officer call him at his Detroit home two or three times a day, and anything short of that was a punishable offense. I had been warned of Wilson's peculiarities. One of his previous general managers told me that during a casual conversation with the owner, he had put his feet on the owner's desk. Wilson fired him for "lack of respect." He fired me for "lack of communication."

Another opportunity appeared soon when an old friend was promoted to president of the Chicago Bears. I called Ted Phillips to congratulate him, and we began discussing the possibility of me coming to Chicago. I did not know at the time whether I even wanted to stay in the League, fresh off the Benson and Wilson debacles. But Phillips was busy trying to get the city of Chicago and state of Illinois to support construction of a new Soldier Field. He asked me to come aboard and run the company while he devoted himself to getting the stadium built.

After a long career in the National Football League, the prospects of going to the founding franchise was like a dream come true. Jim Finks, the man who brought me to New Orleans, had been the general manager of the Bears and had built the team that eventually won the Super Bowl after the 1985 season. Finks, who passed away in 1994, still had many admirers, as well as two of his four sons, in Chicago.

My tenure with the Bears was not nearly as successful as Finks's, but it was not without its stories. One, in particular, involved a future Hall of Famer, linebacker Brian Urlacher.

Urlacher was the Bears' first-round draft choice in 2000, and it was my responsibility to negotiate a contract with his agent. Negotiations for first-round draft choices are a tedious process that traditionally extends to the opening day of training camp or beyond. The outcome is generally predictable, because every agent has a track record, whether it's signing on time, signing a few days into camp or signing after an extensive holdout. It is the club negotiator's job to know the agent's history and conduct negotiations accordingly.

The problem with the Urlacher negotiation was that his agent had never done an NFL contract. Steve Kauffman was a veteran negotiator for National Basketball Association players, but Urlacher would be his first NFL client. I called Jerry Krause, general manager of the Chicago Bulls, to get an idea of what to expect from Kauffman. Krause's response was: "Well, you could do a lot worse." That gave me some confidence that Kauffman would not engage in the dance of posturing and threats that would keep his client out of camp. The Bears' beat writer for the Chicago *Tribune*, John Mullin, had the same impression after talking with me and Kauffman, writing: "Early signs suggest the Bears may not face their third consecutive holdout by a first-round draft pick. Team negotiator Jim Miller will be in Los Angeles in mid-May and expects to begin preliminary contract talks with Steven Kauffman, agent for first-round draft choice Brian Urlacher. This will be one of the earliest starts to negotiations in recent years and reflects the Bears' and Kauffman's belief in not waiting until picks around Urlacher's No. 9 slot set the market."

When I met with Kauffman, he was friendly and appeared eager to hear my take on the process. I did not expect his assertion that he wanted to achieve a contract prior to July 1, a full three weeks before camp opened. Most agents in the first meeting might say they want an early agreement, but that desire normally carries the unspoken clause "as long as you give us what we want." But Kauffman framed his desire in a context that I never had heard before. It appeared Urlacher was betrothed to a woman whom Kauffman believed was an opportunist, and he wanted to protect his client. Under the applicable law, anything that Urlacher brought into the marriage was his property, and anything the woman brought into the marriage was her property. Therefore, Kauffman wanted the deal consummated before the wedding date so Urlacher could keep whatever signing bonus was agreed upon.

Brian Urlacher became the first player in the 2000 NFL draft to sign a contract, on June 15, 2000. The prophecy as written by Steve Kauffman came to pass as Urlacher married, and eventually divorced, the woman. However, he kept his signing bonus.

CHAPTER
5

Ialways thought myself fortunate that I had careers instead of a job. My career in the newspaper business included stops at the Louisville *Courier-Journal* and the Baltimore *Evening Sun*. My next career, in the NFL, included stops at the NFL Management Council in New York, the Saints, the Bills and the Bears. When you have a career, you always have a job, somewhere. The prospect that I might have to look for a job outside my career frightened me to death.

Jean had told me that God would provide an answer, and again she was right. But this time it was Jean, and not me, who received the call. Our brother-in-law, Gary Solomon, employed Jean in one of his businesses prior to her employment with the Saints. He knew her administrative skills and work ethic. She stopped working after our marriage in 1992, but with my prospects uncertain, she was ready to go back to work.

She asked Gary what job he was recommending her for, and he jokingly replied "general manager of the New Orleans Hornets." The Charlotte Hornets of the National Basketball Association had just moved the franchise to New Orleans, and Gary was assisting the transition group to sell suites in the corporate community. Doug Thornton, SMG's general manager of the Louisiana Superdome and New Orleans Arena, had worked tirelessly to get the Hornets to New Orleans. Now, Thornton was tasked with helping the team staff the offices, and Gary recommended his sister-in-law.

Jean interviewed with team president Sam Russo and with team owner George Shinn, who offered her the job on the spot. The Miller family was back in Show Biz, and now Jean was the primary breadwinner.

I relished my new role that fall as Mr. Mom, ferrying the children to school, while keeping in touch with people in the sports industry. I was actively looking, and Gary Solomon again brokered an opportunity. SMG, the facility management conglomerate that managed the Louisiana Superdome and New Orleans Arena, was tasked to sell the naming rights for the buildings. The income was necessary to fulfill the state's obligations to the Hornets and Saints, and SMG wanted a company that had experience selling naming rights.

One of the applicants for the job was Gilco, Inc., a husband-wife team of Sara Gilbertson and David Cope headquartered in Washington, D.C. Coincidentally, we hired Gilco at the Bears to explore naming rights and other marketing opportunities for the new Soldier Field. During the process, Sara, David and I had become fast friends. When SMG put the bid on the streets, David called me asking if I would recommend Gilco for the job. I called Gary and told him of Gilco's qualifications and of our relationship.

The man who would make the decision was Doug Thornton, and Gary suggested Thornton invite Sara and David to New Orleans for an interview. With his prodding, a deal was struck in Gary's suite at a Saints game whereby SMG would hire Gilco, which in turn would hire me as their point man in New Orleans. The opportunity was a blessing for me, because it pulled me back into my career as a sports administrator in the town I wanted to live.

Sara, David and I worked for the next few months making presentations to several companies in New Orleans and elsewhere, trying to persuade them that a connection with two prominent sports venues would give them a dynamic identification that would promote their business. We pitched a dozen companies, but the most memorable presentation was to Bacardi in Miami. Sara was a genius at compiling facts, figures and some pizzazz to support David's dynamic presentation skills. An example was Sara's graphic that overlaid Bacardi's trademark bat on the roof of the Superdome. It was a dazzling appearance, but was not enough to entice the beverage company to come aboard. The trip, however, was significant for another reason.

When we were flying back to New Orleans, I pulled out the copy of the morning *Times-Picayune* that was still unopened in my briefcase. The lead story in the sports page was that the University of New Orleans's athletic director, Bob Brown, was stepping down. A national search would be conducted for a successor, and the head of the search committee was Will Peneguy, an associate vice chancellor who would serve as interim athletic director.

Peneguy was another old newspaper guy and a friend, having been a sports writer at the *Times-Picayune* when I was a reporter at *The Evening Sun*. We did not know each other well in our newspaper days, but we became friends in our second careers, I with the Saints and Peneguy as assistant general manager of the Superdome.

When we arrived back in New Orleans, I called Peneguy and asked him, "What are you looking for?" He responded candidly, "I don't know. Are you interested?" I told him that I might be, and he said to send him a letter of interest along with an updated resume.

The University of New Orleans again had entered the picture. I had talked with Tim Ryan about teaching at UNO, but the athletic director's position encompassed more of the skills I had developed in the NFL. It was about leadership, running an organization, dealing with coaches and athletes and marketing. I *thought* I could teach, but I *knew* I could run a sports business. I sent Peneguy the letter and resume.

From the outside, the position appeared perfect for me, but I did not want to go into it blindly. I called two men whom I knew would give me an honest perspective on the job. Ron Maestri, who was the longest-tenured AD in UNO history, and Wright Waters, commissioner of the Sun Belt Conference, which was based in New Orleans. I had met Maestri back in 1993 when Tom Benson was trying to buy a minor league baseball team. Jim Finks and I visited with Maestri to discuss the possibility of Benson's team playing games at the UNO baseball field. Benson never bought the team, but Maestri and I remained in touch.

When I told Maestri I might have an interest in the UNO job, his first response was "Do you have a death wish?" Maestri was not a fan of then-Chancellor Greg O'Brien, who himself was not a fan of the athletics department. O'Brien admittedly never participated in sports as a child and knew little about athletics.

In fact, O'Brien's lack of sports knowledge took on mythical proportions among the UNO faithful. O'Brien's first athletic event after being named chancellor in 1986 was a baseball game in which the UNO pitcher was striking out the opposing batters at a rapid pace. Some students in the stands dutifully recorded each strikeout by posting a large "K" on the press box. After the third strikeout, O'Brien noticed the display and became enraged. He came down on the playing field and announced loudly to the crowd that as long as he was chancellor, he would not tolerate such racist displays as "KKK." An embarrassed aide pulled him aside quickly and told him the display did not mean "Ku Klux Klan," but was a common baseball reference. O'Brien sheepishly returned to the stands and the game resumed.

According to Maestri, O'Brien's inattention to athletics resulted in less financial support than UNO's peers and led to a deterioration of the athletics facilities. Maestri complained O'Brien did nothing to keep successful coaches like Tim Floyd and Tic Price at the university, which sent a negative message to Privateer fans. As an institution with a large commuter enrollment, it was difficult enough to attract fans without providing evidence that athletics was not important enough to make the investment. Maestri felt he had spent more than a quarter-century at the university playing catch-up against the schools his teams were trying to beat. Maestri's frustrations were evident. It was a conversation that would come back to me many times over the next few years.

Waters's opinion of the UNO situation was not as personal, but not entirely different. He said it was a difficult job considering O'Brien's record of non-support. He said UNO's facilities were the worst in a conference whose members were making investments in their athletic infrastructures. He advised me if it looked like I would be a finalist to make sure O'Brien pledged he would support the program.

It occurred to me that Maestri and Waters were describing a program that in many ways resembled a Mardi Gras masked ball. On the outside, the program appeared robust and competitive but beneath the mask was a program struggling to survive. The coaches wore the masks when they recruited, and those student-athletes who signed with UNO themselves donned the mask when they arrived.

Of course, at the time I had no job, and it probably would not have mattered if Waters and Maestri had told me Greg O'Brien ground the bones of students to make his bread. I recognized the challenges of the job. If I was the guy, I would be leading a program that lagged far behind its peer group in so many ways. It was almost as if I would be leading from behind the eight-ball of non-support, indifference and history.

But I was just confident — or maybe gullible — enough to think I could make a difference and change some attitudes. I knew I had the knowledge and the desire to effect necessary change, but I could not do it alone. This was a job that would require a lot of help, first from the administration but also from alumni and students. To borrow a phrase we used in the NFL, *if I have the ammo, I can deliver the wham-o.* In other words, if I had the tools I could create something new and lasting.

As the process entered the Christmas holidays, O'Brien asked me to lunch with Peneguy and a few other university officials. During lunch, he asked me if I had any more questions, and I said to him: "This program can't be successful unless you are behind it, which means increasing funding to athletics. Are you prepared to do that?"

O'Brien did not hesitate. He said not only would he do that, but athletics would be his next major fund-raising project.

I told him that was all I needed to hear.

I received a phone call on January 10, 2003, from O'Brien, saying he was calling to ask if I would do him a favor. I said I would, and he asked me if I would agree to a four-year contract to be the fifth Director of Intercollegiate Athletics at the University of New Orleans. I readily agreed, excited at the prospects, particularly after his assurances he would support my efforts to build a quality program.

A press conference was hurriedly assembled, and my appointment was well received. I still had positive name recognition through my years with Jim Finks and the Saints, a quality I hoped would bring some credibility to my new program. Jean, who was a UNO graduate, sat with her mother on the first row, next to a beaming Tim Ryan, nattily attired with his trademark multi-hued socks reflecting the light like a disco ball.

Peneguy, head of the search committee, jokingly told me later I was the choice of some search committee members because I had displayed one quality that none of the other candidates possessed. My first interview with members of the committee included lunch, but when we drove up to the selected restaurant, it was closed. Coincidentally, the restaurant was three blocks from my house, so I was the only candidate who could have quickly offered one or two alternative spots, as well as a cautionary note to avoid a huge pothole in the next block. None of the other candidates had that knowledge, so I was their guy.

Whatever the committee's reasoning, I suspect my selection was influenced to some extent by Gary Solomon. Gary's father, T.G., was a huge benefactor of O'Brien and a very close friend. I do not know exactly what was said between T.G., Gary and O'Brien on the subject of my candidacy, but I've always suspected T.G. and Gary had a large role in O'Brien's decision.

Gary's day job is chairman of the board of Crescent Bank & Trust of New Orleans, but he spends most of his time with charitable endeavors such as the New Orleans Children's Museum, the American Red Cross, the Young Leadership Council and another half-dozen organizations seeking to make New Orleans a better place to live.

Gary was always in my corner, and he would become an even greater influence as circumstances would evolve at UNO.

CHAPTER
6

My new role as a college athletic director had many advantages over my NFL positions. I no longer had to worry about agents calling to complain about low pay or playing time for their clients. Nor did I have to juggle the whims of club owners whose delicate dispositions easily could be knocked off balance by a lost game or public comment. More importantly, I believed these impressionable young college athletes still could be influenced positively. In the NFL, I saw many athletes whose attitudes were well established, for better or worse. Now, I had the chance to make a difference.

The one issue in college athletics that was less an advantage, however, was the issue of "funding," which is the collegiate euphemism for "show me the money." In the NFL, money was never the problem. If it would help win games or put fannies in the seats, you spent it and considered it a good investment. In the middle kingdom of mid-major college athletics, you did what you could afford. If you did not have the money to hire another academic counselor, you didn't do it, whether it was necessary or not.

This practice appeared to be ass-backwards to me, especially in the area of revenue generation. Most college athletic programs are expected to raise much of their own support. But if they could not hire the additional sponsorship sales person or a ticket sales person dedicated to athletics, it limited efforts to generate the required income. Fiscal problems became a self-fulfilling prophecy.

To O'Brien's credit, he approved my first request to hire a sponsorship sales person and a fund-raiser, neither of which the department currently employed. Those responsibilities plus that of sports information director and play-by-play man had been invested in one staff member, who could not devote adequate time to any of the tasks.

College athletics posed many other issues that fell under the topic of "Miller's learning curve," but I was fortunate to have inherited an experienced staff to help me navigate through those areas. My associate Athletic Director was Mike Bujol, who came to UNO as a scholarship soccer player when the school sponsored the sport in the early 1980s. After graduation, Bujol was hired in the sports information department and had risen through the ranks to the No. 2 man under both Ron Maestri and his successor, Bob Brown. Mike had been through the wars at UNO, knew how things worked and knew the location and occupant of every unmarked grave.

My assistant athletic director for academic services was Dr. Kathy Keene, a 29-year-old freshly minted UNO PhD who also handled the compliance responsibilities. Kathy knew the strict academic requirements at UNO from first-hand experience, and as such she had a comfortable relationship with the faculty and administrative staff.

The third key member of the organization was Mike Dauenhauer, the assistant AD for business operations. Mike was another 25-year UNO employee, having started as business manager at Lakefront Arena. He was an expert at navigating the myriad rules and regulations thrown at UNO by the state and the LSU System office.

I felt very comfortable that the two Mikes and Kathy, and their ability to run the day-to-day operations, would leave me time to concentrate on raising money and raising awareness for UNO athletics.

One of the strengths I brought to the UNO job was my ability to relate with coaches. Having spent 15 years with NFL clubs, I worked closely with such different personalities as Jim Mora, Marv Levy, Wade Phillips and Dick Jauron. Each had his own style of how to run a program and how to deal with their assistant coaches and administrative staff. I respected each of them and had no major problems with any, so long as I kept in mind their peculiarities and inclinations.

Mora was a "my way or the highway" guy, who could display multiple personalities, depending on whether it was during the season or off-season. Wade Phillips, who was named head coach of the Bills in 1998 after Levy retired, offered a laid-back, cowboy demeanor that belied an extensive knowledge of the game and the ability to hold his coaches and players accountable. Levy and Jauron were very similar in personality and genuinely nice men who were respectful of everyone in the organization and the jobs they were assigned.

Levy's record of taking four teams to the Super Bowl stands on its own, but I credit Levy with the greatest coaching quote I ever heard. When asked by a reporter whether the upcoming game was a "must win" situation, Levy responded: "World War II was a 'must win.' This is a football game."

A couple of the coaches I inherited at UNO had similar qualities. Monte Towe, the men's basketball coach, was like Jim Mora. He wanted only to coach basketball and did not care much for the other responsibilities that came along with the job. He delegated much of the recruiting and academic responsibilities to his assistant coaches, but he was in control at practice and during games. Towe grew up in Indiana as a "gym rat" and had been point guard for the great 1974 North Carolina State Wolfpack team that won the NCAA championship.

Another of my head coaches also had experienced big time success. Randy Bush, who played under Maestri at UNO, had a credible career in Major League Baseball and earned two World Series rings as a member of the 1987 and 1991 Minnesota Twins. Bush was much like Jauron in manner, humble and polite and very respectful of those around him, no matter what job they had to do.

But I saw other areas that needed change. When I took the job, my brother, Jerry, told me a new manager needs to do three things to send a message: (1) Fire somebody, (2) hire somebody, and (3) paint the lobby.

After several months on the job, I targeted a couple of head coaches to fulfill part of that suggestion. I made changes in the sports of tennis and track and field and the following year, women's basketball. I hired new coaches who convinced me they could bring to UNO some of the enthusiasm and credibility that had been missing.

In my first few months on the job, I also hired a new administrative assistant, a new marketing and sales manager and a new director of fund-raising. I had achieved everything I had intended, with one exception. The lobby never got painted.

Only two months into my tenure, I experienced the benefits of big-time college athletics. The university had been selected to host the 2003 NCAA Men's Final Four, and I arrived just in time to enjoy the fruits after all the work had been done. My main duty was to attend meetings and watch how the Greater New Orleans Sports Foundation and the local organizing committee worked with the NCAA staff to put on a major event.

I had been to a dozen Super Bowls during my years in the NFL, and I knew the logistical magnitude of such an event. The buildup for the game occupies more attention than most events, and the half-time show is nearly as anticipated as the game itself. It is doubtless the biggest sporting event of the year.

But there was something different, and very special, about a Final Four. It was college athletics, which still is more grassroots than glitz. Attendees at a Super Bowl are largely corporate because the price of a ticket has risen far beyond the regular fan's reach. But the cheering sections for the Final Four participants, with their large number of students, provide an innocent enthusiasm that is refreshing and encouraging.

The semi-final games on Saturday were mere tune-ups for the winners. Syracuse had little trouble with Texas, while Kansas blew out Marquette.

Three hours before the championship game between Syracuse and Kansas, I was sitting on the Syracuse bench in the empty Superdome talking with former AD Ron Maestri, who was working for the Greater New Orleans Sports Foundation. I told Maestri that so far Chancellor O'Brien had said all the right things, and I was confident we were making progress.

As we sat there, suddenly I felt a drip of water on my head. I looked up, and the Superdome had sprung a leak! A terrific rainstorm was raging outside and a leak had developed in the Superdome's fabric roof. Somehow, I was the target of the first drip. I recalled my years with the Saints when the Superdome maintenance crew would conduct its annual roof sweep to collect buckets full of lead from bullets that had been fired at the Superdome from the nearby housing projects. But we never suffered a leaky roof during a Saints game.

We contacted Superdome maintenance, and a team was dispatched to patch the leak before the game. We were fortunate the leak occurred when it did. If it started dripping on Syracuse Coach Jim Boeheim in the middle of the national championship game, it would have been a major embarrassment for the Superdome and the city.

As it was, Boeheim was spared and Carmelo Anthony led the Orange past Kansas, 81-78, in an exciting championship game.

Another major event in my first year as athletic director was welcomed at the time and would resonate throughout my tenure. In late summer, Greg O'Brien resigned as chancellor over a controversy about using UNO Foundation funds to pay for his two daughters' weddings. O'Brien argued that the guest lists included UNO supporters, his superiors and members of his staff, but the state auditor didn't buy the argument.

Gary Solomon again entered the picture, this time as a UNO alum and a board member of the UNO Foundation. Gary lobbied hard with the president of the LSU System, Dr. William Jenkins, on behalf of Dr. Tim Ryan, dean of the business school, to succeed O'Brien. Ryan was a New Orleans native and UNO graduate who had earned his PhD at Ohio State before returning to UNO as a faculty member in the 1970s.

He was a friend of Gary and a season ticket holder for UNO basketball and baseball. In addition, Ryan continued to play in a competitive over-50 softball league, and he was an avid golfer. With a chancellor whose history reflected a knowledge and support of athletics, I believed UNO athletics had a unique opportunity to reach levels never before imagined. We were positioned to throw off the stereotypes of the commuter school that did not support its athletics program.

Shortly after his appointment, Ryan convened a Sunday morning golf group and invited me to participate. It became a valuable part of our department's ability to move forward, and it strengthened my relationship with other university administrators. Provost Rick Barton, the university's chief academic officer, was an avid supporter of our program, and he was invaluable at helping us achieve our academic commitment to our student-athletes. Dr. Bobby Dupont, the vice chancellor for strategic planning and dean of Metropolitan College, bought radio time on our broadcasts to promote the university's strong night school programs. Dr. Scott Whittenburg was associate vice chancellor of Academic Affairs and still a scratch golfer after playing collegiately at Oregon State University.

If the week's events proved to be too time-consuming, I knew I always could catch Ryan or the others to discuss the issues concerning our department over a couple of beers at the 19th hole.

I was excited about our prospects.

The first 32 months of my tenure as Athletic Director at the University of New Orleans were the most satisfying period of my professional career. College athletics at this level carries an innocence and purity I had not experienced in the NFL. College athletes must be students first because so few of them will ever reach the professional level. The emphasis on academics is noble and just, and it was refreshing to see athletes every day who were enjoying their lives as college students.

It was especially gratifying within this environment to reposition an entire program. In my first year, we added women's swimming to our existing 14 sports to help with our Title IX compliance. I hired as head coach former Olympic champion Ashley Tappin, a New Orleans native who had won two gold medals at Melbourne.

We also launched three major initiatives to enhance the program. A fund-raising drive was aimed at renovating Privateer Park, the baseball stadium. We were working with Daktronics to identify sponsors who would provide a stream of revenue to install new signage for Lakefront Arena, Privateer Park and at key locations around campus. We also signed an agreement with local attorney and sports figure Rob Couhig to build a 26-court tennis center.

Things were not perfect. The program was still seriously underfunded, and ranked last in the Sun Belt Conference in the amount of support that came from the institution. We were making it on a shoestring budget. But I was optimistic that once our initiatives were in place and the improvements to the infrastructure were made, we could improve our sponsorship sales, sell more tickets, increase donations and identify new revenue streams. Most importantly, we had an advocate in a chancellor who supported our efforts.

Our program was headed in a new and definitely positive direction when school opened for the fall semester on August 20, 2005.

CHAPTER
7

The early predictions of when the flood waters would recede were not optimistic. Rumors abounded that New Orleans might never reopen its most devastated neighborhoods. The national news media focused on the Lower Ninth Ward, whose residents were predominantly lower-income black families, but equally hard hit were our own middle class communities of Lakeview and Gentilly, which surrounded UNO like a tarnished necklace. Even if New Orleans could rebuild, the critics said, it would surely take months, or maybe even years to recover sufficiently.

Uncertainty framed our discussions at Gladys and Jim Brown's house in Baton Rouge. Our only certainty was the gradual realization that our lives had been broken into two periods — Before Katrina and After Katrina — probably for many years to come. Our immediate consideration was the children. We had to make the transition as easy as possible for them, which included getting them into school. One of our friends whose children also had attended St. Dominic School in Lakeview told us St. Aloysius Church and School near the LSU campus in Baton Rouge had opened its doors to all parochial school refugees. We made plans to contact the school and get details.

Gary Solomon suggested we might be in Baton Rouge longer than we thought, and we had better prepare. Gary and Martha offered to lend money through their bank for a mortgage to anybody who wished to buy a house rather than rent. It made sense at the time. Other refugees would be making the same decisions, so it was in our best interests to move quickly. On Thursday, three days after Katrina, we started house shopping.

Baton Rouge's pre-Katrina population of 225,000 had doubled with many refugees now staying with friends or looking for housing. Consequently, traveling from one part of town to another was an exercise in patience. Roads were clogged and gas station lines resembled those from the 1970s gas crises.

Making things more difficult was a subtle attitude that we were not welcome. Some locals who were interviewed on television expressed resentment at the intrusion of these evacuees who were suddenly making their lives more complicated. That attitude was a manifestation of a long-standing fissure between mostly Catholic south Louisiana and the mostly Baptist north Louisiana. Baton Rouge was the accepted line of demarcation.

Contributing to the conflict was the fact we didn't want to be there any more than they wanted us there. Frankly, my dear, I'd have rather been back on Vicksburg Street in Lakeview.

Jean's faith only grew stronger during this monumental disruption in our lives. She never complained nor bemoaned the loss of our house or furnishings. Instead, she thanked God for keeping our family safe and intact and for the kindness of friends. At that time, thanks was not the first thing I would have said to God.

We attended services at St. Aloysius the first Sunday morning after Katrina, one week after our evacuation. We saw some Lakeview neighbors and asked them what they'd heard or what they knew, which at that point consisted of sparse facts, speculation and rumors of looters going through Lakeview in stolen motorboats.

I will never forget the prayer that morning by the St. Aloysius parish priest, not so much for the content but for the moment itself. He asked everyone to hold hands and bow our heads. I was sitting with Jean and the kids, all of whom were to my right, so I reached out my left hand to an elderly lady who was seated beside me. The priest thanked God for the safety of all visitors who were sent here by this terrible tragedy. As the priest spoke, the lady squeezed my hand tightly and leaned over to whisper "God bless you and your family."

I did not have time for tears in the previous week, but suddenly I couldn't control them. I didn't want people to feel sorry for us. I was only cognizant of the unanswerable questions that raged. And, by God, I wanted answers.

I shouted to my inner self: *Why the hell is this happening to us?* This is the kind of thing you see on television, to other people, not us. What has happened to us and what will become of us? What effect will this have on our children, such a great tragedy disrupting their short lifetimes of peaceful dependence and harmony? What if the university never opens again and I have to go looking for another job at my age? *God, damn it, why have you done this to us?*

Raised in a devout family, I would never have thought of talking to God the way I was talking to Him now. Tragedy inflames the bubbling lava of our inner selves that may never bubble to the surface otherwise. Was it anger or something more? Was it just panic and confusion or something sinister? When I was little and would lose my temper, my mother would tell me "that's the meanness in you coming out." Well, if that was the meanness coming out, so be it, but I had questions, and I wanted answers.

But there *were* no answers. There were only people around me who had suffered as we had, and others who were willing to help and support us. Jean understood this far better than I ever did, and she gave me the only answer I needed. She hooked her left arm into my right and pulled me close to her. "I love you," she whispered. It was probably the best answer I could have received at that moment.

After services, we waited in line with the other refugees to enroll Layne and Charles Connor in school. The school had a program that provided free uniforms to underprivileged children, and we were directed to that line to get the recycled uniforms. Things that I would never consider doing in normal times, like accepting free used uniforms, became true blessings. Similar examples of kindness throughout those first months gave us our first encouragement that we could endure this tragedy.

Over the next few days, we tried hard to adapt to our new circumstances. We had things to do, like buying clothes to supplement our three-day casual wardrobes. Our cell phones still could not make or receive calls, so we went to the local AT&T store and bought new phones with the Baton Rouge 225 area code.

We also bought a house. In one day. I remember our moves to Buffalo and Chicago and the never-ending house hunting expeditions. Never did we think we could look at three or four houses and buy one in a single day. But after much speculation that New Orleans might not open up again for months or longer, we pulled the trigger on a small three-bedroom house in the city's eastern suburbs closer to New Orleans. Jean's sister Patricia and her husband Schaffer found a house down the block the same day.

The things we were doing usually took weeks or months, not one day. But we had no choice. It was as if we had landed on earth from a distant planet and had 24 hours to assimilate.

Schaffer had a nephew who lived in Baton Rouge and was willing to give up his two-bedroom house for a few weeks, at least until we could take possession of our new houses. So for the next three weeks, four adults, four children and a noble hound named Elmo lived in a small two-bedroom, one-bath house, and we were grateful for it.

Friday morning, I drove over to the LSU campus and joined a dozen UNO deans, vice chancellors and other staff members. When I arrived, I was greeted with hugs that reflected a sense of relief that another one of us had made it through the gunfire to the safety of the bunker. We were soldiers sharing the same foxhole. By their dress, it was obvious most of them had packed as we had, for a short stay. T-shirts, shorts, running shoes or sandals were prevalent, and shaving and makeup were optional.

The LSU System had set up a disaster information phone center in a conference room. A dozen of those present were talking with staff, students and faculty trying to field the various questions about the status of the university and when or if classes would resume. Nobody had answers, but the fact we were restoring some semblance of order gave us all a sense of purpose.

I spent the rest of the day trying to get in touch with our coaches and staff. I discovered that Mike Bujol and Kathy Keene had text messaging ability and had been in touch with our coaches. All of our student-athletes were accounted for, although at the time we did not know the extent of Jeremie Davis's and Wayne Williams's ordeal.

The conversations between phone calls were the same among us all. *Where did you evacuate to? Are your kids okay? Have you heard anything from New Orleans? Where are you staying in Baton Rouge? What are you going to do?* We were all refugees of the same tragedy, with a lot more questions than answers.

Chancellor Tim Ryan's first words to me were soothing and encouraging. He expressed concern about our student-athletes and insisted we use athletics to send a positive signal. Despite the adversity, we were alive and well, and we needed to project that message. The best way to do that was to proceed with a basketball season, showcasing our most visible sport. I thought it fortunate that Ryan and not his predecessor, Greg O'Brien, was chancellor. Ryan clearly wanted to use athletics to help the university endure and rebound, while the tragedy might have been a good excuse for O'Brien to bow to history and drop athletics altogether.

I informed Ryan that our coaches were talking with potential host institutions about taking our teams intact, enrolling them in school and giving them the opportunity to continue working toward their respective seasons. Ryan approved the plan, and he received approval from the LSU system to guarantee remuneration for those institutions. Enrolling our students at LSU would have been the best situation, but the few dorm vacancies already were being scooped up by other displaced students. Our head track coach, Willie Randolph, did a masterful job at finding housing for his students on the LSU campus, along with an agreement with the Tigers' coaches that would allow them to train at LSU facilities.

Our other coaches were busy making similar arrangements for their own teams with amazing success, thanks to the generosity of the intercollegiate family. Baseball coach Tom Walter was talking with several schools until New Mexico State, a former member of our Sun Belt Conference, offered free housing and free tuition. We were only responsible for books and for feeding the players, which seemed like a good idea until we discovered later how much baseball players can eat. Tom had a friend who owned a 40-seat private jet, which picked up his Louisiana-based players in Baton Rouge and flew them to their new temporary home at no cost to us.

Ashley Tappin arranged for her small squad of women swimmers to attend Agnes Scott College in Atlanta and train at Emory University. We had just started the program and had only six swimmers, so it was less of a logistical issue. Ashley had a friend affiliated with an Atlanta church who offered to find host families for the women, at no charge. Jimmy Headrick, our director of golf who coached our women's team, placed his team at Nicholls State University in Houma, Louisiana, while the men's coach, Chris McCarter, enrolled his students at LSU-Shreveport.

One coach who had not made arrangements was Burzis Kanga, our head tennis coach. Most members of the men's and women's teams were internationals, and once Katrina blew through, many of the players returned to their home countries. Kanga said he was talking to all of them, but he was meeting resistance from some who did not want to return.

Women's volleyball had started their season and had won all four of their matches. But because of the uncertainty of our playing venue, I recommended to Ryan that we suspend the program for a year. I had spoken with the NCAA, which agreed to grant our volleyball players an extra year of eligibility. I informed Coach Julie Ibieta of the decision, and she was disappointed but relieved. Cancelling the volleyball season also gave our department time to regroup before basketball season began.

Kathy Keene made arrangements for the men's and women's basketball teams to enroll at the University of Texas at Tyler, Texas, where her own family had evacuated. Her brother was a tennis coach at the Division III school, and he had approached the Tyler athletic director, Dr. Howard Patterson, on our behalf. Our student-athletes and coaches could use the university dining facilities, although we would be required to find off-campus housing, which created some problems.

Women's coach Amy Champion's 12 eligible players reported to Tyler, but they had no place to sleep. The on-campus housing we thought would be available for the women's team would not be available for several days. The temporary solution was to set up Red Cross cots in the team locker room. Megan Kassabian, then a freshman forward, recalled that the players did not seem to mind as much as the parents and coaches, especially Champion. After the cots were delivered, the coach gathered her team in the middle of the locker room and told them to put their arms around each other.

"I want you to know that this is not going to be a permanent situation," the coach said, tears welling up in her eyes. "Tomorrow morning we are going out to find you girls another place to live."

She no longer could contain the tears as they streamed down her cheeks, unable to say anything else. The players took turns hugging their coach whose only objective was to keep her team together amid the turmoil.

"Let's pray...." she told the players.

"Coach Champion was always praying," Kassabian recalled. "Thanking God for all the things she was able to do and asking for strength to do the things she feared we could not overcome."

The men's basketball team reported to Tyler with one notable exception. Not surprisingly, the reluctant holdout was Jeremie Davis.

"Jeremie told my coaches there's no way he's coming back to New Orleans," Towe told Ted Lewis of the *Times-Picayune*. "I haven't talked to him myself, but I understand how he feels. That's why I understood that if he needs a little more time to think about what he's going to do, it's fine. We'd love to have him with us here."

Davis told assistant coach Mark Downey he did not want to come back to New Orleans, let alone play basketball for the Privateers. He was angry the coaches didn't do more to account for each player during the evacuation. He did not want to relive the memories of riding out the hurricane, then being passed around like so much flotsam and jetsam. He was back home in Arcadia, Louisiana, and he wanted UNO to release him so he could go play somewhere else.

But Towe would not release him and instead encouraged him to return. Davis felt trapped, like he had been during the storm. But now, he could not expect the U.S. Navy to fly in and save him. He had nowhere to go and nobody to rescue him.

He still believed basketball was his escape, his way to a better life. He was not yet ready to give up on that dream. With that motivating him, Davis relented and reported to Tyler. It was only a little over two hours from Arcadia, so he'd be close to home. If he was lucky, he thought, maybe their stay in Tyler would be longer and he would never have to go back to New Orleans.

CHAPTER
8

Baseball Coach Tom Walter was entering his second season at UNO. His first team was a patchwork of inherited players and summer signees who slogged to a 20-39 record. His second team, however, recruited through the fall of 2004 and spring of 2005, had the promise of a champion. Walter had beaten out local powers LSU and Tulane for some local prospects, including all-state selections second-baseman Johnny Giavotella of Jesuit High School in New Orleans and right-handed pitcher Ryan O'Shea of Mandeville.

At the first team meeting after they reported for school in August, Walter counted 43 players, including walk-ons. After the events of August 29 and the immediate aftermath, 32 made the trip to Las Cruces, New Mexico. Two more players would leave during their exile, and the 30 survivors would start the season.

Walter kept a diary of the events before and after Katrina. The words are his own but they reflect the common thoughts and concerns of all our coaches. Most performed similarly under the pressure of tragedy and the responsibility of caring for a group of young people who looked to them for answers.

Walter's diary reveals emotions and concerns that ranged from doubt to uncertainty to the false sense of relief before the actual effects of the storm were known. He gave ample credit to his wife Kirsten, who chided Walter to cut short a late-night birthday celebration for one of his coaches, to evacuate.

The native Pennsylvanian who attended Georgetown University and coached at George Washington saw in UNO his best chance to get to Omaha and the College World Series. Coaching and recruiting in the South where players were numerous and the weather provided 12 months of opportunity was a proven formula. Walter soon learned that with the advantages also came the perils of coaching baseball in the Gulf South.

8/26 — Friday — Team meeting to discuss Hurricane possibilities. Make sure all players have a plan, have somewhere to go etc ...

8/27 — Saturday — Kirsten is sure we need to go. I am "doubting Thomas." Go out drinking with coaches to celebrate one of their birthdays. Promise Kirsten I'll be home at 2:00 and actually keep promise.

8/28 — Sunday — Kirsten, as usual, is right. We need to go. Fortunately for us Kirsten has packed kids and herself. We're on the road in about 20 minutes and beat most of the traffic out of town. Unfortunately for us, we pack as though we're going on a long weekend. Could have taken much more, though Kirsten had the foresight to grab (social security) cards, birth certificates, some photos … wedding album. Kirsten once again proves to be hell of a lot smarter than me. How the hell she had one hiccup in her life, which led to her saying yes, I'll never know. Officially evacuate with one coach, Kirsten, the kids, and of course, (dog) Bogey, to my sister's in Atlanta. Glued to CNN/MSNBC. Calling all the players to be certain they have safely evacuated.

8/29 — Hurricane comes through, turns at the last minute; eye missed New Orleans. Not in that bad of shape. Thinking at this point we'll be back in New Orleans in a week tops. Trying to get in touch with all the players. Cell phones down. E-mail down. Out-of-State kids we locate by calling via land line.

8/30 — Still watching CNN/MSNBC … still hopeful of a quick return. Still trying to reach some Louisiana-native players.

Walter soon discovered what all of us had learned. His house was about four blocks from ours in the Lakeview section. Despite the realization of the tragedy's magnitude, Walter keeps his sense of humor when it comes to his dog and the importance of his now submerged 7-wood. After the family is safe, his next challenge is to verify the safety of his players.

8/31 — Levee breech, one mile from house. All the water pours directly into our neighborhood. We're screwed. 15-20 feet of water on our block according to chat room reports. Our only hope is that the water didn't reach our upstairs Master Bedroom or the upstairs office. Everything else is submerged. Grandmother's Rosaries and the 7-wood are the irreplaceables that will be missed most. Immediately make plans to fly Kirsten and the kids (and of course, Bogey) to Michigan. Bogey's seat on the plane was more expensive than all the other tickets. Kirsten makes a few phone calls, (son) Chase to start school on Tuesday after Labor Day.

9/1 — For the past three days I have tried frantically to account for all of our players. Cell phones are down, e-mail is down, finally figure out that text messaging is working. Get in touch with all the players. Tell them to go home, it's going to be a while before we figure this out.

9/2 — One coach and myself go to my parents' (house) in Washington DC. Mostly so I can start to head to Michigan, partly because I need a new cell phone. Old number starting to work more and more each day. Will have both numbers at least until January at which point will dump 703 number … after using all my parents' rollover minutes!

9/3 — Begin to explore options of moving entire team to another school. Labor Day weekend so not able to get into touch with many schools. Dealing mostly with coaches I know, looking for help getting to the right person etc …

9/6 — Communicating with players every day. Looks like leading candidates for team relocation are Central Florida (housing issues), Indiana University of Pennsylvania and Shippensburg in PA (kids hate these two choices, mostly because it's cold). Kirsten speaks with Geno (Walter's college roommate Geno Zamorra was on New Mexico Governor Bill Richardson's staff). At Kirsten's suggestion and unbeknownst to me, Geno calls New Mexico State. He knows the president. Of course, his call is not taken.

9/7 — Coincidentally, I am flipping through my cell phone rolodex and see Rocky Ward's phone number (Head Coach of New Mexico State). I tell him what we are looking for; he says he'll call me back. The president takes his call, and they get the deal done. Rocky calls back and says the school is willing to offer free tuition, free housing on campus and use of all athletic facilities, not to mention they have an academic support person who will help us register for classes etc ... New Mexico State wins for a host of reasons: 1. It has "sex appeal." At this point I have to re-recruit each player. Competing schools are contacting our players about transferring. It is a helluva lot easier to sell New Mexico than Pennsylvania or Tennessee. 2. They have Engineering and a business school — all of our players can stay on track for graduation. 3. They have given us academic support. 4. They have given us the best financial package, which makes my AD very happy. 5. Campus housing is walking distance to classes, cafeteria, weight room and Baseball field.

9/8 — Call players and tell them we are going to New Mexico. Reception was terrific. Call Russ Ramsey (GW baseball alum), who lends us his private plane and stocks it with a "goodie sack" for each player — includes boxers, socks, notebooks, pens, calculators, toiletries and power bars to name a few items. We plan a Saturday departure to New Mexico.

9/9 — Good news. Coach Ward tells me they have separate quarters for myself and the other coaches. Was not looking forward to sharing a community bathroom with the players. I will share a small 4-bedroom apartment with one other coach. Each of our spare bedrooms will be an office. For about the 8th straight day I communicate with each player via text and/or phone.

9/10 — Fly from Dulles to Baton Rouge with Russ Ramsey and Coach (Bill) Cilento. Pick up 13 of our players in Baton Rouge. The remainder of the team is flying commercially. We have players from California to Massachusetts. All flights are on time. No less than five TV cameras meet us when we walk off the Private Plane. By 12:45 pm (El Paso, TX time) we are all on the bus on the way to Las Cruces. Again, TV cameras are waiting for us at the dorm room. We are checked in by 2:00 pm and off to Wal-Mart to purchase the necessities. For the players, that means pooling their money to buy as many TV's as possible — 15 of our players are at checkout with a TV. Two random people ask me if there is a sale on TV's they are missing! Later that evening we have a cookout with the Red Cross and a team meeting to go over some ground rules. The bad news is we are about 20 minutes from Juarez, Mexico. Nothing good can happen there; it is banned for the players. The good news is that we have a bunch of good guys, for the most part.

9/11 — Brunch with the Red Cross followed by an Academic meeting to get class schedules etc ... Later that night dinner with Coach Ward's team at Golden Corral. Each of our players rides over with one of NMSU's players, exchange cell numbers etc ... I'm thrilled about how we are being treated. Again TV cameras follow us around. On an entirely different note, every time I write or see the date "9/11" I get a chill. I'm sure it will be that way forever.

9/12 — First day of class. Some juggling to do, but all in all we are pretty close to having them in the right classes. A bunch of equipment companies are donating bats, balls, gloves etc ... we have nothing. Hoping to start team workouts a week from today. I get a call from a Sorority to set up a "mixer." The players have a whole new set of girls to get blown off by. Outside of Kirsten and the kids being 2,000 miles away, life is good.

9/13 — Russ Ramsey had towels, linens, comforters and pillows delivered from Bed, Bath and Beyond to the team. Russ's generosity as well as the hundreds of calls, text messages etc. that I have received amaze me. I love the fact that I am an American, I love the fact that I have a wonderful family, I love the fact that I have awesome friends. I am in awe of everyone's "character." Drive to Geno's to pick up a car that he set up for me. He and wife look great and their new house is beautiful. All in all, I cannot imagine being in a better situation for the team than we are in right now. The people of New Mexico and NMSU have been awesome and have bent over backwards to give us a new home.

After the players had begun their new routine at New Mexico State, Walter instructed each of them to write a journal of their experiences. The coach believed the exercise would help his players confront the tragedy and perhaps provide a catharsis in moving on to the healing stage. Their stories begin a week before the storm and end when they are safely together again in New Mexico. The journals are as disparate as the group of young men from different parts of the country who would share a common bond forever.

Most expressed concerns about lost belongings or girlfriends or spending free time drinking beer and playing video games. But also included were their concerns, their fears and their resilience after being asked to grow up a little bit quicker than normal. Some treated it like a dreaded homework assignment, and other accounts reflect the whimsy and irreverence of youth. But all understood they were being herded through an experience they never sought yet would never forget.

8/26/05 — We met after class and had the team meeting in the new clubhouse. We got our numbers and Coach Walter told us about study hall and then mentioned we might have to evacuate because of a hurricane. A lot of us didn't know what to think about that.

I was very impressed with the clubhouse. It was much nicer than I had anticipated … As I was leaving the clubhouse, I felt good about being at UNO.

8/27/05 — Woke up very early to do physicals. Took way too long because every athlete was there. We started talking more about the hurricane coming … I heard we had to evacuate … Coach (Dennis) Healy called us and told us to go home. Lesyk and I got in my car and drove 12 hours to Shreveport.

I got a call from Coach Walter telling us to evacuate. So I went home, and my parents and I decided to stay … I can remember we had never evacuated for a storm. So that night I went to bed expecting to confront Katrina the following night.

8/28/05 — My brother woke me up at 6:30 and told me to pack my shit. So, I rolled over and turned on the television to see that Katrina's winds were over 175 mph, a Category 5, and now the experts were saying it was headed right at us … This storm was different from the others … the tension was thick.

8/29/05 — Awoke to newscast talking about tornadoes and ridiculous winds coming through … desperately tried to contact all of our friends and family, some of which had stayed behind. It was a difficult day, but it was only the beginning to the worst week of my life.

At that time the worry and sense of helplessness set in. Knowing some of your family is fighting for their lives without being able to help is a horrible thing.

8/30/05 — We are finally getting some radio stations with the news we didn't want to hear … We drove to my brother's house, not knowing if it was even standing. The one-hour ride mixed with dodging trees on the road and the feeling of loss made it seem like four hours.

Sat in front of the TV all day, watching as everything I grew up with was being destroyed. Where are you, Mr. Bush? No comment!

8/31/05 — Levee breaks. All hell breaks loose. Water steadily rises. The unthinkable happens. FEMA has no response. Does not start patching hole. No fleet of choppers. Looting starts. (Mayor Ray) Nagin realizes he doesn't have control. Bush has yet to come to region.

I find out the 17th St Canal was breached, directly by my home in Lakeview. Just when I thought it couldn't be worse, I lost another home. Now, literally everything I had was gone. The house and parish I was raised in and created all my memories is now completely under water. The house I lived in for a year and planned to be in for my senior year was now also completely underwater. Some good news did come … friends were starting to be accounted for. It was understood that everything was gone, but at least our families and friends were all alive.

9/1/05 — Found out about satellite pictures of the city on the Internet. Checked them all out and it confirmed that my house (in Lakeview) and everything was under a sick 10 or 12 feet of water.

Watched the news back and forth …I remember watching idiots run rampant through the city stealing anything in sight.

9/2/05 - 9/5/05 (Labor Day Weekend) — Went to my cousin's house in Baton Rouge where there was electricity. It felt so nice to have air conditioning again and to have a hot meal. We were able to watch cable for the first time.

9/6/05 — Coach called and told me that we would either finish out the semester in Pennsylvania or Florida. It made me happy to know that I would be able to play baseball for UNO and that I would get out of the dump I was living in.

9/8/05 — Thursday, I found out we would be moving to Las Cruces, New Mexico. I really wasn't too happy about it. My first thought was to … stay back. After talking it over with my parents, I decided to go.

Going to New Mexico? What the hell? I was in complete freakin' shock. I was wondering how I was going to adjust, but whatever. Shockingly, my girlfriend actually didn't blow up.

I was excited to go somewhere to start baseball, no matter where it was.

9/10/05 — Woke up bright and early to head to Baton Rouge to catch the plane for New Mexico State. I wondered who would be there and who wouldn't.

We got our tickets and waited for the plane. That was my first time to fly.

9/11/05 — We met with the academic advisor who gave us our schedules. The team ate with the NMSU team at Golden Corral.

Watched the Saints win. Happy to see Saints and Giants win a game.

9/12/05 — First day of class. Had to get schedule changed. Got ID. Ate dinner at caf with all the guys. I like my schedule now.

They are three weeks ahead of us. My schedule seems pretty hard but hopefully I can adjust.

Went to class. Some hot chicks at NMSU!

CHAPTER
9

Three weeks after the storm New Orleans still was shut down. We were settling into our new house in Baton Rouge, which was mostly furnished by the kindness of others. My brother, Jerry, and his friends George and Jeannie Scott, caravanned from Louisville with an overloaded U-Haul trailer pulled by wife Laura's Toyota Highlander and a flatbed trailer behind Jerry's Subaru Outback. The much-appreciated harvest of help included a couch, a kitchen table and four chairs, a desk, mattresses, bed frames, kitchen utensils, two televisions, a DVD player and assorted knick-knacks. Jerry left the Subaru for my use, and the three Samaritans drove back the following day.

Our only look at our ravaged neighborhood had been the occasional news clip until we discovered a web site that allowed the viewer to zoom in from a satellite view. It did not take long to find our house. Water was up to the roof of the neighbor's one-story house, which meant our first floor was surely inundated.

I blamed myself for not bringing my car with us as we evacuated, but I rationalized that insurance would replace it. Also gone were the folders of genealogical research that I had accumulated over the years on the Miller family that were located in my first-floor home office. Luckily, I had transferred much of it to my laptop, which was with me, and Jerry had duplicates of most every document I had.

However, beyond the reach of insurance and rationalization were irreplaceable memories and artifacts located in my home office. My collection of 33-rpm records I had collected since the 1960s were surely gone, as was a binder containing sets of 1958 through 1960 baseball cards that I collected between the ages of 10 and 12.

But the loss of baseball cards and record albums were minor compared to a cache of precious family heirlooms that had been entrusted to me. They included a dictionary that was given to my great-grandfather, also James Miller, on his 21st birthday in 1873. A family Bible dated 1864 that belonged to my great-great-grandfather. Another Bible dated 1891 that belonged to my grandfather. A book of newspaper clippings from the Nineteenth Century collected by my great-grandmother. A lock of blond hair cut from the head of my grandmother's brother, who died as an infant in 1904. All were stored in my first-floor home office in a Rubbermaid tub behind my desk.

Jerry and I have been collecting information for more than 30 years that we intend to use one day to write the history of our family. I frequently would look at the books and other research we had collected and feel proud of my family and their modest achievements. All of it was stored in my office and was now likely gone because I did not take proper precautions.

Stupid, stupid, stupid!

Gary Solomon used his contacts to secure a pass for us to get through the National Guard roadblocks and into the city. New Orleans still was closed to all residents, particularly the hardest-hit areas. Only emergency personnel were allowed inside the sealed-off perimeter, but Gary said the pass would get us through.

Gary's contacts cautioned that anyone returning should wear a surgical mask, non-porous gloves and high boots. The true dangers were not really known yet, but vulnerable ears turned fears and suggestions into rampant rumors of gas leaks, fetid air and snakes nesting in overturned couches. We went to the nearest Home Depot and loaded up with the necessary armor.

Jean and I joined Patricia and Schaffer as we drove down Interstate 10 from Baton Rouge to New Orleans. The area is largely rural until you cross the Bonnet Carre Spillway leading into New Orleans. It was not until we crossed Loyola Drive, the first major street in the western suburb of Kenner, that we began to understand the level of devastation.

Outdoor advertising signs were blown over like twisted pipe cleaners. Entire sides of buildings were blown away. The three-story northern wall of a storage facility was peeled away, revealing cubicles filled with furniture, boxes and clothing exposed and spilling to the ground.

Traffic slowed to the stop-and-creep of a backed-up tollbooth. We did not know how long it would take us to get to the Canal Boulevard exit on the southern border of Lakeview. We made our way past the Veterans, Clearview and Causeway exits and when traffic slowed even more we exited at Bonnabel Avenue. We wove through city streets until we were stopped by a National Guard roadblock at the Metairie Road underpass to Interstate 10.

It was uncomfortable, waiting there to have our passes checked by a young shavetail from Wyoming who was enjoying the first real authority of his life. He looked at our pass, looked back at us, and asked a few questions that my loquacious brother-in-law bluffed his way through. He waved us in.

We drove down City Park Avenue, hoping to turn north onto Canal Boulevard or Marconi Drive, but both were blocked off. We continued to Wisner Boulevard, which bordered the park on the east. City Park, a 1,300-acre recreational Mecca 50% larger than New York's Central Park now was gray and lifeless. Broken trees were leaning against others in an interruption of their death fall. Power lines were hanging in helpless loops that touched the ground. The grass on the park's three golf courses lay flat, covered with a grayish silt. And there were no animals. No squirrels, no turtles in the pools, no birds in flight. City Park was a dead limb on a dying tree.

We turned left at Filmore Avenue and proceeded back westward toward our house at Vicksburg Street. We noticed that all the houses contained large orange X's with numbers written in the quadrants between the painted lines. We learned later the markings represented the morbid National Guard code designating when the building was entered, which unit went in and if any dead bodies were found inside.

We turned left onto our street and saw our house for the first time. From the outside, it looked intact except for the brown water lines that encircled the house, marking the levels as the water dropped. The highest line was at the top of the porch, indicating that about 14 feet of water had engulfed our neighborhood and about nine feet of it had entered our home.

We parked the car and for the first time smelled the scent of devastation. It was a carbon smell, like burning wires, and it would linger in my nostrils for months. We put on the surgical masks to protect us from any unknown contaminants and started to survey our home. The side fence had blown down, and a soffit was hanging loose, suggesting the damaging gusts had come from the south.

We stood there in disbelief and in total silence. No sounds of traffic, no planes flying overhead, no dogs barking, no music coming from open windows. Nothing.

The front door of our house was swollen shut, and we had to push hard to force it open about a foot. I squeezed inside, and was greeted by the dissonant beeping of a half-dozen smoke detector alarms. I looked around, and my first thought was that a grenade had exploded. The hardwood floors had buckled and resembled a mud-encrusted roller-coaster track. The furniture in our dining room to the left was askew, and the beautiful round table for 12 we had purchased only a few months earlier had buckled like a pancake thrown against the wall.

The damage in the living room was similar. Our baby grand piano had flipped upside down and was lying there like a dead armadillo. My entertainment center with the 50-inch plasma TV had been picked up and floated across the room. The floor was covered with six inches of mud, and we had to be careful lest we lose our footing and fall. Curiously, a wooden snack table appeared intact, a dry legal pad and pen still laying on it. Apparently, the table floated up with the rising water and floated back down as it receded.

My home office to the right of the foyer also was a portrait of chaos. A 300-pound butcher block table had floated from the kitchen, 20 feet away, and settled on top of my desk. A tall bookcase had fallen over, throwing years of collected books into the invading water. Behind my desk, my hutch was buckled, although some of my souvenir footballs from the NFL and other memorabilia remained high and salvageable. Among them was my most prized NFL memory, a football bearing the inscription: "Jim, the years together were great. Pete (Rozelle)."

Up the stairs above the waterline, the second floor was just as we had left it. Beds were unmade, kids' clothes were strewn about and school books were on top of desks where they had been dropped on Friday afternoon nearly a month before. The smell inside was worse than outside, and the heat in the enclosed house was stifling. After about 15 minutes none of us could take any more, and we went back outside.

Our house and the neighborhood more resembled photos of Hiroshima or war-torn Baghdad than of what we remembered as our home. We retrieved what was left of some photo albums, then drove off. We were several miles down the road when I realized I had forgotten to check the tub in my office for the family heirlooms. It was just as well, I thought. After what we had seen, I should just forget about them.

We secured another pass and went back a week later, loaded with trash bags, with the intention of salvaging whatever we could. Jean immediately went to the dining room to collect the silverware we seldom used, and I went to my office to see if I could find anything left of the family records. I thought of little else during the week, blaming myself over and over again for being so stupid to leave these valuables in harm's way.

I moved the fallen bookcase away from the desk so I could walk behind and locate the tub that held my treasures. To my surprise, I saw a manila folder on top of the closed lid. It appeared intact and untouched by the water. I immediately thought of the snack table in the living room I saw the week before. Could the tub have floated up as the water rose? I thought it unlikely, because several pounds of books would have weighted the tub down. Wouldn't they?

I picked up the pad, lifted the lid and was stunned. Against all odds and amid all the devastation around it, the Rubbermaid tub had indeed been picked up gently, its rim staying above the water. The tub protected its priceless contents. The Bibles were intact, the dictionary had not been exposed to the water and my great-grandmother's clippings were crisp. Even a forgotten loose-leaf binder that held my 1958-60 NFL football cards also survived in the tub.

I screamed to Jean, who thought I'd been bitten by a cottonmouth. She came running into the room, and I fell to my knees in relief. She put her arms around me as I cried tears of thanks. God had given me back the one material possession I treasured, even while He allowed the replaceable and unimportant "stuff" to be washed away.

We continued our task as urban archeologists elsewhere in the house with different degrees of success. I tried to open my desk drawers to salvage some papers, but they were so swollen shut they would not budge. I would have to bring back an axe and hack my way into the drawers. My books were strewn about, and my record collection was caked together in a mass of soggy album covers. It was a terrible fate for the Beach Boys, the Kinks, the Rolling Stones and the Beatles, my companions of youth whom I had carted around with me for 40 years.

I did retrieve a leather case of CDs but left behind another case of old cassette tapes that lay on the muddy floor. I retrieved a small box with about 25 silver dollars and some other coins, along with some knickknacks, including a Hopalong Cassidy drinking mug that I'd had since I was a baby.

Meanwhile, Jean collected her silver from a dining room cabinet, and we broke down our bedroom door to retrieve the jewelry she had left in a drawer. Luckily, it was still there in a lambskin bag. I retrieved my grandfather's railroad watch, now rusty and useless, from my closet and a loose-leaf notebook of plastic sleeves that held my baseball card collection from the late 1950s. The cards had been submerged, but I hoped to dry them out and save them. I grabbed a couple of caps that were untouched on a high shelf, but the rest of my wardrobe was wet and putrid.

I wanted to see my car before we left, so I climbed over the fallen side fence to get to the garage. I forced the side door open, and I didn't know whether to laugh or cry at the sight. Our spare refrigerator had floated up and sat atop my car, at an angle between the hood and the roof. The windows of the car had rolled down and the seats had gone flat, which is an anti-drowning feature I did not realize it had. I was proud. She went down fighting!

I tried to retrieve the registration out of the glove compartment, but it was a sodden mess. The trunk also had opened when the water rose, and I pulled out my rancid golf bag, emptied the clubs and was pleased to find them fairly intact. Callaway should trumpet the fact that the graphite shafts on their Big Bertha clubs can withstand a natural disaster! I put the clubs in a garbage bag and took them to the car.

My senior staff still was, literally, all over the map. My associate AD, Mike Bujol, was with his brother in Dallas. Kathy Keene had settled in Tyler, Texas, with her brother's family, while John Barranco, our assistant AD for sales and marketing, was in Birmingham, Alabama, with his parents. Mike Dauenhauer, our business manager, was the only staff member whose house was not damaged. He was home in Marrero, Louisiana, on the west bank of the Mississippi River, no doubt in front of his computer.

We tried hard to create a routine that would reflect some semblance of normalcy. Kathy would monitor the basketball teams and their class work. Mike B. would stay in contact with the rest of the teams. Mike D. would monitor the financial aspects, particularly how we would compensate the other institutions that hosted our students.

Barranco came up with an idea to go on a fund-raising tour with his staff. The father of his marketing assistant was a Cajun cook, and they created a "Get New Orleans Cookin' Again" fund drive. John received permission from several Southeastern Conference schools to set up a tent in prominent tailgate areas of their football stadiums during games to dole out cups of jambalaya in return for donations.

We also began to receive offers of help from other institutions. The University of Kansas offered us $80,000 to bring our men's basketball team up for a game. Southern California, where former UNO Coach Tim Floyd was head coach, sent us a check for

$40,000. Monte Towe's friends sent in several thousand dollars to help his program. Other smaller donations came in as the collegiate community began to rally around a wounded comrade.

Over the months of October and November, I went on tour and visited with each of our teams. My message was to update and re-assure them that Chancellor Ryan's intention was to have the campus open by the spring semester.

Aside from the logistical messages, I also wanted them to know that they were doing something that no other NCAA institution ever had done. They were enduring an extended school-year disruption forced by a natural disaster.

We adopted a slogan "We Will Endure," that we put on hats and t-shirts and sold on the website. We believed we would get through it, although the instruction manual on how was yet to be written.

I was meeting daily with Tim Ryan about the condition of our facilities and the status of our teams. Lakefront Arena suffered similar physical damage as that of the Louisiana Superdome, its fabric roof peeled back, and water damaged much of the interior. It would be closed indefinitely. Fortunately, several months before Katrina, Ryan had agreed to put a new floor into the old Human Performance Center gym, to become the home of UNO Volleyball. The gym was the first basketball facility on the campus, but the floor had not been replaced since the building opened in 1968. The old floor had been removed prior to Katrina, and since water did not get into the building Ryan authorized the project to resume. That enabled us to open an on-campus playing venue for Sun Belt Conference games, which began in January.

Ryan also approved nearly $300,000 for the resurfacing of Maestri Field at Privateer Park, the baseball field which had been heavily damaged in the storm. Constructing began in December, with the hope of completion for the opening game in February. Light poles were knocked down, so day games would be required, but at least we would have baseball games on campus, another sign of normalcy that Ryan wanted desperately to restore.

Despite the positive signs and Ryan's efforts, enrollment largely would dictate what our program would be able to do going forward. Our operating budget in 2005-06 was $4.1 million plus another $850,000 in other institutional support such as out of state tuition waivers and payment of certain staff salaries. About 75% of the $4.1 million came from a dedicated student athletics fee that cost each full-time student $100 per semester.

Spring enrollment was expected to drop precipitously from the fall number of 17,250, which made it a certainly that the entire university, including athletics, would be forced to downsize. The university restored Internet classes by October, and more than 7,000 students registered, which was an encouraging sign. But the mystery remained of how many would re-enroll for the spring semester.

The week before Christmas, Ryan confirmed that a massive budget cut for the

2006-07 academic year would be imposed in the spring. In preparation, he instructed all department heads to prepare options on downsizing every administrative unit on campus. It would not be a pleasant exercise, but we all realized these decisions had to be made if the university was to survive.

Still, it was not like trading baseball cards. We were dealing with the lives of people who had endured great hardship. Most had lost their homes and possessions, and now they would lose the one vehicle they needed to build back, their job.

They all deserved better.

CHAPTER
10

Two pieces of good news made it easy to leave Baton Rouge and return to New Orleans. On October 10, Ryan moved the university's offices from the LSU System office to the Jefferson Center, a building the university owned in Metairie. Also, our children's old school, St. Dominic, reopened at the unoccupied Holy Rosary School building on Esplanade Avenue.

Those two bits of progress meant that after our first — and last — Christmas in Baton Rouge, the Millers would be moving back to New Orleans. We gutted our house on Vicksburg Street, and it passed the tests for structural soundness and mold remediation. Our insurance money was starting to trickle in, and we began talking with a builder. However, we found ourselves at a critical crossroad, and we were not sure which fork to take.

Should we rebuild our house or sell the gutted property and move to a less vulnerable location? It was tempting to leave behind this wounded structure that symbolized such pain and disruption. A lot of our neighbors were selling their properties and moving to safer havens such as Mandeville across the lake or into Metairie. But this was a time when our city needed its citizens to restore their neighborhoods and in doing so help New Orleans recover. Damn the torpedoes! We started rebuilding with gusto.

Before the storm, Lakeview was the most convenient community in New Orleans, where you could get anywhere in town inside 20 minutes. And it would be again. The university was eight minutes away, the kids' school was three blocks and Jean's family lived within 10 minutes of each other. We also believed the lessons taught by Katrina would result in a safer, stronger infrastructure that could better withstand future hurricanes.

While our house was being renovated, Jean's mother Gloria offered to let us move in with her again, as she had done before when I was between jobs. Her home, near UNO in the Lake Terrace section of New Orleans, was two blocks from Lake Pontchartrain and did not experience any rising water.

Patricia and Schaffer's house was only slightly damaged, so they, too, were ready to return. Gloria and Saint lost their townhouse and were looking for a rental while they decided what to do long term. Gary and Martha were content to remain in Baton Rouge for the time being, near Gary's sisters and his father and mother.

Things were starting to look up. The refugees were returning to the city, and whatever was ahead, the "new normal" would be a welcome relief over our "refugee camp" in Baton Rouge.

Christmas was a difficult time for many of our student-athletes, displaced and belea- guered with uncertainty. The preceding four months had been filled with unprec- edented upheaval, and the future held no guarantees when it would get any better. The overriding question on the lips of most student-athletes and their parents: *Do we go back to New Orleans for the spring semester or transfer to another school in a more stable environment?*

The women's basketball team adopted the phrase "The Katrina Curse" to explain everything that seemed to go wrong, particularly with their team. After winning two of their first three games, they lost seven in a row. One player already had quit, and two more did not return after Christmas break. Aside from basketball, they had doubts about coming back to New Orleans and what they would find if they did. The grow- ing concern of returning to a ravaged campus in a dangerous city eclipsed all concerns about basketball.

With little enthusiasm, nine players and their coaches reluctantly traveled to a holi- day tournament at the University of Montana in Missoula. The trip had been scheduled nearly a year before, when a tournament in a location most students had never seen sounded like fun. But recent events had turned the trip into a 4,400-mile, four-day forced march that had lost its luster.

Predictably, the Lady Privateers started the tournament meekly, losing to the host Lady Grizzlies 79 to 43. They were to play South Dakota State the following night in the consolation game. But before that game, the Montana administration arranged for a tribute. Before the tip, the team members and coaching staff were called to center court.

The players stood there wearing their royal blue and silver uniforms with "New Orleans" written across their chest as the public address announcer recounted the rutty road the team had traveled to get there.

After hearing what the coaches and players had endured the past few months, every fan in the sold out Dahlberg Arena rose and gave the Lady Privateers a hearty ovation. Tears fell from the eyes of every player, coach and not a few fans. Without knowing the team members, the fans showed their appreciation for what the women had been through and gave them encouragement to continue the fight.

"Looking back on that night, to me it meant a sign of survival," Megan Kassabian, a freshman forward, would write later. "Somewhere between the first of December and that tournament, we had forgotten why we were still playing. The team members felt they had lost faith. But it was evident the (Montana fans) had not. Our faith was merely overshadowed by a series of unfortunate events. We had to maintain our path of faith, and after that night, faith was restored in our hearts for good."

The repatriation of our student-athletes to New Orleans was the modern day equiv- alent of a medieval voyage into uncharted waters. Columbus or Vespucci certainly had questions about what lay ahead of them, but they did not have to deal with concerned parents who were unconvinced that our destination was a safe one.

One parent wrote a long letter addressed to Tim Ryan and me repeating every sensationalized concern that CNN and the national media were perpetuating. Crime was rampant, the air quality was poor, the dormitories were full of toxic mold, medical care was unavailable and the nearest basic services such as food, drug stores and gas stations were five miles away in Metairie. Some degree of truth existed to all of the concerns, but it was nowhere near the crisis level the national media portrayed. The old axiom of not letting facts get in the way of a good story was alive and well at certain news organizations.

This perception became reality for many parents, and some student-athletes did not return. Women's basketball eventually lost four of their 12 scholarship athletes, including a highly rated transfer from Mississippi State who was leading the team in scoring and rebounding. Two members of the baseball team who had spent the fall semester at New Mexico State chose to transfer, adding to the 11 who decided not to make the trip in the first place. And, most of the men's and women's international tennis team members who had returned to their home countries in the wake of Katrina never returned.

Sadly, the grimy world of college athletics recruiting presented even more repulsive examples of one person's tragedy becoming another person's opportunity. Several schools began contacting our better athletes, encouraging them to transfer. The rumor that UNO athletics was dead or dying traveled quickly, and the vultures started circling to pick our bones. UNO's athletics program was going to shut down, they said, or New Orleans was unsafe or why wouldn't you come to our school where you would be free from all the distractions? They were compelling arguments, logical in the midst of our uncertainty.

A handful of our athletes were prime targets. Therese Nilsson, a prize recruit from Sweden and No. 1 player on our women's golf team, heard the arguments and transferred to Lamar University, where she would become the Southland Conference champion. Bo McCalebb, the star of our men's basketball team, was being recruited heavily by coaches who contacted his mother, Tara. Monte Towe did a good job of re-recruiting Bo, which was facilitated by the fact that McCalebb broke his wrist in the fourth game and was out for the season.

Convincing the majority of student-athletes to return was the first step, but just as challenging was what to do with them when they returned. The Privateer Place apartment complex where most of the student-athletes lived was heavily damaged by wind, rain and looters, but another issue delayed its reopening even further. The loss of service insurance held by Century Campus Housing, owners of the complex, provided full fare reimbursements as long as they were closed. Why open up and encounter all the aggravations of being in business if they could make the same money with less aggravation? With Privateer Place closed while that debate dragged on, the university elected to renovate an aging dormitory named Bienville Hall that was scheduled to be taken out of service. The bottom floors of the dormitory sustained some damage, but the top floors could be brought into use fairly quickly.

It would not be quickly enough for the start of the spring semester, so a stop-gap measure had to be found. Our students normally reported back ahead of the remainder of the student body in order to prepare for the spring seasons of baseball, tennis, golf and track-and-field.

Kathy Keene spearheaded the housing search, along with help from Mike Bujol, John Barranco and fund-raiser Kathleen Gross. Shortly after Katrina, Kathy instructed the coaches to file for FEMA assistance and to have their students do the same. That move was prescient. Much of the available housing in New Orleans was occupied by FEMA workers and others associated with the recovery. We were able to find housing only because our coaches and students all had FEMA numbers, identifying them as evacuees who had been displaced by the storm.

Though available, the housing would not be free, and we had to make certain the university was in concert with our plan. Tim Ryan instructed us to proceed, based on assurances he had received from the state and FEMA that such costs would be reimbursed.

Barranco was an aggressive salesman who could convince you the campfire scene from the movie *Blazing Saddles* was a wind ensemble. He used his power of persuasion with his hotel contacts to identify an adequate number of rooms for our students. Keene and my administrative assistant, Susan Broussard, took over the laborious task of matching up our students and coaches who needed rooms to the available housing.

Our students and coaches split time between the Monteleone Hotel in the French Quarter and the Galleria Hotel in Metairie for at least a month, until Bienville Hall was ready. At the same time, a caravan of FEMA trailers began arriving for use by displaced residents. About 1,000 trailers were brought onto campus and set up on six soccer fields and a parking lot north of Lakefront Arena. Any one of us who had filed for FEMA numbers were eligible for the free housing, although only our golf coach, Chris McCarter, took advantage. McCarter, who has a wry sense of humor, boasted that his compact FEMA trailer was the epitome of convenience. He could lie in bed and watch television, grab a beer from the refrigerator and take a leak, all without leaving the bed.

We proceeded into the spring semester with some amount of trepidation. We were instructed to continue business as usual, but I was struggling with Ryan's directive to give him options on downsizing the department.

Enrollment on the first day of the fall 2005 semester had been 17,250. A week later, nobody knew how many of those students would return when the campus reopened. The more defections UNO had, the less revenue the university would have to support its programs. It was obvious the university was faced with a significant downsizing, but the extent of it would depend on how many students came back.

The LSU System office ordered the university to prepare a request for a declaration of financial exigency, which is the most drastic action a university can take to preserve its academic integrity and mission. Financial exigency, which is not unlike declaring bankruptcy, would allow the university to reallocate available resources and make extreme decisions to fit the circumstances, including such radical measures as elimination of colleges and academic programs and termination of personnel. A realistic projection of enrollment was the first step in the process.

Ryan and his chief academic officers, Provost Rick Barton and assistant director of academic affairs Scott Whittenburg, met with admissions director Ron Maggiore to estimate how many students would return. Ryan's expectation was optimistic, at 15,500, which he had calculated based on a formula of multipliers he used throughout his career as an economist. That number was not shared by his subordinates, who put the estimate at no more than 13,000.

In a budget meeting that included other deans and vice chancellors, Ryan reluctantly compromised and told the participants he would accept a projection of 14,600. However, after the meeting, Ryan, convinced he was right, instructed Linda Robison, the university's chief financial officer, to put the estimate back at 15,500 upon which the current and subsequent years' budgets would be based.

That decision would prove costly, as enrollment never topped 12,000 in the ensuing years. Ryan's estimate provided an artificial expectation of revenue that would never materialize and would saddle the university with programs it would not be able to pay for. The result was that future expenses far exceeded revenues, a condition that would haunt and eventually doom many units on campus in the ensuing years.

For the Department of Intercollegiate Athletics, the practical effect of the downsizing was the certain suspension of sports, the firing of coaches and the elimination of scholarships. Thanks to Mike Dauenhauer, the athletics business manager, we had no fat in our budget, which made it all the more difficult to find areas we could cut painlessly.

It's not an easy task to play God with people's lives, but that is exactly what the project entailed. Which of my staff or coaches would I be forced to terminate? Which student-athletes would hear the news that, despite our recruitment and all the glowing promises we'd made about the University of New Orleans, we are going to pull your scholarship?

After all we had been through, to subject our survivors to such a choice was not easy. I had to separate the logic from the emotion and make hard decisions on which coaches, staff and student-athletes could stay and which ones would be shoveled to the curb like so much storm rubble. Who could best help us move forward, and who were, for all intents and purposes, expendable?

I submitted three options for downsizing the athletics department to Ryan on January 6, 2006. Each option included the elimination of the track and field program, which I estimated would save $427,577. Track and field is a high expense, low revenue sport, but has the benefit of counting as six sports — indoor track, outdoor track and cross country for both men and women. We funded the NCAA maximum equivalent of 18 full scholarships for women and 10.5 (of a maximum allowable 12.6) for men. In addition, the contract of our head coach, Willie Randolph, would expire on June 30, 2006, which reduced liability beyond the current fiscal year.

Track and field also was our only team sport without an on-campus facility. Our home track was the municipal Tad Gormley Stadium, an aging venue built in 1937. The field and restrooms sustained major damage from Katrina and its availability would be unknown for some time. Track and Field was a logical elimination, but it would be an emotional one. Willie was the first head coach I hired after taking the job in 2003, and his sister lived in New Orleans. Willie was a role model and a mentor to a young nephew, and I did not relish a decision that would disrupt his family.

Option 2 also would eliminate men's golf, one full-time administrative position, both managers in men's and women's basketball and would reduce tennis scholarships by three, at a total savings of $623,990. My rationale was that trimming additional staff would not directly impact our ability to generate revenue, and reducing three scholarships in tennis would not affect our ability to field the sport.

Option 3 also would suspend women's swimming and women's golf, for a total savings of $853,333. None of the sports included on the lists were revenue producers. In addition, swimming would cost us more each year as we added scholarships from the current four toward the NCAA maximum of 14. On the flip side, swimming was our newest sport and an important component of our Gender Equity plan. Its athletes were self-starters and motivated toward academics, and the sport had the potential to become a revenue producer. Not many programs have an Olympic champion on staff, and Ashley Tappin gave our program national and international recognition.

As we waited to see what kind of budget we would have for 2006-07, a partial solution came from the unsettled condition of our tennis program. Head Coach Burzis Kanga, who evacuated to New Jersey to be with his ailing father, had been unable to persuade the bulk of his athletes to return to school in the spring. Most of his players were international, and the majority of them returned to their home countries after Katrina struck.

In late December, Burzis called to inform me he was resigning. The news was not shocking, but it was disappointing. After Randolph, Kanga was the next coach I had hired after taking the job in 2003. He was a UNO graduate and was the best tennis player in university history.

Other than his father's health, Burzis had another reason for his decision. His long-time companion, NBC personality Hoda Kotb, was pressuring him to remain in the New York area. Hoda had given Burzis an ultimatum: Either stay in New York and we get married or go back to New Orleans and our relationship is over. Kanga had met Hoda when she was a news anchor for WWL-TV in New Orleans and he was the head tennis pro at Chateau Country Club in suburban Kenner.

Kanga, who was born in Tanzania, was a dead ringer for a young Omar Sharif. He was a strikingly handsome man whose ready smile melted the hearts of many New Orleans women, but Hoda had snared him.

What seemed like every man's dream — having a beautiful, wealthy wife who did not care if you worked or not — was not what Kanga wanted. After a stellar collegiate career at UNO, he had worked hard to make it on the pro tennis circuit. When that dream ended he came back to New Orleans to teach the game. He enjoyed the affluent country club set, but he also had worked hard for what he achieved and was proud of his work ethic. Despite the benefits that Hoda offered, Kanga did not relish the idea of becoming a "kept man."

The question he could not answer was why go back to New Orleans? Katrina had heavily damaged his condominium in the tony West End section. He had no team left since most of his student-athletes had defected. The questions about the viability of the university and athletic department were far from resolution.

In the final analysis, there was not much of a choice to be made. The practical considerations persuaded Kanga to remain in New York, and he and Hoda set a wedding date.

The news was especially disappointing since I had spent much of the previous year perfecting a contract with an investor group to build a 26-court tennis facility at UNO. The lead investor was Rob Couhig, an attorney and former owner of the New Orleans Zephyrs AAA minor league baseball team. The Zephyrs had used the UNO baseball field when the franchise moved from Denver in 1993, and Couhig had a history of supporting the university.

After nearly a year of wrangling with the LSU System office to allow us to initiate the project, construction finally had begun in mid-August. The land, adjacent to Lakefront Arena, was cleared and two hard courts had been laid when Katrina struck. Nobody would have faulted Couhig if he had bailed out of the project at that point, but, to his credit, he saw it through. The University Tennis Center was the first major construction project in New Orleans to be completed after Katrina.

So we had a new 26-court tennis facility and no coach or teams. I believed we still had time to recruit, so I launched a search for a new head coach. I hired Tom Hand, a former assistant at Tulane, but after a short time on the job, he came to me and said recruiting had been far more difficult than he first thought. Recruits and their parents were afraid of New Orleans, and he could not persuade young tennis prospects to come. At that point, I made the decision to suspend the tennis season, and so informed our scheduled opponents in a letter.

I told Hand to continue to try and build a team for the 2006-07 academic year, but after a couple of months, he resigned. I was selfishly upset that Kanga had not persuaded his players to stay, and I was equally upset Hand was unable to fill the gap. But it partially resolved one of my problems. Men's and women's tennis went to the top of the list of sports I would suspend. The decision was all business, with little emotion attached. I would revise my options and wait for Tim Ryan to tell me how much I had to cut.

Meanwhile, the student-athletes who were competing were doing their best to lift our spirits. In the first athletic event in New Orleans since Katrina, our men's basketball team nipped cross-town rival Tulane 50-49 on New Year's Eve. Wayne Williams, who with Jeremie Davis, had spent a frightful few days riding out Katrina, scored the final four points of the game, including two free throws with seconds remaining, to assure the victory.

The game was played before 1,064 fans at the Alario Center, located across the Mississippi River in Marrero. Work had not yet begun on Lakefront Arena and renovation would not be completed on the old on-campus gym until the first Sun Belt Conference home game on January 12. It was worth the wait, however, as the Privateers defeated Troy 79 to 75 behind Williams's 26 points.

The glow of victory was a lonely sliver of light in an otherwise darkened community. No traffic signals worked and blocks upon blocks of housing between the university and Interstate 610, four miles to the south, were uninhabited. The closest gas stations or restaurants were five miles away in Metairie. Night travel in the Gentilly area near the lakefront was dangerous, which made even the modest attendance of 627 an encouraging sign. Nobody knew how many people would take time off from their own problems to attend a basketball game.

The opening of an on-campus athletic facility was a positive step toward recovery, but it was soon offset by more bad news. Williams, who had blossomed into the Privateers' leading scorer after Bo McCalebb was lost for the season, quit the team on January 20 and withdrew from school. Williams was averaging nearly 19 points per game, but he scored only 5 points in limited minutes in a 61 to 52 home loss to Florida International. The next day he told Head Coach Towe he was quitting.

Towe, who was going through the most difficult season of his coaching career, was stoic about this latest setback.

Said Towe: "I think he just couldn't take everything anymore."

Towe had few options in deciding who would take Williams's place in the starting lineup. Jeremie Davis had been a disciplinary problem since he had rejoined the team, and he had scored only 28 points over 16 games. Still, Davis's teammates marveled during practice at the accuracy of his long range jumper.

Towe had no choice. Williams's roommate and fellow Katrina refugee, Jeremie Davis, was moved into the starting lineup.

CHAPTER
11

Barely five months after Katrina, on February 2, I received a telephone call from my next-door neighbor, Jay Sequeira. Jay was a native Nicaraguan who had spent most of his adult life in the United States and had graduated from the UNO College of Business. His son Brandon and our son Charles Connor were the same age and best friends.

"Jim, you'd better come over to your house," Jay said, sounding grave. The builders had started renovating our house, and my first thought was a construction accident or even looters. I did not expect the bad news Jay called to deliver.

"We had a tornado come through here early this morning, and it hit your house."

I couldn't believe my ears. I was stunned with a thousand images racing through my head. *We get ravaged by Katrina, and now a flipping* tornado? *New Orleans doesn't even get tornadoes!* I told Jay I would be right over.

I did not know what to expect, but as I made the eight-minute drive from my mother-in-law's house I saw the damage. A tornado had hopscotched up Canal Boulevard and onto Robert E. Lee, shearing off the outside walls of one house, then skipping several before dropping down to take the roof off another. Two houses a block apart appeared as though they had exploded, with nothing but rubble piled onto the foundation. As I turned onto Vicksburg Street, I could see the right dormer of our house partially blown away. I parked and saw slight damage to the middle dormer and a six-foot-square swatch of shingles stripped away. All four front windows had been blown back into the house.

Our damage was mild compared to some, but it wasn't the extent of damage that hit me. It was the fact we were again victimized by another natural disaster. Most people go their entire lives never being abused by an "act of God," and now we had been whacked twice within five months! I sat down on our front steps and put my head in my hands. I wasn't going to let another tear fall over our troubles, but I needed to talk to somebody. I pulled out my cell phone and called my father.

"Dad, I just can't take any more," I told him in a voice cracking with utter exasperation. "All this that's happened to us is just too much."

My father had been concerned about us since the storm, and I tried to show him a brave front that we were getting through it. But it's always been difficult for me to lie to my father, and he sensed it. He tried to comfort me, although I felt guilty sharing my burden with him. He had just turned 84, and his health had been reasonably good since my mother passed away in 2002. But sitting on the steps talking to my father I felt like it was 50 years ago. I was an eight-year-old kid desperately wanting him to put his arm around me and make it better. I hated feeling sorry for myself, but the things we were experiencing had a good start on equaling the Seven Plagues of Egypt.

I thanked my father for his soothing words and called Jean to give her the bad news. She was typically stoic, which gave me some comfort. We talked a while, and I came to one conclusion. If nothing else, we had just improved our odds against being flattened by a meteor.

The women's basketball team played its final game March 2 in the opening round of the Sun Belt Conference tournament in Murfreesboro, Tennessee. Defections and injuries, which the players attributed to "the Katrina Curse," had reduced the roster to seven available players. The 69 to 46 loss to Florida International was not unexpected, and it ended their season with a record of 3-25.

After the final buzzer, the team shuffled back to the dressing room and sat in front of their lockers, heads down and the disappointment suffocating. It was a season that at times seemed would never end.

Head Coach Amy Champion burst through the door, head high and shoulders pulled back.

"Everyone gather around," she said looking at her players. "Ya'll fought hard tonight. To be honest with you, girls, after Hurricane Katrina I had a lot of schools offer me coaching jobs, but I am right where I want to be. I would not trade a single one of you for anything. And even though the scoreboard may not represent it, you are true winners. You had a chance to give up this season, but you kept working, you kept fighting."

Champion's voice began to crack as she held back the tears. "And I am so proud to have each and every one of you on my team." She took another long pause this time allowing the tears to fall before she commenced her game-ending tradition of reciting the Lord's Prayer. "Let's pray. Our Father…"

Their Katrina Season finally had come to an end. It was time for a new start, a chance at a new year and a new beginning. But I soon would get the news I had dreaded. Would the new beginning signal the beginning of the end?

In early April, the Office of Financial Services informed Mike Dauenhauer that we would be required to cut approximately $800,000 from our 2006-07 budget. That was worse than I had expected, and I immediately went back to the worksheets to modify my earlier Option 3. Suspending the Track and Field program was a given, as was men's and women's tennis. That totaled eight sports, but it did not get us to $800,000. Our only options were to also suspend men's or women's golf or women's swimming.

My first consideration had to be revenue potential. Golf did not provide any revenue upside. You don't charge for admission, it's a relatively small number of athletes and it costs money to rent time at a golf course. On the other hand, I believed swimming would reflect well on our program. Our UNO Aquatic Center in Lakefront Arena was a first class venue that eventually would be restored. We could charge for admission to meets, and we could sell concessions. Swim teams are large, and are expensive to maintain, but swimmers are self-motivated student-athletes whose parents support the program.

The teams that were safe were men's and women's basketball, women's volleyball and baseball. If women's swimming was preserved, that made three women's sports and two men's sports. That left the decision to suspend either men's or women's golf. Keeping men's golf would even it up at three each, and our men's golf team had become one of the top in the Sun Belt Conference. Chris McCarter, although officially an assistant coach to Jimmy Headrick, had done an outstanding job and deserved consideration. Reluctantly, I decided that women's golf would join track and tennis on the chopping block.

The decision portended an especially emotional meeting. Headrick, who supervised the women's team, had been head golf coach for several years and I had known him through the golfing community before I came to UNO. We also shared the personal tragedy of Katrina. Headrick lost his home in Slidell, and he was going through much of the same problems that many New Orleans residents were trying to fight through. More importantly, Headrick had lost a son several years earlier, and he established the Colin Headrick Foundation in his memory. He was a good man who did not deserve what I was forced to do to him. I was going to take his job away, compounding his problems. It was impossible in the post-Katrina world to make business decisions without suffering the collateral damage.

I submitted the plan to Tim Ryan, and then we waited.

On April 25, the first draft of the university's emergency plan for downsizing leaked out of the chancellor's office. It was inadvertent, one of those innocent things that happens when too many people have the information and are trusted to maintain confidentiality. Whoever said, "When more than one person knows a secret, it's no longer a secret," was correct.

The document was expected, but devastating in many ways. Departments were named that were to be eliminated, and positions were identified. While no individuals were listed, it was not difficult to figure out who was gone and who escaped. The document that would remodel the post-Katrina university was out:

> In the aftermath of Hurricane Katrina, the University of New Orleans suffered revenue reversals in both state funding and self-generated revenues. Declining state revenues resulted in statewide cuts to higher educa-

tion. State appropriation to UNO was reduced by $6.47 million, the largest cut administered to any institution in the state. In addition, the physical damages to the Greater New Orleans area and the massive loss of housing resulted in a significant dislocation of population. Pre-Katrina, UNO's fall 2005 enrollment was 17,250; after reopening on October 10th (the only New Orleans university to do so) 7,000 students registered for classes at the Jefferson Center campus, four other satellite locations and online. UNO was able to return to its lakefront campus for the spring 2006 semester. Historically, UNO has taught approximately 16,000 students in spring terms. In spring 2006, however, the enrollment was only 11,600 (73%). Due to the enrollment decline, lost self-generated revenues exceeded $33 million, bringing the total budgetary shortfall to nearly $45 million and requiring sundry economies and extensive federal assistance to bring the 2005-2006 budget into balance.

As the university moves into 2006-2007, it remains in a financially exigent situation, and as such, the LSU Board of Supervisors officially declared UNO in a state of financial exigency at its April 21 meeting. Enrollment analysis indicates that student headcount for fall 2006 is unlikely to exceed 14,500. Assuming the state budget allocation is not restored to its pre-storm levels, the combined self-generated revenue losses of between $8.9 million and $12.1 million (due to projected enrollment decline) leave UNO's general fund with a shortfall of between $15.3 million and $18.5 million, a reduction of between 12% and 14%. This is not a sum that can be cut from the UNO budget by eliminating vacant positions and reducing operating expenditures. The entire university must be resized.

The document further listed the policies and procedures for furloughs and terminations and informed those affected how they would receive notice of their future. Human Resources would work with affected employees to assist them with such things as retirement, insurance, alternative employment and other issues. All of the above was prelude to the chilling reality to come, the listing of who and what would be terminated.

Athletics was mentioned as a department that was downsizing by eliminating sports. Not specifically mentioned in the document was the termination of a number of tenured faculty positions, a rare practice in academe. Although it was a courageous decision and correct under the rules of financial exigency, terminating tenured faculty was a decision that would haunt Ryan and even threaten the existence of the athletics department three years later.

The final section of the document gave some of the terminated units hope that some of the cuts could be restored under certain conditions:

If UNO gains access to additional, unanticipated revenues prior to or, where applicable, during the fiscal year of 2006-2007, the university will attempt to address critical needs such as faculty and staff raises, the re-placement of equipment damaged or destroyed by Hurricane Katrina or the subsequent mold infestation of some of our buildings, research support through the funding of graduate assistant positions, downsized administra-tive support and yawning capital needs including $111.4 million in deferred maintenance.

If unanticipated continuing revenues emerge through an increase (or restoration) of state funding prior to the beginning of the fiscal year 2006-2007, the university will seek to restore the cuts described above...

The priority listing gave the athletics department no reason for optimism. The three groupings were listed as "high," "medium," and "low" priority. The "high" priority group listed 15 reductions or cuts that would first be considered if new money were found, including "Reduce Academic Support Funding," "Downsizing in Campus Ser-vices" and "Reduced Instruction in Computer Science." The "medium" group included 13 items, including "Classical Music Concentration" and "Reduced Instruction in Ital-ian."

The "Low" priority group, which had virtually no chance of having anything re-stored listed 12 reductions or cuts. No. 12 was "Downsizing in Athletics."

At least we had made the list.

The most distasteful part of the downsizing was informing the coaches, five staff members and the student-athletes who were directly affected. I sat down with Wil-lie Randolph and Jimmy Headrick to inform them of the decision, as well as Ken Tra-han, an assistant AD for campus relations and our radio play-by-play man. I told each they would be paid through June 30 and that I would help them any way I could with referrals or phone calls. It was not much consolation, especially for Headrick who was disappointed I would choose to let him go while keeping his assistant, Chris McCarter, the men's coach.

I wasn't worried about Randolph, who was a good young coach and soon landed an assistant's job at the University of Louisville. Trahan was a journeyman newsman in New Orleans who was a survivor in an insecure media market but always seemed to land on his feet.

I asked my chief assistants Mike Bujol and Kathy Keene to meet with the teams. Mike was a veteran administrator who had been at the university as a student and mem-ber of the department for nearly 25 years. Kathy had the NCAA knowledge regarding transfer procedures and knew the student-athletes better than anyone else in the depart-ment. A piece of positive news was that Ryan had agreed to allow any student-athlete who was at least 50% through their degree requirements to remain on scholarship until graduation.

Members of the women's golf team took the news well. Two juniors elected to stay at the university and finish their degrees, while the younger members of the team quickly found other schools ready to offer scholarships. Two members of the tennis team also elected to stay and complete their degrees.

Members of the track and field team did not take the news gracefully. Mike and Kathy almost were assaulted by some members of the women's team who could not understand the decision to terminate their sport when other sports were saved. In retrospect, I should have been there to take the criticism along with Mike and Kathy. I probably would not have said anything differently, but at least they would have had the chance to vent at the guy who made the decision. I apologized to Mike and Kathy and never again asked anybody else to take a bullet meant for me.

Part II
Rebuilding

CHAPTER
12

A few days after the downsizing plan leaked, Sun Belt Conference Commissioner Wright Waters called with an interesting offer. He knew our present state was precarious and our future filled with doubt. If we were willing and the chancellor agreed, the conference would be willing to underwrite a strategic plan for athletics, conducted and written by an impartial, outside group.

Wright had spoken with Bill Carr, the former Florida athletic director who operated one of the premier college athletic consulting and job placement agencies in America. Wright had brought Carr up to speed on our situation, and Carr was eager to help us plot our future. I told Wright I had spoken with Carr once before. Three years earlier and prior to my taking the UNO job, Carr led the search for a new athletic director at Kentucky, and I had applied. I had appreciated his bedside manner in telling me obliquely I wasn't qualified at the time to be an athletic director in the Southeastern Conference and didn't have a chance at the job.

With the Sun Belt Conference office located in New Orleans, Wright had an up-close view of the UNO situation over the years. As commissioner, he had more than a rooting interest that UNO have a successful program. I knew this even before I applied for the job, which is why the only two people outside of UNO whose opinions I solicited were former AD Ron Maestri and Waters.

After I took the job anyway, Wright always lent a sympathetic ear, both as a commissioner and at times when he offered to "let me take off the commissioner's hat and talk to you friend to friend." Wright could be glib, pompous and charming — sometimes in the same sentence — but he was always forthright and appeared concerned about me as much as our program. I valued Wright's opinion and his friendship, and if he thought Bill Carr could help, I was all for it.

Wright arranged a conference call with me and Carr on May 2. Carr laid out an ambitious plan titled "Six-Point Transition Plan for UNO Athletics." The six points were:

> Establish a shared vision for Athletics
> Partner with University's restructuring
> Achieve competitive success in NCAA Division I
> Determine appropriate sports sponsorship
> Provide required infrastructure
> Allocate necessary financial resources

I was excited about the prospects of a third party review. I was frustrated about the modest financial support our program received before Katrina, and this might be the opportunity we needed. The university was restructuring, and having our own strategic plan would position athletics well within the new university.

A view from the outside also would tell us if we would be better served with a different menu of sports going forward. I believed Katrina had given us a one-time opportunity to jettison some sports that did not contribute anything other than numbers to our program. We needed to forget sports like track and field and implement sports that better reflected our community and could generate more interest. Softball was one. Soccer was another.

I also believed if an outside party identified the same problems I had been raising, Ryan would have no recourse but to accept the recommendations. I was not seeking vindication, but I knew it was easier to ignore those with whom you are familiar than an impartial third party. That is the reason kids might not listen to a parent, but when another adult or a peer says the same thing, they take it as gospel.

The downsizing and uncertain prospects for our future soon revealed its first major casualty. In early May, our men's basketball coach of five years, Monte Towe, informed me he had been offered a position as associate head coach at North Carolina State. At first glance, it made little sense for a Division I head coach to quit his job for an assistant coach's position. Most assistant coaches would plot mayhem to become a D-I head coach. But in Towe's case, it made perfect sense.

Towe was point guard on the 1974 N.C. State team that ended UCLA's record seven-year string to win the NCAA title. Teammates David Thompson and Tom Burleson received more attention, but Towe was clearly the sparkplug of that team. More importantly, he still was a legend in Wolfpack nation.

Our prospects for a successful recovery were an obvious concern to him. However, I believed him when he said his primary reason was the attraction of returning to the coliseum "where my jersey is hanging in the rafters." I liked Monte, probably because we talked the same language, that of basketball in the heartland. He knew the players I grew up idolizing in Kentucky, such as my boyhood friend and eventual UK star Mike Casey, and I knew the players who inspired him from Indiana such as Bobby Plump, Jimmy Rayl and Rick Mount.

That bond, plus our mutual admiration of Tom Petty's music, created a warm personal relationship. We had our moments professionally, however. Monte and our women's volleyball coach, Julie Ibieta, mixed like oil and water. I recall coming to the office one summer morning, only to have those two storm into my office shouting at one another. Their summer camps ran back-to-back in our auxiliary gym, and Ibieta's camp ran five minutes long one day.

Towe, who could still be a brat at 50, walked out into the middle of the floor amid the young volleyball players, bouncing a basketball and disrupting her camp. I tried to play Gandhi and calm both of them down, and I sent Ibieta back out on to the floor. I told Monte I was disappointed in the way he handled the situation, and I wanted him to write Julie a letter of apology. It was like I had asked him to spit in the face of his N.C. State mentor, Norm Sloan. But after I dictated the note, he put it on paper.

Towe's win-loss record during his time at UNO was mediocre at 70-78, but I believed he performed his duties admirably and with integrity. That was reflected when it came to a buyout clause in his contract. He did not object to it, and after some negotiation with N.C. State, they agreed to play a game at Lakefront Arena, and Monte paid every cent of the negotiated buyout amount, which exceeded $160,000. He went out like a man.

Towe's decision to leave gave the poachers another shot at trying to convince his players, in particular Bo McCalebb, to transfer. McCalebb's mother had been contacted by coaches from other schools since Katrina, and she was pushing for him to leave. After Towe announced his resignation, Bo's mother called me and asked for a meeting. I met her and Bo in a classroom at the Human Performance Center, where we had set up temporary offices.

She demanded we release Bo from his scholarship. I argued it was not in Bo's best interests, especially because he had broken his wrist in the fourth game of the season and spent the remainder of the season as a medical red shirt. NCAA transfer rules would require him to sit out the next season as well, which was something Bo would not do.

"I told you, Mama," he said adamantly to her. "I don't want to sit any more, I want to play!" The meeting turned into a shouting match between Bo and his mother. I excused myself, and they argued for a while longer and then left. To his credit, Bo stayed at UNO and finished his career in 2008 as the leading all-time scorer in UNO and Sun Belt Conference history.

Towe's departure had a silver lining. I believed it would give us an opportunity for a fresh start, hopefully with an exciting new head coach who would lift us out of our lethargy and toward success. No better cure existed for a university reeling from tragedy than immediate success on a national scale. Basketball could provide that cure. It would be a great story, if it worked.

After word of Towe's departure went public, the phones started ringing. Current head coaches, unemployed former head coaches, assistant coaches, high school coaches and seemingly everybody but the ghost of James Naismith called to apply. Bobby Knight, Tubby Smith, Tim Floyd, Greg Popovich and other prominent head coaches called to recommend assistant coaches or friends. I was gratified at such interest, but I also believed our unique position required me to establish specific parameters for the search.

My first rule was I only would consider coaches who applied for the job. That would convince me they knew of our situation, or at least it would give me the opportunity to fully inform them. In our current state, becoming head coach at the University of New Orleans would not be your typical Division I head coaching job. Our arena was shuttered, and we had no idea when it would be reopened. We had downsized to six sports, from our pre-Katrina total of 15. As such, we were operating under a five-year waiver from the NCAA which, in effect, made us a provisional Division I member until we could restore the minimum number of sports.

I did not want to identify a candidate, pursue him with vigor and finally persuade him to take the job, only to have the effects of Katrina make his job even more difficult than advertised. My mantra to all of the applicants was "it's not perfect, and it could get worse before it gets better."

Over the next few weeks, I talked to many coaches and began to narrow the list of candidates. One of my Sun Belt colleagues, Wood Selig, the athletic director at Western Kentucky, told me of an upcoming meeting I needed to attend. The Villa Seven conference was an annual get together of assistant coaches at prominent programs who were aspiring to be head coaches. Nike sponsored the event at its Beaverton, Oregon, headquarters.

Wood sent me the roster of attendees, and two assistant coaches who had applied — Barry Sanderson of South Carolina and Philip Pearson of Alabama — were attending. Another applicant was Joe Pasternack, a young assistant at California who was a New Orleans native. A swing to Beaverton and then down to Berkeley would accomplish three in person interviews, and maybe a couple more. I made my reservations, not at all expecting what was to happen.

I arrived in Beaverton in time for the opening night cocktail party. I was the only athletic director in attendance, and I was looking for a head coach. In a crowd that included 30 assistant coaches coveting a head coaching job, I quickly felt like the prettiest girl at the high school dance.

One of the organizers of the conference asked me if I had met Buzz Williams, an assistant coach at Texas A&M. I had never heard of Buzz Williams, but I was told he would like to meet me. He was pointed out, and I went over and introduced myself. We spoke for several minutes, and he said he would like to talk about our vacancy. I told him I appreciated his interest, but I cautioned him the job carries some baggage. He said he understood and said he still was interested in discussing it at length.

My schedule at the summit was tight, with the Sanderson and Pearson interviews sandwiched between the coaches' schedule of meetings. Williams said he was leaving the conference early to go recruiting, but I agreed to contact him the following week to pursue our discussion. I flew to San Francisco that night and had dinner with Pasternack before returning to New Orleans. He impressed me immediately with his earnest desire to come back to New Orleans. His parents lived about a mile from us, in Lakeview

South, and lost their home. Pasternack was well attuned to the problems we faced.

The Sun Belt Conference annual meetings in Destin, Florida, took up much of the next week, but I did have a break and decided to call Williams. I was sitting on the balcony of my room at the Sandestin Hilton, looking out at the Gulf of Mexico, notebook on my lap when I placed the call. I had a number of prepared questions, which he answered to my satisfaction. I was impressed by his almost military bearing. His responses were filled with "yes, sir" or "no, sir" and he displayed a discipline that suggested he was extremely organized and focused.

I already had narrowed my list to four candidates and had not expected to add another. However, there was something about Williams I liked. He recruited me hard, and I thought if he can recruit young basketball players like he was recruiting me, he might be our guy. I added his name to a list that included:

Jaren Jackson, a New Orleans high school legend who played at Georgetown before a long and impressive career in the NBA;

Ray Harper, who had forged a long record of success at Kentucky Wesleyan, who was currently head coach at Oklahoma City University;

Jeff Price, head coach at Georgia Southern, who had achieved modest success including an NIT appearance the previous year;

Pasternack, who had been Knight's manager for four years at Indiana before becoming an assistant coach for seven years at Cal-Berkeley.

I formed a search committee, which was required under LSU System and EEOC rules. The committee's authority was fact finding and advisory only. Who would be the next head coach would be my decision. As Tim Ryan confirmed: "I don't want an English professor to make a decision on a head coach for whom you are going to be held accountable." I liked his thinking, and I would have it no other way.

We established the travel schedule and distributed it to the candidates the first week of June. The interviews were to be held the following week, between June 5 and June 10, and I hoped at that time one of the candidates would rise to the top.

I was feeling good about it when Jean and I went to dinner at Ruth's Chris Steak House on Saturday evening, June 3, to celebrate our 14th wedding anniversary. Our anniversary is actually June 6 (getting married on D-Day makes it easy to remember!), but we moved up the dinner because of the busy week ahead.

We ordered two glasses of wine, which had just been delivered when my cell phone buzzed in my pocket. It was my brother Jerry who called with grim news. Our father had fallen and had been taken to the hospital. "They say his heart is shot," Jerry said. "He doesn't have much time left. You need to come home."

Jean and I left the restaurant immediately, and I began packing. If Dad's condition was as severe as Jerry reported, I knew a funeral might be in our immediate future. But Katrina's ugly head reared again. I had lost all my clothing during the ensuing flood. Peter Ruocco, a vice president in labor relations in my old office at the NFL Management

Council, had sent me one of his sport coats and a suit he thought might come in handy until I could restore my wardrobe. At that point, those were the only "dress clothes" I owned.

Rather than trying to get a flight, I told Jean I would sleep a couple of hours, get up about 3 A.M. and then drive to Kentucky, which was about a 10-hour drive. I did not sleep much, and the first hours of the darkened drive up I-59 through the Mississippi pine forests were tiring, at least until the sun came up.

I had too much time to think during that drive. I regretted not taking a stronger stance with Jean on moving to Mandeville on the north shore of Lake Pontchartrain instead of Lakeview. We both loved the north shore, but Lakeview was close to "mama and them." We might have had a tree fall on our house, but that would have been mild compared to what had happened.

I thought about how Katrina had destroyed everything we had owned, including my books and some of my research into the Miller family. I thought about when the tornado in January took off the dormer of our damaged house and blew in our front windows and about how I sat on the steps near tears and called Dad. Then, I had the sudden fear that my call might have contributed to Dad's decline.

CHAPTER
13

Charles Edwin Miller was born in Shelby County, Kentucky on January 19, 1922, the son of Chester C. Miller and Bessie Boswell Miller. He was the fourth of six children that included older brothers Bob and James, a younger brother Bill, an older sister, Dorothy, and a younger sister, Ann.

Charles attended the two-room Clark Station School and then Simpsonville schools, graduating in 1940. He went to work in the general store in Clark Station that his father had operated since 1926. World War II intervened, and Charles went into the U.S. Army Signal Corps and trained as a radio operator. He was shipped overseas in 1943, attached to the communications vessel, the *U.S.S. Mount McKinley*.

After the war, he came home to marry his high school sweetheart, Emily Connor, in 1945. Charles and his brother Bill bought a milk truck route, and for the next 39 years hauled milk from Shelby County's numerous dairy farms into the processing plants of Louisville.

In the meantime, he and Emily were blessed with two sons. Jim, named after Charles's brother James who died in a California chemical plant explosion in 1942, was born in 1948. In 1951 came Jerry, who was named by big brother Jim after his favorite television character, puppet Jerry Mahoney.

On Charles 62nd birthday, in 1984, he retired. I was working in New York at the time and commemorated his retirement with a front page printed at a Times Square headline shop that announced: "Miller Parks Truck, Bids Bovines Adieu." The front page adorned the wall of Charles's and Emily's TV room for years thereafter.

Retirement was good. Charles and Emily enjoyed bowling and traveling with their senior group, and in the summer months, Charles grew the finest garden in that part of Shelby County. Corn, tomatoes, broccoli, eggplant, carrots, beans and okra were daily bounty, and strawberries, blueberries, blackberries and grapes were turned into juices, jellies and jams. Despite Emily's protests that "I hate that damned garden," she dutifully turned its yield into sumptuous meals and canned and frozen goods that they could eat all winter. They were devout members of the Fisherville Church of Christ, which Charles served as treasurer for many years.

And, they were die hard Kentucky Wildcats basketball fans. Emily hated the rival Louisville Cardinals almost as much as she loved her Wildcats. Once, when she was putting gas in her car at the community filling station, she almost went apoplectic when she noticed at the next pump Denny Crum, the Cardinals coach who lived nearby. She finished her purchase and drove away quickly, fuming at the nerve of that man.

Charles also was a long-suffering Red Sox fan. He had watched as the Louisville Colonels of the Forties and Fifties sent their best players to Boston, and he passed on that love of the Red Sox to his two sons.

Charles's and Emily's decline started in 1997, when they were both 75 and appeared in the best of health. Emily sustained a complication from a childhood bout with rheumatic fever that required heart surgery. According to the website of the American Heart Association: "Anyone can get acute rheumatic fever, but it usually occurs in children five to 15 years old. The rheumatic heart disease that results can last for life."

Emily's surgery triggered mild dementia, a condition that had affected one of her mother's sisters. Her deterioration now thrust Charles, whom Emily had waited on faithfully for 52 years, into the role of caregiver. Predictably, he slid down his own rabbit hole into a dark sea of depression. His pendulum swung from tolerance at best to considerations of suicide. At one time, he gave Jerry his car keys and his 16-gauge shotgun to reduce the temptations of closing up the garage and starting the car, or something more violent.

But since Emily's death in 2002, Charles seemed to be doing well. He terribly missed Emily, whom he affectionately called "my buddy," but he was functioning. He began attending church regularly again, and with Jerry and Laura 10 minutes away, he knew he had a safe haven. When Jerry and Laura would take a trip, I would come up and spend a few days with him.

The only time Charles was left without a safety net was in January 2005, when Jerry and I took the wives to Spain for 10 days. We didn't dare tell Charles we would be out of the country at the same time. Instead, we made regular phone calls to check on him and even made sure we both called on his birthday January 19, separately, from adjoining hotel rooms near Seville.

Charles had been doing so well the past two years that he even suggested he might feel good enough to visit us in New Orleans once our house was renovated, something he had not done since Emily became ill. But on the morning of June 3, he walked out to the end of the driveway to check his mailbox, and he collapsed.

I arrived at the Humana Jefferson East hospital complex around 1 P.M., and greeted a waiting room full of family members. Dad's brother Bill and wife Juanita and his sister Ann and her husband Allen Purnell were there, along with some of our Miller and Purnell cousins and some family friends.

I went in to see Dad, and Jerry was standing beside his bed. Dad was alert, although looking very tired. He smiled when he saw me and seemed surprised. "Well, hello, Jim." I gave him a hug and we exchanged the uncomfortable pleasantries that seem to come out at times like these.

Not unexpectedly, he asked if I'd been watching the Red Sox, who were in a series that very night with the hated Yankees. The Red Sox and Kentucky basketball always had been our favorite subjects of conversation, spanning the differences in age or interests between fathers and sons. Ted Williams and Adolph Rupp and all of their contemporaries were subjects that we could talk about for hours. I thought then about when I moved to New Orleans and became friends with Mel Parnell, a native New Orleanian and probably the greatest left-hander in Red Sox history. I regretted not fulfilling a promise to get Mel and Dad together for lunch one day.

But here he was, in his last hours, and the talk was the same that we had enjoyed during a lifetime together.

We watched the Yankees and Red Sox on television Monday night, and the Sox were pounded 13-5. Dad watched and commented on some of the action, giving us hope he would pull through this. He began deteriorating the next day, however, and the doctor told us he wouldn't last much longer. Jerry and I agreed Dad would not let his last Red Sox game be a Yankees' blowout.

The following day, his lucid moments became fewer and fewer. He was concerned that we needed to "go downstairs and turn the thermostat up." Then he would go back to sleep. He slept through that night's baseball game, another Yankees win, 2-1.

On Wednesday, June 7, the doctor told us if any family members wanted to pay their last respects, they should come. Dad's brother Bill and sister Ann and their spouses came as did eight or ten of our cousins. Also there was a man I had not seen in nearly 40 years. Theodore Todd was the minister of a small African-American church in Shelby County. But when I was young, he was "Tut" Todd, who worked on the farm of Mr. J. L. Coots, where I spent summers pitching hay bales and setting tobacco. Tut's respect for Dad reflected a bond of racial invisibility which Dad had taught us. Dad's measure of a person was never color, but whether he "worked hard" and was a "good person." Reverend Todd was generous with his praise of Dad and with words of comfort for us, before we turned the visit into a joyful recollection of hauling hay and cutting tobacco at two cents per stick.

That night was bittersweet. Family members tried to keep our spirits up with stories about the past, which is what families always talk about when they get together. Every one of them went in to tell Dad farewell. When they left, Jerry and I decided to go home and get some sleep and come back early in the morning.

But Dad's heart would not last, and at 2 A.M. a nurse called to say that Dad had died peacefully. Jerry and I went back to the hospital and kissed Dad good-bye, and we shared our final tears. We went to the funeral home the next morning to finalize the details, which Jerry and Dad already had framed out a couple of years earlier.

The viewing was an uplifting event, celebrating Dad's life with family and friends. Such an occasion always is somber, but the stories and the visiting with those who were important in his life, and ours, was a good thing. To top it off, as we were saying good-bye to the last visitors, we learned the Red Sox beat the Yankees that night, 9-3. My childhood friend, Mike Casey, was still there and said Dad would have rubbed it in since he knew Casey was a Yankees fan. Dad could now rest easy.

Once again, brother-in-law Gary Solomon was by our side when we needed him. Gary flew Jean and the kids up in an airplane he leased with some fellow executives. Lindsay flew in from Washington, D.C., and she, Layne, Charles Connor and my older son Rich all provided great support. Layne flew back to New Orleans late that evening with Gary and Martha, but C.C. and Lindsay stayed with Jean and me for the funeral. Dad was very special to C.C., not only because he was the namesake, but because I believe he understood the concept of family and how moments like these are events to be treasured.

Jerry and I agreed the best tribute we could give to Dad would be eulogies to our parents. When Mom died in 2002, we did not give a eulogy, a fact we both regretted. So Jerry's eulogy would be about Mom and Dad, while mine focused mainly on how my relationship with Dad has shaped my relationship with my son:

> A son looking back at the life of his father first remembers the common bonds they share. Most are positive such as the bond of *faith,* which helped mold the father and in turn helped him mold the son, and the bond of *family,* which is the strongest emotional and enduring bond.
>
> Some bonds Dad and I shared weren't always peaceful ones … such as Politics.
>
> In my infallible youth, I was appalled that Dad was so unenlightened that he couldn't understand my reasoning for voting for McGovern. But, to paraphrase Mark Twain, by the time I was past 30, and we both had voted for Reagan, I was amazed at how much Dad had learned.
>
> But for Dad and me, the bond that we always could return to was sports. I remember him throwing the ball to me when we lived in the house that Madge Stucker lives in now, and I remember the basketball goal he built for Jerry and me out of scrap lumber when we moved up to our new house "on the hill." I remember the makeshift ball field we carved in the backyard, which closed permanently the day I hit a ball through Uncle Billy's bedroom window next door.
>
> That's about the time that Mike Casey moved to Clark Station and Dad *watched* and I'm sure *hoped* that his chubby little boy would somehow keep up with the Natural. Mike and I shared a lot in our youth, including playing in my dad's last softball game in a church league at Eastwood when Dad was playing his customary left field and a routine fly ball somehow missed his glove, came down and broke his glasses. He was only 42 or 43, but he knew it was time to turn the playing of games over to his sons.

That certainly didn't put a damper on his enthusiasm, though, and Kentucky basketball and Red Sox baseball were always the prime subjects of discussion after jobs took me away from Kentucky and we'd talk frequently on the phone.

This past week when he was still conversant he said the best trip he ever took was when Jerry and I took him to Fenway Park to celebrate his 70th birthday. Even in his final 48 hours, when he was coming in and out of consciousness, the last questions he asked were (1) Did the Red Sox win? (2) Are they still in first place? (3) Who's pitching tonight?

I truly believe that after the Red Sox won the World Series in 2004, he was ready to go, but I wish the last game he ever watched was a little better than that 13-5 Yankee win Monday night. Another reason to hate the Yankees.

I'm hoping to pass that special bond on to my son, Charles Connor. In fact, we've had a bet for the past four years that if he catches a ball in the outfield during a game, I'd give him $100. It's been the safest bet I'd ever made.

Then last night, after Billy and Ann and their children had made their last visit to Dad and said their last good-bye, I got a call from Charles Connor. "Dad," he said, "we won tonight, and I caught a fly ball in left field." And I caught it for Granddad. "And you know what else?" I said, "What?" He said, "You owe me a hundred bucks."

I never got to tell Dad, but I think he knows.

We buried Dad with his blue Kentucky baseball cap with the white "K" on it and his Red Sox cap that he had bought when Jerry and I took him to Fenway Park. He would have liked that.

CHAPTER
14

It was not easy getting back into the work mode after an emotionally taxing week, but I had to find a new basketball coach. I rescheduled the candidates' visits and prepared a new timetable for their meetings with the search committee. Over the next week, as the candidates came and went, I kept going back and forth between all of them. All had great qualities, and each one excelled in one category or another.

After the final candidate left, I polled the search committee to get their opinions. Consensus among the committee members favored Buzz Williams, and I agreed. He had success at a high level, was a relentless recruiter, had great energy and I thought had the qualities we needed. He was a little rough around the edges, but I did not think that would hurt him in New Orleans. Especially if he were winning.

Provost Rick Barton was the only committee member who did not have Buzz Williams in his top two. Barton knew college basketball. He had played at Davidson College under legendary head coach Lefty Driesell, then transferred to Valparaiso where he played for another respected head coach, Gene Bartow. Barton became a professor of English, specializing in creative writing, and basketball was a common theme in his eight books.

Despite Barton's dissent, I called Williams on Friday to offer him the job. It appeared as though he was visibly touched. He hesitated for a moment, and it sounded like he was weeping. He said he was just so thankful for the opportunity, and he wouldn't let me down. We flew him in, and we had our press conference the following day. He again teared up at the podium, but everybody in attendance was taken by his apparent sincerity and welcomed him warmly.

I believed even more strongly then we would get our program jump-started through men's basketball. Williams inherited some returning talent, and Bo McCalebb and 6-10 Ben Elias would be back from their season lost to injuries. Williams also knew of several other players he believed would be available to bolster the lineup.

It was important to Williams also to upgrade the bottom of the lineup, which would improve the depth necessary to win. It was a new coach's prerogative to terminate scholarships of players he did not think fit into his program. But since the NCAA instituted the Academic Progress Rate as a measurement of academic success, wholesale changes could have disastrous effects on our APR scores, which could lead to loss of scholarships and other penalties.

The APR measurement is a mathematical calculation that awards each student-athlete two points per semester, one for eligibility and one for retention. If a student makes his grades and is eligible for the following semester, he gets one point for eligibility. If he returns to the program the following semester, he gets an additional point for retention. A four-for-four is good, but if the new coach runs off three or four players, you lose the retention points.

I cautioned Williams, who pointed to his record at Texas A&M as proof he could weather a one time blip and build a stronger program for the long term.

He was the head coach, and I deferred to his judgment.

Jeremie Davis finished his classes the spring semester, and he returned to Arcadia when he learned Towe had resigned. That was good news to Davis. He had not gotten along with the head coach, and he believed a fresh start with a new head coach would be good for him.

After Wayne Williams left, Davis moved into the starting lineup and became the "go-to" guy, averaging 17.1 points over the last 12 games. With that body of work to build on, he could pick up where he left off and have an even better year next season. After all, Bo would be back, and teams could not guard both of them.

In mid-June Davis heard that Buzz Williams, an assistant coach at Texas A&M, had been hired as the Privateers' new head coach. Davis felt he was the same type of player and maybe a better shooter than A&M's outstanding guard Acie Law. If Coach Williams wanted somebody like Law who could complement Bo, then he was the guy.

Unfortunately, the new coach had other plans. Davis was back at UNO taking summer classes when Kathy Keene informed him that Williams would not renew his scholarship. The new head coach already had decided not to renew the scholarships of Towe holdovers Sami Badawi, Dusty Driggs and Eric Hipolito. Those three did not play much and the action was understandable, but Davis had been the team's leading scorer after Wayne Williams had left, and how can you cut the team's leading scorer?

No member of the new coaching staff called with any definitive word on his status, but as summer school wound to a close Davis had his answer. He was angry he was not given a quick answer so he could make some inquiries and possibly get into school somewhere else. But now it was too late even for that.

The rejection left Davis in total despair. He had survived the hurricane and experienced even more hell on an overpass with no toilet or food or water and his life in danger. *They owe me for that. Why did I even come back here? But I did come back and led the team in scoring and was the best player on the floor when I finally got to play, and this is how they thank me? To hell with it! If basketball doesn't need me, then I don't need basketball.*

Davis decided to quit school and get a job. No more coaches telling him what to do. No more classes whose subjects he didn't understand or care about. No more New Orleans with the memories of thinking he was going to die in a storm and dodging looters only to be rescued and dropped on an overpass where people were fighting over cots.

No more basketball was a high price, but he would be away from those bad memories, and that had value. Besides, this wasn't the game that he had played for fun as a kid. Basketball had become a business and one he no longer wanted to be a part of.

It was time to move on.

CHAPTER
15

I considered the first summer after Katrina "the Summer of the Phoenix." Our department had been reduced to ashes, and Bill Carr and his team were working to help us resurrect it. Like the mythical bird reborn, I believed the strategic plan exercise would result in a dynamic new attitude that would help us create a healthy and sustaining program.

Our department, like every other one on campus, was depleted of resources. We were sitting in the ashes of financial exigency, slashed budgets, collective downsizing and damaged facilities. But Katrina had given us the chance to fix it. As difficult as it was to realize as we looked around at our situation, we had been given a gift that would not have come along if we had not been so devastated. Neither individuals nor institutions change unless forced to do so, and Katrina had forced us to recover or die. If we planned strategically and could generate support from our constituents, we could throw off the yoke as the lowest funded athletic program in the conference, the one with the worst facilities, the one with the fewest number of coaches and support staff.

The first step toward recovery in my mind was to identify those pockets of revenue potential, then provide them with the weapons to raise more money. The simple term is ROI — return on investment. Among all departments in a university, athletics is uniquely positioned to achieve the dual tasks of "fund-raising" and "friend-raising," generating revenue while keeping the university's name in the public eye. I argued if the university would allow me to hire more ticket sellers, more sponsorship sales people and more fund-raisers and seed their activities with advertised initiatives — the dollars generated would increase proportionally to the dollars invested. In addition, each activity, game or campaign would serve to burnish the university's brand with the public. It takes money to make money.

I was counting on Bill Carr to preach the same sermon. If Tim Ryan accepted it, we had a chance to rise out of the ashes and produce a program that would properly service our student-athletes, furnish a greater percentage of our own support and reflect positively on the university as a whole.

Carr commenced the process by bringing his team members to the campus between July 10-13. Accompanying Carr were Gerald O'Dell, former athletic director at the University of Cincinnati, and Richard Konzem, athletic director at Benedictine College in Kansas. O'Dell was the authority on program assessment, while Konzem was the financial expert. It was a good mix of big school/small school experience to analyze our little corner of the athletics universe.

To prepare for the first meetings, Carr made a request for certain materials that his group could use as a first step toward understanding our current situation. They were taking a thorough approach. The list of documents they wanted to see was three pages long and encompassed every aspect of the athletic department and the university.

Among the requested materials were university policy documents to include the institutional mission statement and administrative structure, descriptions of any university committees dealing with athletics and information on our faculty athletics representative. Carr also wanted to see the university's strategic plan and any additional planning documents developed since Katrina. In addition, he requested documents that could provide an overview of the current situation on the UNO campus, the neighborhoods surrounding UNO, the situation across town at Tulane University and the city's restoration efforts.

Other requested documents included everything possibly associated with our department for the last three years, including financial statements, NCAA financial and academic reports, Title IX status reports, media guides, ticket sales and fund-raising numbers, sponsorships, capital projects, university and Sun Belt Conference reports and data that pertained to our athletic department. After digesting all that, Carr's group would have a good idea of the challenges we were facing.

I scheduled the appropriate individuals to meet with Carr's team over the three-day period. I was first up for about 90 minutes, followed by Ryan for an hour. We took a break, and I conducted a brief tour of our facilities, including our baseball stadium and our still shuttered arena. After the tour, the Carr team delved into the university infrastructure with two more days of interviews with all the top university administrators, boosters, university alumni and with members of our department.

Carr followed his initial visit with a request for supplemental information to fill holes the team discovered: coaches and administrative salaries, additional information on the athletics budget and further information on the Board of Regents athletic cap which may affect strategic decisions. The cap was an albatross created in the 1990s as a method to control the athletic spending of Louisiana's colleges. It was championed by former Chancellor Greg O'Brien, who was engaged in an annual budget battle with then AD Ron Maestri. The chancellor did not want to spend any money on athletics that he could devote to projects that would keep the university and O'Brien in the public eye. What better way to achieve that purpose than to implement a rule to limit athletic spending?

While I was trying to concentrate on the strategic planning process, the "Katrina Curse" continued to plague our department. Julie Ibieta, our volleyball coach, resigned to become head volleyball coach at Metairie Park Country Day High School.

Much like the Towe situation, it would appear odd that a Division I head coach would resign to become a head coach at a high school. However, in Julie's view it made sense.

Women coaches who are married have different priorities than do men coaches: family first, job second. Julie had three young children, and she did not want to spend any more time on the road recruiting or traveling with her team. That was a good reason, but finances were an even better reason. Julie was making around $45,000 as our head coach. She could take the job at Country Day for less money, but she would more than make up the difference as her three children would qualify for significant discounts to Country Day's annual tuition, which was $15,000 in 2006.

It was a reasonable decision, and I applauded her for it.

Making the decision less painful was the fact that Julie's top assistant, Dana Launey, was eager for the opportunity to be a head coach. I informed Tim Ryan of Julie's resignation and my intention to promote Dana, and he was fine with it.

Two other changes would resound far more significantly that summer than losing a head coach.

In June, Mike Dauenhauer, the athletics business manager and one of the rocks I inherited, was offered the job as university bursar, in charge of student billing and revenue collection. Mike started in the business office at Lakefront Arena in 1982 and had been the athletics' CFO for nearly two decades. He was an expert at navigating the myriad rules and regulations regarding state and campus finances, and he was liked and respected throughout the university.

The other blow came in July when Dr. Kathy Keene informed me that my good friend Wright Waters had offered her the position of associate commissioner in charge of compliance for the Sun Belt Conference. It was a wonderful tribute to Kathy and a significant promotion with an accompanying salary increase.

Mike recommended as his replacement Ola Adegboye, a former sprinter with the UNO track-and-field team who was chief financial officer with the Department of Recreation and Intramural Services. Ola had achieved his MBA at UNO and was anxious to get back to athletics in some way. He appeared to have the experience to navigate the murky financial waters at UNO, and he wanted to be here.

Kathy recommended my administrative assistant, Susan Broussard, as her replacement to oversee compliance and academics. I wasn't enthusiastic about the idea at first simply because Susan lacked experience in those two critical areas. But Susan was a hard worker and assisted Kathy the previous three years on compliance and academic issues. She was a former student-athlete herself, having been team captain of the Alabama-Birmingham golf team for three years. She was bright and aggressive, and was looking to climb the athletics administration ladder. And, like Mike, she wanted to be here.

In the post-Katrina world, the No. 1 quality of a job candidate was often their mere presence. They were here already, which suggested they had come to grips with the city's post-Katrina problems. That suggested further they would not be looking to leave any time soon. A seamless transition with minimal disruption was my first goal, and both Susan and Ola gave me some assurance we could achieve it.

Still, the sturdy three-legged stool I had inherited, with Kathy, Mike and Mike Bujol, had just had two of its legs kicked out from under it. I was happy for Kathy and Mike, but their losses tempered my optimism for a summer of recovery.

After a month of analyzing the first collection of data, Bill Carr was ready for a follow-up visit, between September 6-8. The meetings went extremely well. The constituents were candid in their viewpoints, and Carr believed he had his arms around our issues. The information gathered and the conclusions reached throughout the process were the same things I had been saying to Chancellor Ryan: If you want to have an outstanding athletic program, you must support it financially.

My only concern was whether Ryan would adopt the plan and allow us to implement the recommendations. I recalled a conversation with David Walker, the street smart athletic director at the University of Louisiana in Lafayette, who had gone through a similar process with Carr's team.

"We gave them parameters, we gave them all the information they asked for, we paid them their money, and they returned a beautiful plan," he said. "The president looked at what it was going to cost to implement the recommendations, and he told me 'thank you for your work,' and he put it in the bottom drawer. I never saw it again."

I did not believe that would happen to us. Ryan had expressed his enthusiasm for the Carr involvement, and he participated vigorously in the sessions. Carr must have been reading my mind when he asked Ryan in one of the final sessions if he would support the findings.

"I do not want an athletic department just to have an athletic department," Ryan told Carr. "I want an athletic department that will be a credit to this university, and I will support it."

Ryan said exactly what I wanted to hear, and I couldn't have been more excited. Finally, we would have a chance to create a program that would be an asset to the university, would provide much-needed positive attention and could help us compete in the Sun Belt Conference and the NCAA.

"Triumph from Tragedy" is a common theme in literature, medicine, business and the movies (see *We Are Marshall*). I believed our program had the same opportunity now. To take a common post-Katrina theme, the storm effectively stripped our program "down to the studs" and allowed us to build something new and exciting. It washed away the old and ineffective and gave us a clean foundation upon which to build a program that was dynamic, responsive to our community and an effective marketing vehicle for the university.

The tragedy that was Katrina had given us the opportunity for triumph. All we had to do was to grasp it and take it where it would lead us.

CHAPTER
16

On the first anniversary of Katrina, August 29, 2006, we moved back into our house on Vicksburg Street. We had spent four months in Baton Rouge and eight months with Jean's mother, Gloria, and now we would be living in our house for the first time since we evacuated.

In the real estate sales vernacular, "move-in" condition does not mean "finished" condition, and that was certainly the case with our house. It was very much a work in progress. We prodded the contractor to finish the upstairs first so we could at least move into our house while renovation continued downstairs. The upstairs had new carpet and fresh paint, and the plumbing and electrical services were in working order.

Layne and Charles Connor were excited about moving back into their own bedrooms after sharing a bedroom at their grandmother's house for eight months. Jean and I moved into the guest bedroom upstairs since the master bedroom downstairs was not ready. A small common area, which overlooked the great room below, had been a play area for the kids, but now would be our temporary kitchen. The regular kitchen downstairs was not finished, and the new appliances had not been installed. Our kitchen for the next several months would consist of a microwave, a toaster, a coffee pot, an ice chest and a card table with four chairs.

With other amenities such as cable television and Internet service not back to the neighborhood yet, we told Layne and C.C. we were granting their long-standing wish to go camping. As one who considers a Holiday Inn "roughing it," I told the kids that instead of "camping out" outdoors, they would be "camping in" in our own home.

Only Elmo the beagle, with his back yard intact, had all the comforts he had known before. Jean always has kidded me that Elmo is really not the kids' dog, but mine, and I couldn't argue. Beagles always triggered fond memories for me. I grew up with a succession of beagles that stemmed from my own father's love of rabbit hunting. When the weather cooled, Dad would pull out his briar-proof brown hunting jacket and pants and run an oiled rag through the barrel of his .16-gauge Browning shotgun, a brand that enjoyed a high reputation among World War II veterans. I carried my grandfather's antique .22-caliber rifle, which made me feel very much the hunter. No matter that Dad would not put a bullet into the rifle's chamber until "we see one sittin'." We must have had very impatient rabbits in Shelby County because I don't recall ever firing that rifle at a living thing.

But that was not the point. Dad was teaching me and Jerry lessons that fathers teach their sons. We would take the dogs into the fields and cedar forests around our home and walk along fence lines or thickets of brush and tree limbs, where rabbits nested. We learned that once the dogs picked up a scent we merely had to crouch down patiently and listen for the signature call — *Ah-Roo! Ah-Roo! Ah-Roo!* The sounds faded in the outbound chase before growing louder as the dogs circled the rabbit back into range.

I still can name every beagle we ever had and recall characteristics of each. Spot was the first dog I remember, and Dad always said he was the best hunter, while Queenie was more of a pet than a hunter. Jack was memorable if for nothing else than the fact he survived three run-ins with moving vehicles. Jack came to us when I was six, and when he died 10 years later, I cried as I buried him out behind the barn. Max was half basset hound with long ears and a stomach set low to the ground, and Sam just showed up one day and adopted us.

Sometime after I left for college, Sam died and Dad lost his interest in hunting. But he imparted his love of a good beagle hound to me, and I have done the same for my children. Jean resisted a dog for the first few years of our marriage, but after Layne and Charles Connor were born I knew at some point I would cultivate their votes and she would be hopelessly outnumbered. Sure enough, when we decided to move back to New Orleans from Chicago, I used the offer of a dog to bribe the children into leaving their friends with little protest.

Although Elmo would enjoy the chase, hunting rabbits was not on his resume. He is affectionate, loyal and a great watchdog to a fault, barking at everything from a crow flying overhead to a lizard's sneeze. Elmo also is a grand excavator, and quickly turned his old back yard into a replica of the Baghdad airport within hours.

It was important for all of us to restore the veneer of our pre-Katrina life, but we were doing so on a lonely street. The day we moved back in, only our next door neighbors, Jay and Anne Marie Sequeira, were in their home.

Prior to Katrina, the 6600 block of Vicksburg Street consisted of 19 single family residences, two separate townhouse duplexes and one vacant lot. When we moved back into our house, that landscape had changed, literally. In addition to our house and the Sequeiras, six of the single family houses and the two duplexes were in various stages of being gutted or renovated. Four of the other houses had been torn down and two others soon would come down. The other six were gutted and boarded up. It was an early indication that our city would reflect a post-disaster "jack-o-lantern effect" whereby renovated houses would exist between gaps of boarded up houses and vacant lots.

Vicksburg Street was reflective of the entire city's snail's pace to recovery, one year after the storm. Many reasons existed, led by the ongoing insurance wars and the slow execution of applications for governmental relief. But historical reasons also factored into the equation.

A construction mentality driven by geography developed in New Orleans during the latter part of the 20th century. Most urban areas expand outward, with ring after ring of fresh, new suburban growth radiating from the center of the city. This occurs because most urban areas are surrounded predominantly by buildable land. New Orleans, on the other hand, is landlocked on the north by Lake Pontchartrain and on the south and west by the Mississippi River, a phenomenon which prevents contiguous expansion. Enterprising builders figured out the only way to build and market a new house in New Orleans was to buy an existing house, tear it down and build anew on the same site. Other cities employ the device to restore the grandeur of once vibrant urban areas. In New Orleans, it is the predominant way to create new construction.

Lakeview was a perfect example of the tear-down-and-build method. On most streets, strings of small one-story bungalows that were built in the 1940s or 1950s frequently are interrupted by one or more modern two-story structures built on one or two existing lots. Our house was built in 2001 by a builder who bought two smaller houses and tore them down. But most of our neighbors still lived in the original houses, some of them for years, which led to one of the impediments to recovery, the lack of flood insurance.

Any of the original homeowners who carried mortgages had paid them off long ago. Only mortgage lenders required an owner to purchase flood insurance, to protect the lender's investment. Therefore, long-time residents who owned their homes free and clear did not buy flood insurance. Homeowners would not voluntarily incur the expense when New Orleans had avoided major flooding for 40 years. The problem was that homeowners insurance covers wind and blown rain damage, but not damage from rising water. Most of the damage from Katrina came from rising water flooding the homes.

After Katrina, homeowners who did not have flood insurance had no way to recover their loss. Their only outlet was to apply for governmental assistance that was erratically handled through "Governor Blanco's Road Home Program," in which the state administered federal disaster relief money. The Road Home program became a disaster in and of itself. The application of the program was inconsistent and resulted in a paperwork morass that fueled Governor Kathleen Blanco's decision not to run for a second term.

Even the possession of flood insurance did not mean the homeowner would necessarily be made whole. The National Flood Insurance Program, a federal program administered by the insurance companies, limits recovery to $250,000 for the structure, no matter how big the house, and $100,000 for contents, no matter how extensive your personal property. After adding up the total costs of restoring our house, we were about $100,000 short of the structural renovation costs for our house of 3,400 square feet. In addition, we only had $50,000 in personal property coverage, despite losses that totaled $187,588 when we submitted them to our insurance company. Our attempts to bridge the gap through the Road Home program was rejected, which pointed up the inconsistency of the appraisal method. Many of our neighbors with similar damage to a similar-sized house with similar insurance coverage received as much as $150,000 in federal assistance.

We were fortunate we had the financial wherewithal to withstand the losses, but many of our neighbors did not. Even so, moving back into the neighborhood carried with it other concerns.

The city's water and sewer lines were leaking 50 million gallons of water a day because of a collapsed infrastructure. Corroding salt water contributed to broken pipes and water main breaks that threatened the huge water pumps that controlled the 3,200-mile system. A drastic drop in water pressure could allow raw sewage or other pollutants to back up into the water system. The city reported tap water was safe to drink, although few residents drank from the tap before Katrina and fewer would do so now. Many residents who were restoring their homes purchased expensive water filtration systems to assure the purity.

The electrical infrastructure also was problematic. One year after Katrina, no streetlights were working in Lakeview, and only a few stoplights had returned to service. Residents wishing to return were required to notify Entergy, the local power company, to send a crew to perform the on-site adjustments that would assure electrical service. It was a patchwork plan that would continue to hamper the recovery.

Another valid issue was safety and security. Many of our neighbors who locked valuables in what they thought was a secure room in their vacant house often came back to find doors or even walls knocked down and their belongings taken. Adding to the threat was an influx of foreign laborers who streamed into the city to meet the growing demand for construction work. Many of the laborers were from Mexico, and soon graffiti began to appear on abandoned buildings in Lakeview touting the colors and logos of various gangs. Fortunately, National Guard patrols supplemented a depleted New Orleans Police force in Lakeview and other areas. Elmo probably was our best deterrent, frequently barking day or night at some unknown threat to his realm.

It was into this cauldron of concerns that we and our neighbors were returning. Our next door neighbor, Anne Marie Sequeira, whom we affectionately dubbed the "Mayor of Vicksburg Street," kept us posted on our neighbors' progress and intentions. I had not taken the time to meet or get to know many of our neighbors since we bought the house in July 2003. I recognized most only by the nicknames we had given them. Anne Marie reported that Big Bob, her next door neighbor on the other side, had started to build back his home and would return soon. Mr. Frank, the elderly man across the street from her, was going to sell his house and would not return. Miss Linda and her family, on the other side of us, were in Texas and she did not know if they were coming back. Juan the cop down the street was going to renovate his house when he received his insurance money. Anne Marie told us most of our neighbors had survived the storm and were making plans to come back. But, chillingly, not all of them.

Margarita and Manuel Romero, an elderly brother and sister, lived in the little white bungalow directly across the street from us. Manuel was 85 and bedridden, and his sister, although three years older, still was able to care for him. Jean had spoken with Margarita on occasion but did not know much about them or their rich history.

Their parents moved from Mexico after World War I and established a market on Claiborne Avenue where the family members worked. Their father, also Manuel, was a cabinetmaker and during the war worked on the project to build the Higgins boats that would become famous as the Allied landing craft at Normandy.

The family moved to the fast growing suburban community of Lakeview in 1956. After he moved in, Manuel Sr. created a shop in the garage and used his woodworking skills to create beautiful molding and fine furniture for his new house.

Manuel Jr. studied music at Loyola University and became a music teacher in the Orleans Parish public school system. Manuel and a high school friend, Joseph Guerra, formed an orchestra that played at weddings and other events. Margarita worked for a medical clinic as a secretary and translator for Spanish-speaking patients. After the clinic closed, she also went to work for the Orleans Parish school system. Manuel had married, but after his wife died in 1996, he moved into the family home with Margarita who had remained in the house after their parents died.

Margarita had never married, but when Joseph Guerra and his wife had a baby girl, she asked to be godmother. The Guerras named their daughter Sara, and years later, Sara heard a special calling to help her godmother. She was devoted to their welfare, but as time passed and events fell into their natural order, Sara married and moved away to Denver in 1998.

As Manuel and Margarita declined in health, friends would come in and help with the laundry and personal needs. One friend, Howard Gonzalez, ran errands for the couple, and the Lakeview Presbyterian Church would send meals to their home. Patricia Peyton, a real estate agent, became especially attached to the couple. It was Peyton who had reserved a hotel room for Manuel and Margarita when the threat of Katrina became known. But Peyton called Sara to tell her Manuel and Margarita would not leave their home.

They had stayed in the house through Camille and Betsy, which were the worst hurricanes ever to hit the Gulf Coast, and what could be worse than those? They did not want to go to a new place in unfamiliar surroundings and maybe become disoriented, or worse, separated. They did not want to go through all that. They reasoned it was better to ride it out at home.

Sara persuaded her own parents to evacuate to Denver with her and husband Don Rooney, a broadcast engineer.

After Katrina wreaked its devastation, a month went by with no word from the Romeros. Then on September 28, Sara and Don Rooney went back to New Orleans to find some answers. Sara contacted the Red Cross, Coast Guard, FEMA, local hospitals and the National Guard to check their lists of dead, but the Romeros' names were not found.

The Rooneys' first visit to the house across the street showed the National Guard's ominous "X" on the front door. A zero in the bottom quadrant suggested the house had been searched and no bodies found. That appeared to be good news, until Sara learned that in the early days of the search for bodies, laws on the books prevented even the National Guard from forcibly entering a house. The front door legend reflected that searchers had been to the house, but it did not prove that an extensive search had been conducted.

Sara and Don walked around the house and saw that, despite the markings, nobody ever had entered the house. They did not try to break in right away, and instead spent the rest of the day trying to salvage furniture or other memories at her parents' house a few blocks away on Louisville Street.

The whereabouts of Manuel and Margarita was still a mystery.

Sara and Don returned to the house the next day, intent on entering and searching it thoroughly. The house was shut tight, and when they broke in the rancid air inside did not allow them to stay for long. They opened up the windows to enable some circulation, and tried to make their way about, but the explosion of debris prevented free movement.

They tried to move the rubble so they could walk around. Sara saw the elaborate moldings that Manuel's father had created, and remnants of the fine furniture he had crafted, now tossed about in a random heap. Everything was still there, and Sara knew how much Manuel and Margarita loved every piece of it. Sara knew Manuel and Margarita would not leave their house and that they were there, too, somewhere.

Don's work required that he return to Denver, so Sara's next trip to the house was alone. She was trying to move the debris in the front rooms in order to get to the bedrooms, which is where she expected to find Manuel and Margarita. As she moved slowly through, she saw sofas turned upside down, and the piano turned over and crumbling.

Sara made her way into the first bedroom and then backed out. She returned to the porch, afraid of what she might find but equally fearful she would find nothing. She took a deep breath to steel her courage and went back inside. She entered through the living room that opened to a hallway that led to the kitchen.

In the living room, she noticed a beautiful black lamp on the floor that she did not remember. Bob Stout, the neighbor on the other side of the Sequeiras, had black Arabian lamps where the bust and shade comes out of the head. The lamps were favorites of Bob's wife, Mary, Sara's close friend who had died four years earlier. Sara made a mental note to save the lamp for Bob and planned to return the next day. Before she left, she opened the doors to increase the flow of air through the house.

Sara brought Patricia Peyton back with her the following day to continue the search. It was Sara's third visit into the house, and she told Peyton to brace herself for the emotion she surely would feel in her first time through.

The two followed the pathway through the debris that Sara had carved the day before. They were careful to avoid broken glass as Sara harbored thoughts that the couple had been pulled from the house and died on the interstate or anonymously in an unknown shelter.

They had just about exhausted all search possibilities when Sara told Peyton about the lamp she had found the day before. But when they went to the spot where Sara first saw the lamp, she realized it was not a lamp. The increased flow of air overnight had revealed that the beautiful black lamp she thought she had seen was a body. A table lamp under the body with metal pole and lampshade gave the appearance that the body was part of a larger lamp.

Sara called 911, and the coroner's office and New Orleans police came quickly. The body she had found was Manuel. The searchers soon found Margarita's body under more debris in the bedroom. The grim discovery provided closure, but the moment carried special significance for Sara.

Sara was on the porch when the coroner came for Manuel and Margarita. It was then she realized she had been there before in a similar time. She was standing on the porch of Manuel and Margarita's house when the coroner had come for her friend Mary Stout four years earlier.

Sara smiled and thought it a beautiful moment.

CHAPTER
17

Bill Carr delivered the final draft of our Strategic Plan on December 18, 2006. Titled "Redefining UNO Athletics," it identified our history, our issues, our challenges and contained a blueprint for achieving the following "Intended Outcomes":

- A plan that is consistent with the Mission and Vision of both the university and Athletics Department.
- Blend Athletics planning with the *University of New Orleans Restructuring Plan 2006-2007*.
- The development of an Athletics Department Vision Statement and a redesign of the Department's Mission Statement.
- An analysis of the Athletics Department's operating environment; particularly the impact of Hurricane Katrina on the Department's infrastructure, sports sponsorship, facilities and funding mechanisms. Identify significant issues essential to determining the Department's strategic direction; this includes internal strengths and weaknesses along with external threats and opportunities.
- A seven-year plan that includes specific incremental strategies for meeting NCAA Division I membership and Sun Belt Conference requirements.
- Key goals and strategies that are market driven, research based and constituency supported.
- Assignment of staff responsibilities, due dates, resource requirements, measurable objectives and strategies for each key goal.
- NCAA Division I resource requirements (personnel, facilities, equipment and budget) for the Athletics Department's infrastructure and sports teams, including appropriate financial pro formas.
- Appropriate benchmarks in the Sun Belt Conference, selected peer universities and Division I intercollegiate athletics nationally.
- Participation by university and Athletics Department internal and external constituencies that encourages stakeholder advocacy for the Department's strategic direction.
- Identification of opportunities for the Athletics Department to collaborate with university campus service providers along with city and community agencies.

The key to the 46-page document was the section on funding the program, which began on page 19 under the topic "Athletics Funding Philosophy."

> UNO Athletics has historically operated with funding levels at or near the bottom of the Sun Belt Conference and with I-AAA peers. Athletics' revenues have primarily come from institutional support in the form of Student Fees, forcing the Department to manage by enrollment. This reliance, coupled with a modest State of Louisiana institutional funding cap for athletics, has created an unrealistic funding model of UNO athletics, which has dramatically hindered UNO's ability to compete in NCAA Division I.
>
> While UNO has followed other Sun Belt Conference schools in Louisiana by funding Compliance personnel from institutional revenues, it has not absorbed the costs of other Athletics support systems such as Athletics Academic Services. This broader funding is consistent with a national trend to strengthen institutional control and has allowed Louisiana Division I Athletics Programs to maximize funding cap revenues. Some Division I models also show expenses for Athletics business operations and fundraising assigned to the institution's financial affairs and development/foundations units, respectively.
>
> The practicality of UNO's Athletics model is further hindered by weak ticket sales in Men's Basketball and Baseball and an immature fund-raising program (Privateer Athletic Foundation). Revenues from university auxiliaries also have not been available recently to supplement or relieve the Athletics budget.
>
> Athletics' funding dilemma is exacerbated by an annual operating debt service payment of $250,000, which is automatically subtracted from Athletics' Institutional Support. The university is discussing a continuation of this debt service to cover Athletics' unfulfilled revenues resulting from Katrina.

The report generously characterized UNO's facilities as "modest in comparison to those of other SBC members" and recommended the university "commission a facilities master plan for long term benefit." Carr also identified "one of the greatest challenges facing UNO athletics is redefining itself in the greater New Orleans area as well as on the regional and national levels. This is described as branding."

Demerits were issued because the department had not achieved a complete menu of student-athlete welfare programs and had conducted our academic support services "without an appropriate level of staffing and services." Other shortcomings included the lack of adequate on campus dining facilities and contemporary housing which make it "difficult for athletics to consistently attract and retain top student-athletes."

Carr's Goals & Strategies were very well laid out. It reminded me of how Coach Marv Levy described winning to his Buffalo Bills team: "It's simple but not easy." Among the goals listed were the following:

"Enhance Athletics' Competitive Position"

"Maximize External Revenue"

"Provide Championship Facilities"

"Strengthen the UNO Athletics Brand"

"Allocate Sufficient Institutional Revenue"

These and other recommendations all required more funding, which was no mystery. The analysis also validated what I had been saying all along: We could enhance our competitive position if we could increase our recruiting budgets or improve our infrastructure comparable to the institutions we are trying to beat. We could raise more external revenue if we had more people selling tickets and sponsorships. We could strengthen our brand if we had the money to advertise and market our products. We could provide championship facilities if we had more money.

Carr laid out the elements of ROI — Return on Investment. Make the investment and experience the return.

I did not expect this to be an easy bit of persuasion. Even if his intentions were to give us everything he could, Tim Ryan had a lot of mouths to feed on a wounded campus. His ability to funnel funding into athletics would be scrutinized. Would he want to do it or could he do it? I did not consider at the time the political and emotional ramifications of unfettered support to athletics. The statement that continued to drive me was Ryan's assurance to Carr that he wanted a successful athletic program and he would support it.

If I had to carry a copy of the Carr report around with me from that day forward, I was going to remind Ryan of his pledge and give him the opportunity to fulfill it.

At the time the Carr Report was released to the public on January 7, 2007, Ryan was assembling a committee to create a Strategic Plan for the entire university. The committee would interview faculty members, staff members from every current department and students. The purpose was to create a consensus on what kind of a university would best respond to the challenges of the future. Katrina had, in effect, purged the university's closet and provided the opportunity to refill it with a new and modern wardrobe.

Ryan chose Dr. Scott Whittenburg to chair the committee. That was good news. Scott was a member of our Sunday morning golf group and had become a close friend. So far, Ryan had been consistent in his actions that athletics would be a part of the university going forward. I interpreted his appointment of Whittenburg as further confirmation.

On February 16, I was asked to appear before Whittenburg's committee to state why I believed athletics was an integral part of university life. I knew some members of the committee, including Dr. Russ Trahan, dean of the College of Engineering, and Dr. Al Merlin, a physician who served on the UNO Foundation Board. I did not know some of the other committee members, but I did know my message, and I delivered it enthusiastically.

The committee members were cordial and asked several questions after my presentation. Dr. Trahan endorsed my points to the committee and said he believed athletics was a valuable component of a successful university, and, therefore, deserved inclusion into the university's Strategic Plan.

Unfortunately, all the constituencies on campus did not agree. Subsequent polling conducted by the committee showed that athletics ranked at or near the bottom of nearly every list of departments or initiatives that were considered essential to a strong university. It reflected a longstanding attitude that was not actively anti-athletics but more that athletics was a nonentity. To most students, faculty and staff on campus, athletics was like the azalea bush that bloomed brightly for a short time and then sat ignored the rest of the year.

Athletics as it existed at UNO did not arouse passion among the student body, a fact that was reflected in poor student attendance at athletic events. Everybody had his or her own theory on why this was the case. Some suggested that the demise began with the development of the East Campus around 1980 that moved baseball and basketball from the main campus to a new site nearly a mile away. Students who did not have transportation would not bother to make the trip. Others suggested the large percentage of part time commuter students had full time jobs and did not have time for athletic events. Still others cited the shortage of on campus housing, whose students would be more interested in attending campus events.

The low marks from all constituencies were understandable, because they were judging a department that never had been supported properly. Ron Maestri theorized that so many years of non-support alienated a generation of students and led to apathy. It was the only athletic department they knew, and they had no idea what a properly supported program, like the aspirational one recommended in the Carr Report, would be like.

After the polling results became public, I was asked to appear again before the committee. I was fortunate because the day before my appearance, our baseball team rode a six-run inning to defeat archrival Tulane. Fortunately, the next day's *Times-Picayune* ran the story across the top of its front sports page with the headline: "Quick six carries Privateers past Wave." I carried a copy of the sports page into the meeting, and I told the committee members they could never achieve such positive publicity without an athletics program. In addition, we broadcast 40 men's and women's basketball games and 50 baseball games on radio, and we televised a handful of basketball and baseball games on the Cox Sports Network, which carried UNO's name across a network that ranged from

Gainesville, Florida, to Lubbock, Texas. Prospective students across the I-10 corridor may be hearing of the university for the first time because of those broadcasts. That introduction through an athletics event just might prompt them to dig deeper into our wealth of academic offerings.

Furthering that point, I attached two articles showing how basketball success at George Mason University and Butler University led to increased enrollment, more examples of school spirit, enhanced alumni participation, increased donations and higher sales of tickets and merchandise.

My appearances must have made a positive impression, because when the plan was published, athletics made the cut. Most encouraging was the plan's two objectives that pertained to athletics, which suggested support for restoring sports and for providing additional academic assistance for the student-athletes.

Objective 1.8 stated "The Athletics Department will meet all NCAA Division I and Sun Belt Conference (SBC) standards, including sports sponsorship, compliance with Title IX, and SBC sports competition." That appeared to commit the university to restore our sports to the minimum number for a non-football, Division I school within the NCAA's five-year waiver that would expire with the 2009-10 academic year.

Objective 2.6 stated, "The Athletics Department will meet NCAA metrics of academic success." Objective 2.6 was a pledge to bolster our academic support, which was essential in the era of the Academic Progress Rate, the NCAA's measurement of academic success. Also included was support of the NCAA's CHAMPS life skills program ("Challenging Athletes' Minds for Personal Success") directed at preparing students to meet social and career challenges. Other parts of the plan included additional support for summer school and the fifth year program that gave student-athletes an additional year of financial aid to achieve their degrees.

The good news was we were in the university's plan for the future. The implementation of these objectives would be the first tangible signs that the university would see the Carr Report as our blueprint for restoration. Just what kind of department we would have beyond this depended on how much of the Carr plan Tim Ryan was willing to adopt.

I immediately began supplying Ryan with ammunition to reinforce his support of the Carr recommendations. I believed he wanted UNO to have an athletic program, but I also realized that resources were limited and priorities would need to be made. The best thing I could do was to provide him with information, data and arguments that would help him make the case for athletics to some of his reluctant staff or faculty members.

I sent Ryan a memo titled "Institutional Support" in which I gave him the results of a telephone and e-mail poll of about 20 similar institutions I had conducted in conjunction with the Carr Report. The results revealed that athletics is not a profitable venture among institutions in the university's peer group. Deficits are expected and dealt with on an annual basis, either absorbed by their university's general fund or by a specific source such as their Foundation or Auxiliaries.

While athletics is self-supporting only among 20 or so major football schools, the great majority of institutions believe their athletics department is worthy of support. I wrote that our goal always should be to generate enough revenue to produce a profit, but the evidence suggests the true value of an Athletic Department to an institution is not measured in budgetary terms. Whether athletics is viewed as a valuable element of student life or as the public's window to the institution, most schools believe that supporting their athletics department produces a tangible benefit.

I received no response from that message, but that was not unusual. Ryan was notorious among his senior staff for not responding immediately, if ever, to e-mails. I assumed he read them.

Over the next year, I sent Ryan memos every three months on various aspects of the plan. On March 23, I sent a three-page memo endorsing Carr's recommendations to add necessary staff positions to achieve academic and revenue goals. I wrote we were limited by (1) our ability to generate outside revenue, and (2) the university's willingness to adopt certain proposals that are common in the industry but are not common practice here. I encouraged him to adopt Carr's proposed strategies.

The centerpiece of Carr's recommendations on revenue enhancement was the reopening of Lakefront Arena for basketball. "You only get to open a new building once," Carr said, encouraging us to take full advantage of it. However, we had just learned that our timetable for opening the Arena would be pushed back one year from the 2007-08 season to the 2008-09 season. The delay reflected a bigger issue that was troublesome to the entire university. The state's office of Facility Planning and Control had established a priority schedule on which of the 1,500 damaged state buildings would be fixed first. The Louisiana Superdome was at the top of the list, while Lakefront Arena was lumped with other buildings deemed "nonessential." In other words, they would fix it when they got to it, and not before.

I reminded Ryan that the inactivity of our primary revenue-producing venue severely hindered our revenue growth model and suggested that either new revenue streams or new methods of absorbing expenses into the general fund must be considered. The reality was that athletics had no chance of supporting itself until we were fully staffed and our primary revenue engine restored.

Again, I received no response.

The two-headed dragon that continued to breathe fire in our faces were the lack of revenue production and the lack of academic support. Provost Rick Barton and his assistants in Academic Affairs, Whittenburg and Dr. Dennis McSeveney, supported our efforts, but we needed actual bodies to help counsel and tutor our student-athletes. I pleaded with Ryan to allow us to add an academic support position recommended in the university's Strategic Plan. The position had been vacant since the spring 2006 downsizing. If we did not meet certain goals required by the NCAA's new academic yardstick, the Academic Progress Rate (APR), we could face sanctions of limited scholarships or lost post season opportunities.

In order to enhance our revenue, I requested two positions essential to any operation but absent from ours: A ticket manager who was charged with the selling and accountability of tickets to athletic events and a clerical person.

As incredible as it may seem, UNO athletics never had employed a person whose job included selling tickets. Our ticket operation had been handled on a part time basis by an employee of Lakefront Arena. Her primary task was to take orders for ticket sales of Arena events such as a Wiggles concert or Disney on Ice show. A ticket person dedicated to our department could actively sell part of the day and then work on the accounting and implementation the rest of the day.

Another staff vacancy was that of administrative assistant, which was frozen after Susan Broussard moved to the compliance and academic position. We probably were the only unit on campus that did not have any clerical help, but we could not afford the luxury. Callers to the department did not hear a voice but a recording that referred them to an employee directory.

I always had written my own letters, so not having a secretary was not a big deal to me. I recalled Tom Benson regaling his officers at the Saints for making their own copies when the Saints paid secretaries to do that job. "I don't pay you to make copies or type letters," he would say. We didn't pay our coaches to make copies or type letters either, but if they didn't do it, it would not get done.

Aside from the clerical duties, we needed a traffic cop to direct the suffocating paperwork required by the university. Travel reimbursements, time slips for tutors, leave slips for vacations and sick days, human resources debris and the myriad forms thrown into the pot created a sour gumbo that bubbled up daily. Several of us were trying to piecemeal these responsibilities, but those efforts resulted in inconsistencies and errors. Our good intentions exacerbated a deteriorating relationship with other university departments.

For example, if we made a mistake on a travel reimbursement form, the accounting office would reject it and throw it on a stack. We would not know it was rejected until the coaches complained that their credit card bills had arrived, and they needed reimbursement. We finally would track it down, resubmit it and then have to follow up to make sure it was in the pipeline.

We were a nuisance to the offices of financial services, purchasing and accounts payable, because we did not have anyone specializing in their procedures. The attitude trickled down from the top, where sat Linda Robison, the vice chancellor for financial services and CFO. She was a career state employee who bathed daily in the molasses bowl of procedures. Her knowledge of that quagmire made her indispensable. She survived not by solving any problems but by knowing the procedures with which to navigate around and through them.

On athletics issues, Robison could be wheedled only by another career state employee, Mike Dauenhauer. When Mike left the athletics department to become university bursar, his young replacement, Ola Adegboye, was thrown into the breach with little preparation. It would take any new employee at least one annual cycle to become familiar with the peculiarities of the system, but Robison was short staffed in her own office and could not afford time to help train him. Ola's inexperience with the procedures made him an impediment to Robison and her staff. That gave her even more reason to complain to anyone who would listen that athletics was a drain on the university; its personnel were incompetent and the university would be better off without any of us.

While I was fighting the funding and administrative battles, our teams were doing their best to put a positive face on UNO athletics. Our men's golf team under Chris McCarter had become one of the top three teams in the Sun Belt Conference. The year before, the team won two tournaments and had six top three finishes, and McCarter was named conference Coach of the Year.

In 2007, the team had eight top five finishes, including two runner-up finishes in the spring. Privateer medalist Jose Toledo was named Louisiana College Golfer of the Year. Still, it was a near miss in the conference tournament that again raised the fear of "the Katrina Curse."

UNO led the field by four strokes in the final round with one hole to go when Privateer Anthony Cantu pulled his drive into the water. McCarter was walking with Cantu, who had to take a drop on a steep embankment. When Cantu dropped the ball, it began rolling downhill toward the water. McCarter instinctively reached down to save the ball, but touched it before it reached the hazard line. Impeding progress of the ball was a 2-stroke penalty. Cantu took an 8 on the hole, and the team missed a playoff by one stroke.

The best news from the playing field was that Tom Walter's baseball team was having its most successful year since UNO won the Sun Belt Conference tournament in 2000. The team's record of 38-26 included two-of-three over Tulane and a split with LSU. UNO entered the conference tournament seeded fourth but turned the tournament on its ear. The Privateers defeated Western Kentucky and Middle Tennessee before suffering their first loss in a rematch with Middle. UNO and Middle would play an elimination game on Saturday morning with the winner taking on top seed Louisiana-Lafayette for the championship that afternoon.

UNO pounded out a 10 to 4 win in the morning to send the Blue Raiders home and then shocked the Ragin' Cajuns with an 8 to 2 walkover for the championship.

The team's success reflected the battle tested toughness of its core players. Twenty members of the team, including seven of eight starting position players, the three top starting pitchers and the closer all had endured Katrina's hardships and the exile to Las Cruces, New Mexico, after the storm.

The excitement of UNO's first NCAA tournament appearance in seven years was a welcome relief from the hard times. People were excited about something good happening to us after so much frustration. We threw a party in the ballroom of the alumni center to watch the site selection show on ESPN. A big cheer went up when we learned we would be headed to Wichita as the No. 3 seed in that regional. We would face the No. 2 seed Shockers in the opening game.

Tim Ryan flew up for the tournament to show his support of the program as did Sybil Boudreau, our faculty athletics representative.

Walter's team continued to enchant in the opening game, upsetting the Shockers 7 to 6 with a thrilling ninth inning comeback. The second game, against No. 1 seed Arizona, also was set for a storybook ending. But all American second baseman Johnny Giavotella's deep fly ball to right center field with the winning runs on base was run down by the Wildcats' center fielder with his back to home plate.

That sent the Privateers into an elimination match against Wichita, but the magic had run out. New Orleans was out of pitching and the bats went silent as the home team prevailed, 7 to 3.

Even the loss could not detract from the fact that UNO athletics was enjoying national prominence. It was our first major achievement since I became Athletic Director, and it could not have come at a better time. We proved we could produce high quality competitive teams with little budgetary support. It was a logical argument that with sufficient financial support we could do the same with all of our teams.

On June 27, I sent Ryan a follow-up to my March request for additional support, which had not been answered. I streamlined the previous request to include only those positions that were suspended or were frozen after resignations: the academic support person, athletics ticket manager, administrative assistant, another sales person, assistant business manager, and to make our part time broadcast play-by-play man a full time employee.

I told him the other positions requested in the previous memo were no less important to our long term growth and restoration, but giving us back the suspended positions would allow us to maintain "minimum standards" for a Division I program.

A few days later, on June 29, I sent another memo that was in accordance with one of the goals in the Carr Report, a recommendation that the university transfer certain athletics expenses to other departments. For example, many universities take the athletics business manager salary out of the athletics budget and put it in the university's Financial Services budget. The sports information director might be reallocated to the university advancement or marketing department. It is a common practice to relieve the burden on the athletics budget. This practice is termed "institutional support."

To bolster the argument, I included some recently published information that showed only 22 of 313 Division I athletic departments were self-sustaining, and all 22 had robust football programs. Since athletics programs such as ours do not generate the cash flow to support themselves, it is incumbent upon the institution to determine the value of its athletic program and allocate sufficient revenue to support it. Reallocating expenses to other university entities was essential if the department of intercollegiate athletics was to fulfill its academic and athletic mission and its commitment to our student-athletes. Specifically, the Carr report recommended that the following areas of expense be absorbed into the comparable university office: academic services, business operations, fund-raising, compliance and marketing and promotions.

I had not received a response before another crisis intervened a few days later. Once again, something positive such as the baseball championship was about to be offset by more bad news. This was one I had foreseen and was satisfied I had done all I could do to avoid. That is why it was the last thing I expected to hit us now.

CHAPTER
18

B uzz Williams walked into my office on Monday, July 2, and informed me he had been offered an assistant coach's position at Marquette, and he was considering it. He had done the same thing a month earlier when he told me his former head coach at Texas A&M, Billy Gillispie, had called to see if he wanted to join Gillispie at Kentucky. Since UK was my alma mater, I jokingly told Williams if they had a spot for me, we'd make it a package deal. I did not believe Williams was interested, and I heard no more about it.

But this was different. I could tell Williams was serious, because he wasn't joking about it. I've been in this business too long to be surprised by much, but I was extremely disappointed. If I did one thing during the search for a head coach, I made it clear to all candidates that our situation was not normal and could get worse before it got better. As part of his recruiting pitch, Williams convinced me he understood our situation and would get through it. Now he was trying to get out of his commitment.

Williams told me he had to do "what was best for my family." Apparently he thought leaving a Division I head coaching job for an assistant coaching position would help him do that. I reminded him he had a healthy buyout in his contract and if he left, we would pursue it vigorously.

He asked me to give him Chancellor Ryan's number so he could discuss the situation with him. At the time, Ryan was in Innsbruck, Austria, where UNO has an active international program. I cautioned Williams if he called Ryan, to be considerate of the change in time zones. Here I was talking about international time zones to a guy who over the past year showed he did not know that all hurricanes were given names or that President George W. Bush was a Republican.

True to form, Ryan said later Williams woke him around 1 A.M. Innsbruck time and stayed on the phone for 45 minutes. Ryan said the conversation was disjointed, going from statements about doing what was right for his family to his chance to join a "top ten" program. Ryan said Williams did bring up the buyout, and Ryan told him we would not waive it.

Steve Cottingham, the acting athletic director at Marquette, called me to confirm they were interested in hiring Williams. I told him Williams's contract contained a buyout of $300,000, and we would expect Williams to honor it. He asked if we could negotiate it through guarantee games, and I deferred to our university counsel, Patricia Adams. The previous year, during our negotiations on Monte Towe's buyout, the attorney for the LSU System informed Adams we did not have the right to negotiate away a "state asset" such as a buyout. We eventually reached an agreement with Towe, but that situation was fresh in my mind. I did not want to give the impression I would or could negotiate it.

On Wednesday evening, Williams came by my house. He walked in the door, saw our piano and sat down to play a few notes, which surprised me because he appeared relaxed. We moved to my television room, and I closed the French doors for privacy. Much like his conversation with Ryan, he repeated his two major reasons. He said this might be his last opportunity to get to a "top ten" program and that he had to do what was best for his family.

When he saw I was not giving in to any of his arguments, he put his head in his hands, giving the impression he was agonizing over his decision. I suspected later that this, too, was part of his act. If he was truly agonizing, it was not because of a tough decision but because we would not release him from the buyout.

I tried some tough love and told him to "grow some balls," be a man about it and fulfill his obligations. I told him if his ultimate goal was to be a head coach at a major Division I school, the best way to get there was have success here. If I were an athletic director at a large school, I would be reluctant to hire a head coach who did not have previous head coaching experience and, preferably, with success.

I did not hear anything more for 24 hours, until I received a call Thursday from a local attorney I knew, Bill Becknell. Bill had represented the Saints before I joined the team, but I had been with him on occasion and liked him. He called to say Buzz had asked him to represent him on negotiating the buyout. I knew Becknell had done some legal work with former Coach Tim Floyd, but I did not ask how he became involved with Williams. I told Becknell the same thing; if Williams left, we would demand he pay the buyout in full.

Friday morning, Williams came into my office and handed me a letter of resignation. I told him I was very disappointed, and I had nothing more to say to him.

The resignation was a terrible blow to our program, both perceptually and literally. Williams had come in and generated interest and true enthusiasm for the future of our men's basketball program. For him to resign abruptly was a message that, despite my warnings to Williams and the other candidates that things could get worse before they got better, a negative pall continued to hang over our program.

Two years and two new head coaches also created problems for the team's academic standing with the NCAA. Williams ran off four players who did not fit his mold, and I feared a new coach might try and do the same. Wholesale changes lower the academic progress rate and could trigger penalties. Loss of scholarships and no chance at post season opportunities can doom a program.

The NCAA recognizes a coaching change can seriously affect the APR measurement, but they have not yet given the victimized schools any relief. With a new head coach and new expectations, it was apparent our men's basketball APR score would be a major problem for years.

That was just another dilemma that I threw on the stack with the rest of them.

Williams was the third head coach to resign from our program in the space of six weeks. Our swimming coach, Ashley Tappin, had just gotten married, and she wanted to be free to travel with her husband who was a concert promoter. Dana Launey, my volleyball coach of one year, resigned to become an assistant high school volleyball coach under our former coach, Julie Ibieta, at Metairie Park Country Day. Dana also had a young family, and the prospects of educating them at a discount at a premier high school was worth more than her salary at UNO.

Frankly, I was more concerned about filling the volleyball and swimming vacancies than the basketball vacancy. We were only nine months past the extensive search that produced Williams, and the candidates were still fresh in my mind. During the week of playing hide-and-seek with Williams, I decided to offer the job to Joe Pasternack, the Bobby Knight disciple and young assistant at Cal-Berkeley who grew up in New Orleans. Pasternack was impressive in the interviews the year before, and I believed he and Williams were very close in coaching and recruiting ability. At 34, Williams had a slight edge in experience over the 30-year-old Pasternack.

In retrospect, the New Orleans connection should have carried more weight in my initial deliberations. It was one thing to present to the candidates just how difficult things were and how much Katrina had affected our program. However, it was quite another thing when the candidates themselves had been affected.

Pasternack's parents had lost their home, which gave him a shareholder's stake in what we had gone through and what we would need to recover. Williams had talked a good game, but he never understood the impact of Katrina on the university and our community. He was a master recruiter who was accustomed to persuading immature young basketball players that his institution was the best for them. Accordingly, he had done a good job conning at least one athletic director. It was obvious I had grossly overestimated his toughness and ability to overcome obstacles, even ones he had been warned about.

About two hours after Williams left my office, the phone rang. It was Pasternack who had heard the news on the coaches' grapevine. He asked me what I was going to do about a head coach, and I asked him, "When can you start?"

Pasternack came to New Orleans the next day, and his feet did not touch the ground for months. He graduated from Metairie Park Country Day School, the same school where our two former volleyball head coaches now worked. He was truly thankful to be home, coaching at the school where he was a regular attendee during the Tim Floyd and Tic Price coaching eras.

As a recent outsider, he also said UNO was the talk of the coaches' grapevine. If the federal government could harness the coaches' gossip line, they could save trillions on an early warning defense system. Coaches love to talk about which jobs are open, which jobs are going to be open and which coaches are leaving their current jobs to take the new jobs. The only rule of the coaches' grapevine is if you haven't heard a good rumor by noon, you are obligated to start one. Facts are optional.

Pasternack said the hot gossip of the moment was that UNO athletics was going to shut down in another year. Buzz Williams knew it, they said, and that's why he bailed out. Williams would avoid the buyout, they said, because he would fight it until there was no program left to buy out of. The rumors compounded the problems for Pasternack, who was trying to hire assistant coaches. Every coach in America had heard the stories, and when Pasternack called, they said, unless you were desperate you should not take his call.

It was more evidence that Katrina was the gift that keeps on giving.

Despite the rumors, Pasternack's hire was the first of a solid trifecta that included Joszef Forman to coach volleyball and Randy Horner to coach the swimming and diving team. Forman was an assistant at Mississippi State and had a good reputation as a recruiter. Horner was a long-time assistant at Missouri State, which swam as part of the combined Sun Belt Conference/Missouri Valley Conference championships. Horner knew our conference, was enthusiastic and was ready to head up his own program.

I was excited going into the 2007-08 academic year. Anticipation is a great motivator and one reason we stay in this business a lifetime. You always have hope that this season will be that special one you will remember fondly forever. If the season does not turn out well, wait until the last game of the season when you're undefeated again and waiting 'til next year. Brooklyn Dodgers fans popularized the saying, but in sports there is always another chance.

Pasternack, Horner and Forman would join our existing group, which I considered solid. Tom Walter's baseball team was the defending Sun Belt Conference baseball champion and Chris McCarter's golfers resolved to win the championship that narrowly escaped them the previous spring. Amy Champion's basketball team showed gradual improvement with nine wins the previous year. But Amy had experienced more difficulties with Katrina's aftermath than any of our other coaches. I believed in her, and as long as I was AD she would be my women's coach.

Pasternack seemed to be everywhere, trying to sign players, raise money and build awareness for his team. His young face and slight build would get him mistaken for the team manager in his first season, but once the game began his bearing and control would leave no doubt who was in charge.

Rick Mello, the Sun Belt's assistant commissioner, thought Pasternack needed a nickname, and came up with "Hopscotch." I thought it was okay, but it did not truly reflect Pasternack's ability to bounce from one task to the next. From that point on, when Mello and I would discuss "Ricochet" we knew who we were talking about.

Pasternack signed two new players, including a 6-11 freshman from Yugoslavia, Jaroslav Tyrna, who was eligible immediately. The coach took a chance on signing Jeremy Johnson, a high school player who had not qualified yet academically but who Pasternack said was the best point guard in the state. If he had to sit a year, that would not be a bad thing because it would allow him to focus on academics.

Pasternack also persuaded former Privateer Coach Tim Floyd, then head coach at Southern California, to come back for a charity roast to benefit the men's basketball program. It would be the highlight of the fall sports calendar. The proceeds would fund a "bonding" trip to a Cancun tournament the following August 2008, when Pasternack's second team would feature as many as nine new faces.

I spent much of the summer hiring the three new coaches, valuable time that could have been spent restoring some of our sports. It was essential we begin to restore sports during the 2007-08 academic year, which was the third year in our five-year waiver granted by the NCAA. We needed to start showing some progress toward regaining our full Division I status. Which sports would come back first was not a difficult decision.

My old tennis coach, Burzis Kanga, had called to express an interest in returning. I told him I was disappointed in the way things turned out before, and he acknowledged his own disappointment in the situation and his own reaction to it. He explained his marriage to NBC superstar Hoda Kotb was not working out, and they soon would divorce. He wanted to leave New York and return to New Orleans to finish what he had started when I hired him in 2003.

Men's and women's tennis were priorities since the new 26-court University Tennis Center was completed and open for play. I rehired Kanga at the end of the first semester, and he began recruiting his teams for the following academic year.

I also told Horner I intended on adding men's swimming to our menu, and he could immediately start recruiting male swimmers for the following year. I knew men's swimming was not a growing sport and, in fact, was often sacrificed when schools needed to add women's programs to satisfy Title IX requirements. Horner took that as an advantage, reasoning that fewer men's programs meant more quality swimmers were available. Our program could rise to national prominence quickly.

Men's swimming was logical, because we had coaches in place, we could utilize our existing facility, and swimmers as a rule are good students. New Orleans also had an enthusiastic swimming community whose club teams could serve as a feeder system and a source of outside income for our coaches.

We learned later of another benefit. I did not intend for the addition of men's swimming to be particularly groundbreaking, but it turned out to be significant. We received national recognition for being the first Division I school in more than 30 years to add men's swimming.

It was further evidence that genius often is accidental.

About two weeks into the fall, 2007, semester, I asked for a meeting with Chancellor Ryan. I had not received any significant feedback on my proposals to add staff or to reallocate our expenses, and my suspicions were growing. The university plan included some positive suggestions that help was on the way. However, I also knew enrollment for the fall semester again was a disappointment, which meant we could not expect any new revenue through student fees.

I wanted to know if we were going to follow the Carr plan or if current circumstances would dictate otherwise. Ryan was receptive to my concern. He even made one positive suggestion, offering to forego the annual $250,000 deficit reduction payment. The deficit reduction payment was the product of a 2001 agreement between the LSU Board of Supervisors and the university's former Chancellor, Greg O'Brien. The Board agreed to increase the athletics student fee from $60 per semester to $100, but required that $250,000 of the new money would go annually to service the accumulated deficit. Although nobody mentioned it during the interview process, I inherited a $3 million debt the LSU System expected to be paid off. Unlike most schools that absorb a departmental debt, the athletics debt had been accumulating and compounding over the years because athletics was an auxiliary enterprise, which included the bookstore and food service. The university used the auxiliaries' profit to fund special projects, but the athletics deficit ate into the profits of the bookstore and food service. Athletics was expected to pay off the debt that also included a buyout of former AD Ron Maestri's contract.

Ryan's willingness to put that money to active use was positive news. We could use the money to fund critical positions we needed. Ryan asked me to submit a proposal on what positions I would add back if he could persuade the LSU System office to forego the payment. I went back to my office and prepared a memo requesting that the money be put toward hiring a tennis coach, an academic support person, a ticket manager and to bring our broadcaster, Mike Wagenheim, aboard as a full time employee.

To his credit, Ryan approved the plan, and we proceeded to hire the individuals listed in the memo. We still were operating short of minimum standards, but Ryan was showing a willingness to help us. At that point, I would take anything I could get.

Other progress was being made to the action items on the Carr timeline. The most prominent was the assignment of the old Alumni and Development Center to become the standalone Athletics Administration Building. We would have to wait for the building to be renovated since, like Lakefront Arena, it was considered "nonessential" in the state renovation priority. The fact that the athletics department for the first time would get its own building, whenever it was ready, was a huge step forward for our program.

Before Katrina, athletics had occupied a warren of offices in Lakefront Arena. After we returned from Baton Rouge, we set up shop in the 40-year-old Human Performance Center, first in a classroom and then in the offices of terminated faculty. We soon would be moving again, to a single floor in the renovated dormitory, Bienville Hall. It provided more offices to accommodate our staff, but it was stark and looked like an old building. To further darken the picture, a student had been murdered in the building the semester following Katrina in a crime that was never solved. McCarter, our droll golf coach, dubbed our new offices "Shawshank," after the Morgan Freeman prison movie, and the name stuck.

On September 13, Ryan invited me to a meeting introducing the new president of the LSU System, Dr. John Lombardi. All vice chancellors, deans and department heads were asked to submit a one-page summary of their department and be prepared to give Lombardi a short oral presentation.

The attendees were seated in a horseshoe configuration with Lombardi and Ryan at the head. As luck would have it, I was seated next to Linda Robison, the university's chief financial officer and a major critic of our program. The reports began on our side of the table, to Lombardi and Ryan's right. When Robison's turn came, she gave a short summary of Financial Services and closed with a statement that her job would be perfect if not for some departments that kept running an annual deficit. With that, she turned to her right, away from Lombardi, and stared pointedly at me.

In her world, she probably thought she was being clever, but it was an uncomfortable moment. Lombardi had not been around long enough to know the details or the personalities involved. Ryan was smiling through gritted teeth, not knowing what to say. The other 25 or so individuals fidgeted uncomfortably. I was offended, appalled and furious that Robison would stage such a show at my expense. However, I told her simply "turn around and maybe you'll learn something" while I told the new system president that UNO athletics was standing tall and prepared to move forward.

Lombardi smiled, nodded his approval and moved on to the next person.

If we did not have enough challenges with the people and events around us, we soon were haunted by a specter from the past. Our attorney, Patricia Adams, sent Buzz Williams a letter reminding him he was in default of the buyout clause in his contract and demanded payment, which amounted to a bit less than $300,000. Williams responded to the demand with a lawsuit in Civil District Court for Orleans Parish against the university to have the contract declared null and void.

The fact that Williams was trying to avoid paying the buyout was not a surprise. Between his crocodile tears of wanting to do "what's best for my family," he kept alluding to the buyout clause as if it were a secondary consideration. Most disappointing was that the substance of his allegations was forewarned in my Katrina disclaimer to the candidates: *"It's not perfect, and it could get worse before it gets better."* Williams came in here knowing we had problems, because we told him so up front. We warned him it could get worse.

He seemed to be the only head coach who could not handle the situation. Tom Walter never complained and won a conference championship. Amy Champion endured more defections than any other head coach, but she didn't complain.

The other coaches displayed the same resilience and commitment to their student-athletes despite the problems. The coaches who remained used the tools at their disposal and did their best because of their high integrity and character. Those qualities are difficult to measure in a few interviews.

CHAPTER
19

The men's basketball team would have an early test to gauge how much the coaching change from Williams to Pasternack would affect their performance. Pasternack's first significant game as head coach would be at North Carolina State as part of the buyout agreement with Monte Towe. The Wolfpack was rated No. 19 in one top 25 preseason poll, and they recruited one of the top high school players in the nation in J. J. Hickson, who would be an NBA Lottery selection the following spring.

I flew to Raleigh with the team to show my support and also to visit with Monte and his wife P.D. They took me to dinner on Friday night and I could tell how happy they both were to be back in Raleigh. Monte was coaching at his alma mater and P.D. was near her sister who lived there. After dinner, they took me by the basketball offices to show me how "the other half" lived.

The Curtis & Jacqueline Dail Basketball Complex was three years old, but it looked as if it had just been taken out of the box. It included practice courts, locker room, coaches' offices, meeting rooms, a player lounge, weight room and a study center. It was opulent. What impressionable recruit wouldn't want to spend four years in this building? In comparison to what we could show our recruits, it made me want to cry.

I was glad our players would not see the complex, and I hoped they would not feel overwhelmed the next night when we arrived at the RBC Center. Walking onto the floor, I felt like the Christians walking into the Roman Coliseum. Nearly 20,000 red seats surrounded the playing floor at two levels. The 1,500 courtside seats reserved for students were already two-thirds filled, already surpassing UNO's average home crowd. Hanging in the rafters were banners from the Wolfpack's 1974 and 1983 national championship teams, and another from the 2002 Carolina Hurricane Stanley Cup finalist.

Also hanging in the rafters was Monte Towe's No. 25 jersey alongside those honoring David Thompson, Tom Burleson, Jimmy Valvano and other Wolfpack legends.

Once the game began, however, our players saw their big time ACC opponents as just five guys on the other team confined by the same 94-foot by 50-foot rectangle. Our team showed some jitters at first, falling behind by nine points early, but Pasternack would not let them quit, pushing them and convincing them they could compete.

The rookie coach looked as though he'd done this for years, roaming back and forth in front of the bench, shouting instructions and challenging his players. At halftime, I was pleased we were trailing by only 30 to 28. I feared a repeat of past performances at Florida State and LSU when it almost seemed like we were down by 30 points when we got off the bus.

The home team stretched the lead to 11 by the first TV time-out of the second half, and I thought here is where they make their run. But the plucky Privateers came back from a time-out to score the next eight points and were right back in the game.

We were not shooting the ball well, but N.C. State's guards were having problems with the quickness of Bo McCalebb. Our big men, 6-10 senior Ben Elias and 6-11 freshman Jaroslav Tyrna, competed evenly on the boards against the more highly recruited Wolfpack players.

UNO took the lead for the first time, 44-43, on a jumper by guard Shawn Reynolds with 9:44 remaining. I never deluded myself into thinking we would hold it, especially after N.C. State quickly regained the lead and stretched it to 61 to 54 with 1:55 remaining. I was proud of our guys already, but I did not imagine how much prouder I would become.

McCalebb drove for a lay-up to cut the lead to 61 to 56 with 1:47 left. The teams swapped possessions until McCalebb was fouled and sank two free throws to make it 61 to 58 with 57 seconds remaining. A quick State turnover gave UNO the ball again, and Kyndall Dykes hit a driving lay-up to cut the margin to one. N.C. State could have milked the clock, waiting for a foul, but inexplicably went right for the basket and missed a lay-up at the other end. McCalebb was fouled on the rebound.

Bo never had distinguished himself as a great shooter, and he had struggled on the foul line throughout his career. But this night he was nearly perfect. He hit both free throws, his ninth in ten attempts, to give the Privateers a 62 to 61 lead with 14 seconds remaining. The Wolfpack went down the floor quickly again, and this time Gavin Grant nailed a lay-up with seven seconds to go.

Pasternack preferred to let his offense operate and not give N.C. State a chance to regroup defensively. McCalebb was bringing the ball quickly up the floor as the clock ticked past five seconds. I saw a pass into the top of the key, but from my vantage point on the end zone press table, I could not see who caught the ball. I only recall seeing the greatest shot in Privateer basketball history arc high and come down through the nets with less than two seconds on the clock.

Unlikely hero T.J. Worley had given UNO a 65 to 63 win and its most improbable victory ever over a former national champion and one of the top teams in one of the best basketball conferences in the nation.

I jumped in the air with my arms high as most of the coliseum fell into a dead, stunned silence. I ran onto the floor and hugged the first player I saw, who was James Parlow. I followed the team into the locker room for the celebration. Pasternack, who had a shell-shocked look on his own face, was grinning broadly and shouted above the celebration for the players to pay attention.

"That is what you can do with rebounding and defense," he told his giddy players. "Enjoy it tonight, and then let's get back to business tomorrow."

That game ignited a brief flurry of national recognition for UNO athletics. Stories in the *New York Times* and *Sports Illustrated* paid tribute to a program that still was wounded from Katrina but was competing at the highest level of college basketball. It wasn't *Glory Road,* parts of which coincidentally were filmed at pre-Katrina UNO Lakefront Arena, but it still was a feel-good story. America likes the underdog, especially when the underdog overcomes the odds and beats the big guy.

The win over N.C. State was a great moment in Privateers sports history. I only hoped and prayed that moments like this and the NCAA appearance by our baseball team would become the platform we needed to generate more interest, put more fannies in the seats and inject some much needed revenue into the coffers.

CHAPTER
20

John Barranco, my assistant AD for business development, poked his head in my door and asked if I had a minute. I've always encouraged open communication with my staff, and motioned for him to come in. John nodded slightly, then turned to shut the door behind him.

His action was familiar, one that I had seen too many times the past two years, and rarely resulting in anything I wanted to hear. Only recently, Susan Broussard, my administrative assistant whom I had promoted to assistant AD, followed the same pattern when she came in and told me she was taking another job at the university. More money, shorter hours, less stress. Employees come and usually go because of a bigger carrot someone is dangling in front of them. I didn't like it, but I understood it.

I was prepared for déjà vu, but John gave me a pleasant surprise. "I want you to know that I'm not leaving," he said first. John had been with me almost from the beginning, and he was a valuable member of the staff. He was a consummate salesman, hard worker and was dedicated to helping us recover. I sat and waited for his next words.

"You've treated me good, and I've got no complaints," he said, as his eyes looked away from me and toward the floor. "I'm just afraid I'm losing it, and I think I'm going to have to see somebody, get some help. I just wanted you to know."

John sat before me, looking embarrassed about revealing a vulnerability he never had seen in himself before. Normal, well-adjusted people aren't supposed to turn themselves inside-out before strangers. This was a confident, sometimes cocky, individual who would walk through the office, spouting bromides from motivational speakers such as Zig Ziglar, Julio Molero and Jim Collins.

I knew he had experienced some serious family issues with a parent's illness and the recent death of a grandparent, but his job performance had not suffered.

He said he was discouraged that despite our efforts so little good had happened to us. He said he kept hoping he'd come to the office one day and be greeted with good news instead of the usual problems and frustrations. Despite the occasional joyful blip such as the win at N.C. State, we were fighting the everyday struggles of a still shuttered Lakefront Arena, reduced staff and suffocating budgetary restraints caused by lower enrollment.

"I hate to come to work," he said. "But as much as I hate it, if I had lost my house, I'd have …. I don't know how *you* have done it."

I was extremely touched by John's candor and his thoughtfulness. I had asked myself the same questions many times. No matter how hard we worked or what we did to overcome this massive disruption to our careers and our personal lives, it just seemed the water kept rising.

I smiled and thanked him for his concern and told him sometimes a boss doesn't have the luxury of worrying about himself. My main concern when I walk through the door in the morning is how can I motivate these good people to perform beyond their capability or desires just one more day? Let's get through today, and maybe tomorrow will be the day that something good happens.

John's comments made me think about how my work habits had changed since Katrina. I didn't feel guilty about leaving work early to pick up my children at school or going home for lunch and leisurely watching the midday news before returning to work.

Family had become the most important thing in reality rather than ideally. We always say "family comes first," as we spend 12-hour days at the office or miss our child's soccer game because of a meeting that could be held tomorrow. This post-Katrina revelation might simply be a manifestation of the age-old concept of *mañana* that New Orleanians have perfected over the years. It's just that now we had an excuse.

We sat there for a few seconds, looking at each other but neither of us speaking. "I just wanted to say thank you and not to worry about me," he said finally. "I just needed to talk about it."

I had no response but to smile and nod. I knew what he meant.

CHAPTER
21

Propelled by its big win over North Carolina State, Pasternack's basketball team continued to play well. The team won 11 of its first 13 games and received votes for the top 25 in America. The fact that something good was finally happening lifted the attitudes of our staff and gave us hope that things were turning the corner. But the daily frustrations continued.

We did not have a budget for advertising, so we could not take advantage of our success. We hoped the increased coverage in the *Times-Picayune* and on local television would help. But we were right in the middle of the Saints' season. The loyalty of the New Orleans sporting public to the Saints compelled media outlets to devote most of their time and space to the Black and Gold. The NBA Hornets had started strong and were taking the bulk of the remaining media attention.

We were treated like the little brother who came home with an "A" on his report card. We got a pat on the head, a brief "atta boy," and then things returned to normal. We did not have the luxury of riding one big victory or one event to prosperity. We had to do it over and over again until the public and the press took notice and added us to their priority list.

It was no mystery that men's basketball would be our best vehicle to rebuild our revenue base and restore the program. The uncontrollable variable was the performance of the team. Now that we had a team playing well, that alone was not enough. We had to work to sell tickets, preferably through some form of targeted awareness, which costs money. At the very least, we needed to buy advertising in the newspaper and on radio and television, and we needed ticket sellers calling businesses to sell group plans.

I was talking to everyone I could and challenging our staff and coaches to do the same. Michael Sapera, the enthusiastic president of the Privateer Athletic Foundation, was trying to enlist his board to sell tickets. But the results from part time selling would never be the same as employing a full time selling strategy.

I had seen what the strategic channeling of resources could produce. When I was at the NFL Management Council, NFL Properties maintained a "hot markets" division. Every year, one NFL team that was not expected to do well would get off to a hot start. Properties would dispatch a team of aggressive young marketing and sales wizards to the hot market to implement sales plans, provide marketing assistance and suggest community service initiatives to arouse the public and take advantage of the team's performance. That strategy matured to the point that every team in the NFL and the rest of professional sports now has sufficient staff on hand to promote the product year-round.

We needed to do the same thing, to grab the public by the collar and make them look at us. Instead, we were forced to sit back and hope the team would continue playing well until somebody noticed. But few outside of our loyal core ever did notice. As a result, our home attendance at the Human Performance Center during that nationally prominent run averaged only about 700.

We lost a major opportunity because we could not afford to take advantage of what we had. It was another frustration, knowing what we needed to do to help ourselves but not having the resources to do it. My patience pot was beginning to boil.

Unfortunately, men's basketball leveled off after its hot start and finished with a 19-12 record. With the early victories and Bo McCalebb closing out a great career, we had hoped for an NIT berth, but we were ignored when the selections were made.

McCalebb's skill elicited one cliché after another, but simply he was just fun to watch. Listed generously at 6-feet, he had an unorthodox two-handed jump/set shot with a sideways rotation that was not always effective. But around the basket he was a marvel. His ability to score from underneath, despite the number or size of the opponents was truly a delight. His body control while in mid-air gave him the appearance of a feather, falling softly to earth before being blown upward by a gust of grit.

I saw skills in Bo that many cornerbacks in the NFL do not possess. His speed, leaping ability, great hands and bodily control could have made him a first round draft choice if he had focused on football earlier. But he was a basketball player, and he was ours. If the Privateers were within a point or two in the final seconds, McCalebb would find a way to win the game, whether scoring on a coast-to-coast off balance bank shot or a turnaround three pointer as time expired.

He also was a solid defensive player and quick enough to lead the conference in steals two years in a row. His erratic shooting from outside prevented him from being drafted by the NBA, but global basketball provided many lucrative options that might someday lead back to the big leagues.

McCalebb's finale in a Privateers' uniform was the 2008 Sun Belt Conference tournament, played at the University of South Alabama in Mobile. He went out in typical fashion, scoring 25 points, but while driving for the go-ahead basket in the final minute he was called for charging, and the Privateers were sent home by the host Jaguars, 81 to 77.

Although we were "one and done," the tournament gave our department a modicum of hope for another, unintended reason.

The conference was using every strategy it could to make the tournament more of an event in order to increase attendance. A new feature at the 2008 tournament was a Battle of the Bands, with bands and spirit squads from all the participating schools performing. Also scheduled was an event on the *U.S.S. Alabama* in Mobile Bay for alumni of the participating schools.

The most serious aspect of tournament weekend was a one-day Academic Summit. The issues were APR, graduation rates and best practices such as task based study halls. Every school sent their chief academic officers, and a few send their provost, the university's chief academic officer. In the UNO contingent was Provost Rick Barton, who was a member of our Sunday morning golf group and a good friend. We had planned to attend the academic summit on the first day of festivities then attend the Battle of the Bands that night.

The entertainment proved to be just as the conference had hoped, an animated conglomeration of bands, cheerleaders, dance teams and mascots all running around trying to outdo one another. It was a terrific evening, at least until the UNO representatives took the stage. Our pep band consisted of six horn players, and they were professional, but their number paled sadly to those of the other schools. It was worse with our spirit squad, which consisted of eight cheerleaders. They, too, tried hard, but they were up against schools that featured 20-member cheerleading squads plus 20-member dance teams. And all were backed by bands big enough to perform at their football teams' halftime shows, which most of them did.

Barton was embarrassed by the showing. He immediately began asking how we could send only a handful of people to an event where all the member schools were expected to put their best show forward? I responded it was another area where we were under funded, and we could not afford large squads or individuals to coach them. Our spirit squads raised their own money to attend camps and paid for their own travel to the tournament. Their coaches and supervisors were all volunteers. I told Barton it was to their credit, and not ours, that they were even there at all.

"I promise you I'm going to do something about this," he told me, and I believed him. Barton already had used money from his office of Academic Affairs to hire two graduate students to help tutor student-athletes, so I knew his word was good. When we returned to campus, Barton met with the individuals responsible for student life and on campus events. He offered to find funding to enhance our spirit groups. Next basketball season, he promised, things would be different.

Things would be different, but it would not be the difference that Barton intended. Later that year, Barton would resign as provost after a policy disagreement with Chancellor Ryan. We had friends on campus, but few could cut through the bureaucracy and get things done as effectively as the provost.

Barton's initiative would be implemented partially, and some additional funding was provided for the spirit groups for one year. But the initiative had lost its major advocate, and the funding eventually disappeared. It was nice to have a champion, if only for a little while.

Barton's actions did send a message to me. If the goal is considered worthwhile, even on a funding strapped college campus, ways can be found to achieve it.

On March 24, 2008, I sent the NCAA my annual report on our sports sponsorship status, a requirement of our five-year waiver. The NCAA had been extremely understanding of our situation, and they said as long as we kept their staff informed, they would work with us, even if it meant we did not have funding to bring back sports within the period of the initial waiver.

The report outlined my intention to hire coaches during the 2008-09 academic year to restore women's golf and men's and women's cross-country the following year despite our continuing problems. Enrollment numbers continued to languish around 11,500, down from the 17,250 we enjoyed before Katrina, creating financial problems all over campus. Also, funding for restoration of university facilities still was mired in the bureaucracy between FEMA and the state on priority spending.

I did point to some snippets of good news in my report, particularly that work had begun on Lakefront Arena and the first public event, a Disney ice show, was scheduled for May 2, 2008. Work also had begun on converting a university building adjacent to Lakefront Arena into a new Athletics Administration Building.

I did not include it in my letter to the NCAA, but we would need a financial miracle to restore the minimum number of sports within the waiver period. With enrollment flat and other revenues static, adding additional sports within our current budget limitations would be impossible. Our miracle would be the reopening of Lakefront Arena. We were counting heavily on a major spike in ticket sales after drawing only about 700 or so at the Human Performance Center. Attendance in the new arena should double or even triple those numbers. The new building also would provide improved sponsorship opportunities, including a new LED scoreboard that would generate additional revenue.

On the expense side, I still felt confident Ryan would utilize some of the mechanisms recommended in the Carr Report to spread our liability to other units on campus. I had prepared a proposal that would shift about $950,000 out of athletics and into such departments as Academic Affairs, Financial Services, Development, Compliance and Marketing.

However, as with the previous memos I had sent on the same subject, I never received a response.

Despite the financial uncertainty, our spring sports continued to perform well. The golf team won three tournaments, including the inaugural Texas Cup, defeating the nationally ranked Longhorns. The team also finished second in the conference tournament, which marked the best finish in school history. Medalist Jose Toledo was named Louisiana Player of the Year for the second year in a row and was selected to play in the NCAA Regionals.

Tom Walter's defending conference champion baseball team was the preseason conference favorite and looked the part. Led by preseason all America second baseman Johnny Giavotella, the Privateers took two of three from Tulane and defeated LSU in their first two meetings. They also swept Alabama in Tuscaloosa and split a home and home with powerful Southern Mississippi.

UNO was ranked in the top 30 nationally, and held a 38-13 record when things began to go sour, of all places, in Baton Rouge. The Privateers were riding a 13-game winning streak on May 13 when they faced the resurgent Tigers, which themselves had won 15 in a row. Neither team gave ground as the score went back and forth through regulation and on into extra innings. In the 15th inning, LSU pushed across the winning run for a 7 to 6 victory.

That game took something away from the Privateers, who were swept in their final three-game conference series, against Louisiana Lafayette. They returned to Lafayette as the No. 1 seed in the conference tournament, but were embarrassed in the opening game, losing to South Alabama 14 to 2. On a five-game losing streak and facing elimination, Walter's team took Troy into the tenth inning before surviving 7 to 6. They again had to face South Alabama, but this time turned the tables with a 14 to 4 thumping to eliminate the Jaguars. Things seemed to be headed back in the right direction.

That put UNO into the championship round against the host Ragin' Cajuns on Saturday morning. Walter's men had to sweep ULL on its home field twice in one day in order to advance to the championship game. In the morning game, UNO continued its hot hitting with a 10 to 0 blowout. In the second game, sophomore first baseman Nick Schwaner's two home runs enabled the Privateers to pull off the upset, nipping the Cajuns 6 to 5.

The championship game against Western Kentucky on Sunday was anticlimactic. The Privateer pitching staff was down to its eighth or ninth option, and the Hilltoppers rocked six New Orleans pitchers for 21 hits in a 17 to 5 pasting.

The season record and the tournament runner-up spot was enough for UNO to be selected for its second consecutive NCAA tournament berth, this time back in the familiar confines of LSU's Alex Box Stadium. The Privateers desperately wanted to take on the home team they had beaten two of three during the season. However, they couldn't get past Southern Mississippi. The Golden Eagles beat UNO 13 to 6 in the opener, and after eliminating Texas Southern, the Privateers fell again to USM, 8 to 2.

The final 43-21 record was UNO's best in 20 years, and at the end of the season, eight players signed pro contracts. Giavotella was drafted by Kansas City in the supplemental portion of the first round, the highest a Privateer had been picked since Texas selected pitcher Thomas Diamond as the tenth player overall in 2004.

Walter received some interest from other schools looking for a head coach, but it was essential that we do everything we could to retain our most successful coach. I still had Ron Maestri's words in my head that former chancellor Greg O'Brien never would give him the money to retain successful coaches.

A new contract for Walter was obvious, but a renovation of the baseball facility was just as important. Since before Katrina, we had been trying to raise money for improvements to Privateer Park that included revenue enhancing luxury seating and new dugouts. If we could get it done, I believed Walter would stay.

I went to Ryan and found a sympathetic ear. Ryan already had shown a desire to help, and we had been meeting with Joel Chatelain, the university's vice chancellor for facilities, on how we could get the project off the ground. Chatelain's staff gave us good news that the project did not have to be submitted to the state as a capital outlay project. Capital outlay was utilized for projects the state would fund totally, and, therefore, those projects often were caught in the political bog of similar requests from all over the state. Lakefront Arena was one such project, which sat on the state's capital outlay list for eight years before it was finally completed in 1982.

Because our department would contribute some of the funding, the project could be streamlined and completed under Louisiana Legislative Act 959 of 2003. Act 959 provided that under certain conditions, self-generated projects costing less than $5 million and without incurring debt may be performed and administered by an institution, thus avoiding the capital outlay process.

Walter had worked with Sizeler Architects of New Orleans to obtain an estimate of $2.5 million to construct new dugouts and 1,200 new chair back seats between the dugouts. Ryan already had paid for the new playing surface, and FEMA funding would provide for new lighting to replace the old lights that were damaged by Katrina. Under the plan, athletics would come up with about $1 million through current donations, additional fund-raising and pledged sponsorship agreements. Ryan agreed to come up with the rest, about $1.5 million.

The project still was subject to approval from the LSU Board of Supervisors and would fall under the policies and procedures of the state office of Facility Planning and Control. But at least we had a plan and Ryan's support.

Another facility project that was not moving as well was the renovation of the Aquatic Center, located in Lakefront Arena. Prior to Katrina, the UNO Aquatic Center was a community asset. Nearly 100,000 recreational, high school and club swimmers used the facility annually. In addition, in summer 2005 the university had signed a three year agreement with the Louisiana State High School Athletic Association to conduct its annual state swimming championships at UNO.

The intention was to restore that prominence, but the stifling bureaucratic delays between FEMA and the state once again impeded our plans. The reopening of the aquatic center, which had been anticipated in the summer of 2008, was put off indefinitely. There was no urgency to resurrect the aquatic center, as there had been with the main arena, which hosted lucrative shows and concerts. That left the UNO swimming team still without a home pool.

Since Katrina, we utilized smaller pools in the area to accommodate our 12 to 14 women swimmers. However, we were adding men's swimming, based on our belief the pool would be completed sooner. Adding a men's team doubled the numbers and doubled the space and pool time needed. Only two Olympic-sized pools suitable for collegiate competition existed in New Orleans, the other located at Tulane University in the uptown section, 30 minutes from our campus.

Our budget did not include funds to cover rental fees, transportation and other expenses associated with off-site training. I discussed the issue with Ryan, who again was sympathetic whenever the issue was student welfare. He instructed me to proceed but to do it as cost efficiently as possible. Head Coach Randy Horner used his best negotiating skills to obtain a favorable arrangement with Tulane to rent their pool for training and for the occasional meet.

Training at an off campus site also raised liability issues. Our student-athletes and coaches would be on the road an hour in the morning and again in the evening. I made a decision that burnished my reputation as a spendthrift when I told Randy to schedule a bus, and I would fight the budget battle later. I informed Ryan, and he again told us to go ahead and schedule the bus. We agreed if the decision was between our student-athletes' safety and welfare and another budget overrun, then there was no decision to be made.

CHAPTER
22

Jeremie Davis's fall was a logical one. He knew when he returned to Arcadia he would be close to his mother and two brothers. And, he would have time to return to music, the only outlet he had to express the anger at how he was treated in New Orleans. He also could work on his grandfather's construction crew, pouring concrete and fixing roofs. That would give his mother and his watchdog older brother Antoine the impression the money he always seemed to flash around came from honest labor.

But Antoine could not shoot the head off every serpent that crawled through the streets of Arcadia, and Jeremie's money actually came from dealing drugs. It wasn't a big deal to Jeremie. Besides, nobody in Arcadia expected any more of him.

Jeremie's grandfather spent his early life hauling pulp wood for an hourly wage, paid in cash at the end of the day. The cash was his grandfather's escape which he would spend on cheap wine and craps until the money ran out and he'd have to borrow to feed his family. Jeremie's mother, Barbara Davis, gave birth to three boys, all of whom grew up with her last name because she never married any of their fathers. Antoine was the oldest, then came Demaryo. The youngest, Jeremie, was born on July 18, 1985.

It was difficult providing for her sons with menial jobs or domestic work, and when it became impossible, Barbara sent Antoine and Demaryo to live with her mother, Arlene. Jeremie stayed with his mother in a one-room shack on Washington Street, a blighted area where drugs, prostitution and other criminal mischief were common. After school he would go to his grandmother's house until his mother came home from work. Older brothers being what they are, Antoine and Demaryo wanted nothing to do with young Jeremie. While they played video games, his only form of entertainment was the radio, and music became his escape. He especially liked rappers, like Jay-Z, who plumbed the reality of the street life but offered hope that a young man with resolve could rise above it and achieve success.

Barbara tried to improve her son's opportunities by moving out of the shack they occupied and into public housing. Although well-intentioned, the move had the opposite effect, throwing young Jeremie into the briar patch of a violent, lawless culture even worse than Washington Street. Drugs were bought and bartered like candy, and human life was often the price of a casual remark that demanded reprisal.

Jeremie tried to withdraw into his music, but he could not escape the frequent fights, the midnight gunfire and the intimidation. Such an environment was not foreign to the Davis family, whose members had long been involved in the retail side of the drug culture. Hustling, dealing, murders and incarceration were as familiar to the Davis family as steady jobs, family dinners and church socials were to the outside world. Even Jeremie's oldest aunt, Margie Perry, moved back to Arcadia from Shreveport, to enter "the family business" of selling narcotics.

Jeremie's grandmother Arlene did her best to insulate her daughter and grandchildren from the evil around them. She enrolled Jeremie in pee-wee sports leagues and tried to take them on short trips to show them a world outside of Arcadia. And for a time her buffer allowed Jeremie to pull the covers over his head and be alone with his music.

That plan came tumbling down when Arlene Davis died in 1999. Jeremie was 14 when her death left the rest of the family vulnerable and the needle on their moral compass spinning wildly out of control. Jeremie never knew his biological father and now had lost the only person with the strength to influence him in a positive manner. Older brother Antoine attempted to fill the void by dropping out of school at 18 and taking a job at a chicken processing plant to help support his brothers. But long days at minimum wage limited Antoine's available time and left Jeremie with too many idle hours and not enough money to fill them legitimately.

Antoine encouraged his brothers to pursue success outside of Arcadia, but challenged them that it would not come without dedication and hard work. Indeed, Demaryo excelled on the football field and had several college scholarship opportunities, finally choosing to attend nearby Grambling State University.

Jeremie was left with his music. School was the law and not a choice, so Jeremie endured the interminable academic classes each day waiting for lunch break when he and other would-be musicians met in the music cipher. The ability to express himself orally made rap a logical nesting place. The art form fueled his creativity, gave him an outlet to tell his story and offered hope that some day he could ride it out of town, far away from the streets of Arcadia.

Unbeknownst to Jeremie, while he was concentrating on rapping, he was being watched closely by the first man who would become a positive influence in his life. Basketball coach Oswald Townsend saw a gangly youngster who displayed raw talent on the playground, and for the first time Davis was being recruited. Townsend was rebuffed at first when Jeremie rebelled at the structure of daily practices only to slide back easily into music and marijuana.

But Townsend would not give up, and in his sophomore year Jeremie Davis began to turn heads. His game developed, and the playground scouts and bird dogs who watch for such prodigies took notice and began to pass his name around. He did not have the money to attend the prestigious summer camps that could assure a young player widespread recognition and a possible college scholarship, so he honed his skills on the blacktop courts of Arcadia.

While Jeremie's athletic star was rising, Demaryo's headed in the other direction.

After one semester at Grambling, he and his childhood friend Trent Sampson quit school and came back home. Sampson drifted back to the streets and soon became a prominent distributor of illegal substances.

Jeremie finished his senior year with a 24.3 scoring average, capped by an impressive performance in a losing effort to powerful Grambling Lab High School, led by eventual NBA player Paul Millsap. Davis made all-state and was one of the Top 25 guards in Louisiana, but his questionable academic record scared off the big schools.

He had his diploma, albeit a special education diploma that basketball players could earn so they could stay eligible. His high school grades and test scores would not get him into a four-year college, and the hope of major college offers dwindled to a single scholarship offer from Spoon River Community College in Canton, Illinois.

Jeremie was reluctant to leave home, but Antoine and mother Barbara saw what might be his only chance to get away from Arcadia. They forced him to accept it.

Canton, Illinois, touts itself as a "vibrant, thriving city rich in history and full of traditions ... the legacies of the Spoon and Illinois Rivers run deep here, immortalized by poet Edgar Lee Masters in the *Spoon River Anthology* ... a jumping off point for dozens of day trips that will bring you close to all of the natural beauty that exists in abundance in and around the Canton area."

But to a poor black kid from north Louisiana, Canton, Illinois, was an alien outpost 750 miles from home. Jeremie Davis had never seen snow accumulate and could not understand why students still had to attend classes when it did. Homesickness compelled him to take the train home regularly, and usually he came back with several pounds of marijuana.

Dealing and sampling the product soon replaced regular class attendance, and his grades predictably suffered. It wasn't that Jeremie was stupid. He scored a respectable 19 on his ACT test, but he never had been tested for ADD or ADHD or any of the other potential disorders that could affect attention and grades. There also is no metric that tests motivation to excel in the classroom, and Jeremie simply had better things to do.

On the court, he averaged 16.5 points and 3.8 rebounds per game as a sophomore, and the big schools began to notice. He received attention from Louisiana Tech, Wichita, Illinois State and the University of Nevada at Las Vegas, which had won a national championship. You can't get any bigger than that.

But his prowess on the basketball court again was devalued by poor grades, and coaches of four-year schools trolling for junior college prospects began to peel off. A good basketball player who could not stay eligible was of no use. It would take a team with a desperate need for warm bodies to take a chance.

Mark Downey, an assistant coach with the University of New Orleans, stuck around. He told Davis that UNO needed a shooter, and God knows Jeremie Davis could shoot the ball. He could come back to his home state and get a chance to play right away, which is coin of the realm for any recruit. He moved into the UNO dormitory eight days before Katrina hit New Orleans.

A lot had happened to Davis in the year since, the events of which prompted raging conflict. Should he try to play someplace else or just give it up? An unfettered mind might have leaned toward the game, but his was poisoned by the emotions of what he had been through. Thoughts of the storm, the flirtation with death, the treatment he received from the old coaches, the rejection by a new coach. They all were fresh and simmering. Davis knew if he left basketball he was sinking toward a bad ending, but basketball had brought nothing but pain, and he wanted it out of his life. Davis convinced himself he could be content with his lot, to live in Arcadia making music, hammering nails and selling drugs.

Demaryo's entrepreneurial friend from Grambling, Trent Sampson, always could use another salesman, and when Jeremie Davis came home from New Orleans he began working for Sampson. Dealing during the day and partying during the night relegated basketball to a distant memory in a troubled life.

That life soon would come crashing down. The attention Davis had received from college recruiters was replaced by increased scrutiny from the Bienville Parish sheriff's department. He was picked up and questioned about the murder of a high school senior whose body was found in a freezer. Davis wasn't a suspect and told the deputies he did not know who committed the murder, but his belligerent attitude did not win him any chits from the sheriff's department.

On December 5, 2006, just six months after he left New Orleans, Davis was arrested for "unauthorized entry of an inhabited dwelling." His clean record up to that time earned him probation, but the life he had chosen soon resulted in another, more serious arrest.

Authorities suspected the freezer murder was probably a drug deal gone bad and launched a massive crackdown on drug trafficking in the entire region. More than 200 indictments were handed down and arrests made. Those caught in the net included Jeremie Davis and his aunt, Margie Perry.

On August 28, 2007, Davis was convicted of distribution of a Schedule II controlled dangerous substance for selling cocaine to an undercover police officer. He received a sentence of five years at hard labor. All but two years of the sentence was suspended, and he began serving his term at the Claiborne Parish Detention Center on February 19, 2008.

When the doors of the center slammed shut behind him, Jeremie was in denial at what had happened. He fully expected his mother to come down and bring him home, and things would be okay. After all, it was just a game, like a casual fisherman playing catch-and-release on the bank of a stream. But reality soon set in with the daily routine of prison life.

The Claiborne Parish Detention Center was not the television version of a prison with tiered concrete cellblocks and inmates rattling tin cups across the bars. It was a building the size of a small gym that could accommodate 90 inmates dormitory style. The complex was surrounded by a 15-foot fence whose top was ringed with razor sharp concertina wire.

Inmates spent 23 hours per day in lockdown, usually watching television in the small lounge area or playing cards or dominoes with other inmates. The remaining one hour was spent in the yard to get some fresh air or to use the limited recreation facilities. CPDC was no spa, but it did have basketball goals on concrete courts. At first, Davis went outside just to enjoy the warm sun on his face, but his reputation spread among the other inmates, and he was asked to join the basketball team.

Why not? The perks were good, including extra food and more time outside, so Jeremie Davis began to spend his one hour outside every day, shooting basket after basket after basket. It was easy to excel over the other inmates, who seldom had seen the game come so easy to one of their own. But something else happened while he was dunking over the 5-foot-6 burglar or dribbling circles around the 300-pound arsonist. Davis slowly began to enjoy the game again. When he held the slick rubber ball in his hand and squinted into the sun to shoot at the bare hoop, it brought back the halcyon days of his childhood when basketball was simple and not encumbered by painful memories.

Those were the days before the high school coach talked a gangly ninth grader into joining the team. It was before the pressure of having to put out hard every practice and every game. It was long before rules and obligations and structure took the delight out of the game. At CPDC he was back to playing outside just for fun with nobody yelling at him to pass the ball or set a pick or get low on defense.

More importantly, the ease at which he glided around the court or made a 25-footer look simple made him realize what an advantage he had over the other inmates. Their options were so much more limited than his, and he had thrown his best one away.

Once I realized how good I had it, and I had blown it, that became the hurting point!

After his epiphany, every day became a countdown to when he would be released and could pursue basketball again. He would use his phone time to call coaches who had recruited him. He would call players he had played against. He would call anybody who could help him get another chance. One more chance is all he wanted. Just one more time playing in a gym on a polished floor with nets on the baskets and a crowd to cheer his every shot. That sweet squeak-squeak-squeak melody of sneaker against hardwood as he dribbled the tacky leather basketball was as intoxicating as any substance that could earn you jail time. And he wanted another hit of it like nothing he had wanted his entire life.

If he got that chance, Jeremie Davis promised himself, he wouldn't screw it up again.

.

Part III
The Final Breach

CHAPTER
23

Optimism is a fickle mistress, as I began to discover in the summer of 2008. Ever since Katrina, I had been hopeful our program would withstand the havoc until we could restore it to full Division I standards. I took encouragement from the little victories and downplayed the setbacks.

We will endure!

But my optimism began to fade during the budget discussions in May and June. For the first time, I had serious doubts about the future of our program.

I submitted a series of proposals for the 2008-09 fiscal year with the primary purpose of restoring sports. I believed I had ample ammunition in the Carr Report, which suggested a means to achieve every initiative I now promoted. Underlying it all was my continuing belief that Tim Ryan meant it when he pledged to support the Carr recommendations.

On May 16, I submitted an operating budget of $5 million for 2008-09, which included funds to support men's and women's tennis and men's swimming, the first sports added since Katrina. It was a significant increase over the $4.1 million in expenditures of the previous year, but it was based partly on the university's 2007-10 Strategic Plan. Objective 1.8 stated: "The Athletics Department will meet all NCAA Division I and Sun Belt standards, including sports sponsorship, compliance with Title IX and SBC sports competition."

That objective was a clear commitment to restoring sports within the initial five-year waiver. In the first two years after Katrina, we had not added any of the eight sports we were required to add, so the addition of tennis and men's swimming this year and women's golf and cross country next year would be a positive step toward restoring our full Division I status. My budget proposal, though aggressive, reflected that intention.

Ryan and I had dinner at the Sun Belt Conference spring meetings in Destin, Florida, to discuss my proposal. We sat at a table littered with beer bottles and empty plates as we went line-by-line over the budget. Ryan seemed focused on why my estimates for team transportation costs were so high. He drew reference to our team travel costs from our pre-Katrina budget of 2004-05, when we traveled 15 sports. He asked why we were proposing to spend more to travel nine teams in 2008-09?

I thought it was a rather naïve question considering the sharp increase of gasoline prices and other costs over the previous four years. I reminded Ryan that although track & field counted as six sports under the NCAA sport sponsorship math, it was one team.

The only other team that traveled then was women's golf, and their travel costs were insignificant.

I tried to make the distinction that travel costs were not "out of control," but many were out of *our* control. The first culprit was the rising costs of transportation. Gasoline was $2.25 per gallon in 2005 compared with the $4 plus per gallon at that time of our discussion. In addition, as members of a conference, we were not in total control of our travel schedules. Our basketball teams were required to play at the University of Denver during ski season when air travel costs were highest. The conference might schedule our baseball team to play at Florida International in Miami one weekend and then return to play Florida Atlantic in Boca Raton two weeks later. Those trips cost between $16,000 and $18,000 each.

In addition, contract amounts for game officials are voted on by the conference athletic directors. I voted against the increases every year, because I think it's excessive to pay each basketball official an average of $1,000 a game plus expenses, and we pay three of them per game. We sometimes had crowds so sparse our gate did not cover cost of officials. Despite my feelings, the ADs as a group voted for the increases on the premise that the Sun Belt had to keep up with fees paid by other conferences or we would not get the better officials. I gave Ryan other examples that simply reflected the cost of doing business as an NCAA Division I member.

I reprised the argument that no Division I non-football schools break even, according to statistics confirmed by the NCAA. How could we be expected to be any different? Ryan was sympathetic, but would not accept the budget. He asked me to revise it and supply more detail.

On June 26, I submitted an amended plan but continued to make the previous points. The bulk of the proposed increase in expenses was directly attributable to restoring our department to full NCAA Division I standards. The increase in sports not only meant an increased number of coaches and student-athletes, but more support staff to accommodate academic and athletic needs of more athletes.

Despite the anticipated increases over the next three years, the athletics budget still would lag far behind our peer average and a distant last in the Sun Belt Conference. As Carr Sports Associates stated in our strategic plan, the average expense of a Division I program without football was $8 million in 2004-05. I did not anticipate getting to that expense level until 2013.

The argument of how far we were behind our peer group did not score any points with Ryan. The prevailing underdog mentality at UNO required every unit on campus to believe they could achieve superior performance with less support than their peers. That attitude provided some motivation and a sense of camaraderie, but it was not one that could be applied to every unit. Especially athletics.

Recruiting alone separates athletics from other campus units. That does not mean academic departments do not recruit, because the better ones do. However, recruiting high quality student-athletes is far more competitive and more expensive than recruiting other students. Today's student-athletes and their parents have multiple opportunities for college, and they are shopping for the best situation. High quality housing and facilities, new uniforms every year instead of every other year, six pair of sneakers a year instead of three, playing an attractive schedule, having a chance to win. All are factors that can make a difference on why a student-athlete selects one school over another.

Never try to convince a coach that he or she "can do more with less." Coaches are the ones on the front lines who have to explain to a prospective student-athlete why a full athletic scholarship to UNO does not include certain university fees or why we have only one full time academic adviser for 140 student-athletes or why we are taking a bus nine hours instead of flying. Without proper ammunition, our coaches cannot win the recruiting battles.

Quality coaches, high academic standards, outstanding facilities and adequate support are the four-legged stool of successful recruiting. To be short on one or two puts you in second place. My old boss at the Saints, Jim Finks, had a favorite expression when we lost a game: "We came in second." I have used that many times over the years when people would ask how our team did. My response that "we came in second" elicits an initial reaction that second place isn't too bad. It quickly sinks in that second is not good in a two horse race. Today's student-athletes and their parents do not have to settle for second place.

Ryan had more immediate problems than the athletics budget. Enrollment was static, and the university's revenue had not kept pace with rising expenses. Money was not available to improve the infrastructure which, added to the delay of recovery funds, resulted in a campus that appeared shabby and unkempt. The University Center's food service area and bookstore were open, but a few offices and the second floor ballroom and meeting space lay dormant. A dormitory for married students had not been re-opened, nor had "The Cove," a popular sandwich and beverage hangout.

Part of Ryan's frustration came from the fact that UNO's smaller neighbor across the street was basking in federal assistance. Up to that point, the predominantly black Southern University of New Orleans, located on Press Drive across from UNO's East Campus, had received more than $92 million in federal aid, despite claiming only 3,000 students. That compared with less than $60 million sent to UNO. The aid-to-student ratios showed that UNO received about $5,000 in federal disaster funds for each student, while SUNO received more than $30,000 per student. The equation would be comical if it weren't patently unfair.

Ryan also was on the defensive from a withering fire from the home office. Some key staff members in the LSU System office were hostile to Ryan and UNO in general. They delighted in springing surprise visits on UNO, and one regularly met with faculty and staff about the conditions of the university, sometimes without the administration's knowledge.

I was less sympathetic to Ryan's plight than I should have been, because I was concerned solely about moving our program forward. Until the 2008 budget meetings, I truly believed Ryan would do whatever it took to help us restore our program. And, he may have done so if all things were equal. But all things were not equal.

Ryan felt he had stuck his neck out in 2006 when under his watch 26 tenured faculty positions were eliminated and athletics was asked only to trim its budget. The more adamant faculty members would never let Ryan forget that he saved athletics while terminating their colleagues. He had stood up for athletics, and we repaid him with lack of understanding and demands for more money.

Whatever the reasons, Ryan was clearly less sympathetic to athletics' perceived plight during the 2008 budget meetings. I heard fewer words of encouragement from him and more comments about the growing athletics deficit, a favorite refrain of CFO Linda Robison. Other units on campus were expected to work within the parameters of their budget, and athletics would be expected to do the same. It did not matter whether or not the administration understood the cost of doing business as a Division I institution.

I also began to sense a disconnect with Ryan on the issue of the Carr Report and its recommendations. My budget proposal and planning were fueled by Ryan's comment to Bill Carr that he wanted a successful athletic program and would support the recommendations to get there. That assurance to Carr at one of our final meetings was not expressed with strings attached. However, when it came to my execution of the plan, it carried with it the unspoken asterisk "if we can afford it."

Ryan received the budget revision I provided and then informed me that our 2008-09 operating budget would not be increased. Instead, it would be rolled back to the level of the 2006-07 budget, or to about $3.6 million. I was furious. That directive was a major setback. It would be impossible to take any steps toward restoring the program and difficult to even maintain what we had. The budget in 2007-08 was $3.7 million, and although we had cut every corner, we spent more than $4.1 million. In 2008-09, we were adding three sports — men's tennis, women's tennis and men's swimming and diving — all with the chancellor's knowledge and blessing. And now we were supposed to cut the budget?

After he informed me of our proposed budget, I asked Ryan pointedly: "Did it ever occur to you that we might not be able to afford Division I?" Ryan, however, had no enthusiasm for an alternative. He said it was not in the university's best interests to play teams of institutions that he deemed clearly inferior academically to UNO. It was Division I or bust, which for the first time appeared to be a real possibility.

As we debated the issue the next few weeks, my doubts about our ability to survive only grew. If the university was not going to make the commitment to support the program, it would be impossible to compete, and if we could not compete we would not survive. I told Ryan I could not continue to demand that my coaches recruit high quality student-athletes, graduate them and expect them to win championships when we only provided a fraction of the resources of our peers. It wasn't fair to the coaches or to the student-athletes. Expectations must be bolstered with adequate support.

We already were the red headed stepchild of the conference. I was embarrassed at meetings of conference athletic directors when we'd go around the table talking about best practices or the good things our schools were doing. North Texas and Florida International were building new football stadiums. Arkansas-Little Rock had received a $25 million gift from a donor to build a new basketball arena. Middle Tennessee and Troy were building or renovating their baseball stadiums.

When it was my turn to talk about UNO, I would usually make a joke, such as talking about the new order of office supplies that were successfully delivered the previous week. It was embarrassing and demeaning.

Commissioner Wright Waters and the other athletic directors understood and expressed their concern and support. But to sit there and see what others were doing, knowing we had so far to travel before we even arrived at their level was depressing. If nothing else, the UNO conundrum made them appreciate their own situations much better.

As the deadline for budget submission approached, Ryan appeared adamant and inflexible in his position that I had to cut our budget. I pondered the alternatives. My initial contract had expired the year before, on June 30, 2007, and Ryan had ignored my efforts to secure a new one. My coaches had been asking about my contract status for the past year, but I always told them jokingly that Ryan and I would get it done one Sunday morning on the golf course. However, I began to wonder if that ever would happen.

If he was not going to support our restoration plan, and even backtrack on it, then maybe he needed to make a change. I wrote a letter of resignation in which I stated I did not believe he was sincere in his stated desire to sponsor a competitive Division I program. To have a Division I program just to say you were D-I and not support it was a gross disservice to the student-athletes, our coaches and our fans. I felt if he was trying to run our program on a shoestring, he would be better served with an accountant in my chair instead of an athletic director.

I took the letter to the office the following morning, fully intending to deliver it. I told Jean to prepare for the worst, and, as always, she was supportive.

When I arrived at the office, Mike Dauenhauer, my old business manager and now the university bursar, called to tell me Ryan had asked him to intervene. We discussed several options, and finally Mike delivered a budget that hit Ryan's number. To get there, Mike did not cut drastically, but instead adopted some of the recommendations in the Carr Report to divert certain expense items to other units at the university.

Also, for the first time, our revenue would include some game day concessions revenue from Lakefront Arena. As tenants at Lakefront Arena, we did not share in game day revenue, which went directly to the university. The rationale was that the revenue covered utilities and staffing at the games, and athletics was not charged rent for their offices in the Arena.

That maneuver got the budget through the approval process. I was grateful that Mike D. stepped in, but I still was skeptical. Why hadn't these adjustments been made when Carr recommended them initially? Why hadn't they been made when I continued to remind the chancellor of them? The budget debate was contentious and caused ill feelings. Why did we have to get to this point before a solution, which existed all along, was adopted?

UNO's tenured hobgoblin, the lack of resources, was crawling out of the shadows.

CHAPTER
24

Our department suffered another major blow in August when John Barranco left to become general sales manager at the local Cox Communications office. It was a good promotion for Barranco, who had done an outstanding job under trying circumstances. He was a born salesman, and he was a positive thinker and self-motivated employee.

Barranco had consummated the two biggest sponsorship deals in department history. A five-year agreement with Ochsner Health Care was worth $108,000 annually, while the other, with Capital One Bank, was worth $80,000 annually. In addition to a long term deal with Coca-Cola that was bringing in $122,500 per year, we had a core of sponsorships that would lay a foundation for growth.

But it was the small business sponsorships that Barranco loved. He enjoyed reeling in a $1,500 sponsorship for a bar tab at a French Quarter hotel as much as a $25,000 sponsorship with O'Reilly Auto Parts or a $20,000 deal with the Louisiana Department of Public Safety. He enjoyed dealing with smaller companies and their lone sponsorship person, because he took great pleasure in the personal give-and-take.

Barranco's departure had a major immediate impact on our revenue production, because, like most of our departments, sponsorship sales was a one-man show. I had been lobbying for a second sales person, because according to the well tested formula the more sales people you have, the more you sell. When the only sales person on a one-man sales staff leaves, that equals no sales.

It would have been easy to try and fill the void quickly, but two considerations compelled me to take a more deliberate approach. First, I wanted to avoid the impediment of hiring issues that were dictated by budgetary limitations or the continual state hiring freezes. If we needed more sales people, I wanted the ability to add them without interference. Also, I wanted to expand our revenue potential by attracting more national sponsors outside of our immediate market. To achieve both goals, I was convinced our best course of action was to outsource our multimedia rights and sponsorship sales to a national group.

Several other reasons favored that approach, not the least of which was the backward thinking expense first mindset that permeated UNO. The concept of return on investment starts with the investment. You invest $1 to make $3. At UNO, you were never given approval to invest the dollar because it constituted another expenditure. The fact that this basic premise of business success was taught in our College of Business but not practiced by the university business office was an incomprehensible irony.

My way around that obstacle was to contract with a third party vendor in which the expenses were not solely ours but became the responsibility of the third party. Expenses would be paid by the third party, deducted from revenue, and the partners would split the profit.

That direction required that we prepare an RFP, or request for proposal. I discussed the issue with Harriett Reynolds, the university's purchasing director and a big Privateer baseball fan. She told me she and her skeleton staff were too backed up with work to help me. She was preoccupied with an RFP for a food service provider on campus. If I wanted an RFP written, I would have to do it myself.

My only experience with RFP's was when I assisted with one that produced our University Tennis Center, prior to Katrina. I did not know anything about writing an RFP from scratch, but I did know LSU had gone through a similar process a couple years earlier. I called my friend, Herb Vincent, an assistant AD at LSU, to see if he would give me some direction. I had learned if the Mothership had done something to great effect, it was easier for little old UNO to cite the precedent to get it through the state censors. Herb was very helpful, even to the extent of providing copies of LSU's original RFP and the final contract.

We could not be without a sales component for very long, and I wanted to expedite the process. For the next two months, much of my time was spent in writing, editing and adapting a document intended to secure a multimedia rights partner. We went through the process, entertained proposals and scored a winner, Nelligan Sports Management. Nelligan, headquartered in New Jersey, was well respected in the industry and was the marketing and sales partner for Rutgers, West Virginia and Louisville, as well as Middle Tennessee and Florida Atlantic of the Sun Belt.

I had put together a draft of a contract I was ready to send out to Nelligan to begin the negotiations. However, Ryan informed me I was not to proceed on a contract without the input of Steve Kolz, the university's contracts manager, and purchasing director Reynolds. This would seriously delay my plans to jump-start sponsorship and media sales.

Kolz was extremely detailed and known for picking fly specks out of pepper. But he did not understand multimedia rights and would have to be brought up to speed on the entire culture before I could expect him to understand the nuances. He had other contracts to pore over, and I would be just another one at the end of the line. Reynolds, who was retired from the military, also was a stickler for state procedures who had never seen a multimedia rights contract.

I knew then it would take months perfecting even a first draft that would satisfy both. Then, after the draft was completed, Ryan wanted to approve it. All this would have to occur before we could present anything to Nelligan and start negotiating.

My hopes for a quick resolution were fading, which meant our sales would remain static.

The fall semester had been under way one week when we received an eerie reminder of our recent past. Another hurricane was developing in the Caribbean, and early reports suggested it would be of the Katrina magnitude. Hurricane Gustav left behind much damage in Haiti and by the time it reached Cuba it had intensified to Category 4 strength with maximum sustained winds of 150 mph. It was headed on a northwesterly path that predicted landfall in south Louisiana.

On the third anniversary of Katrina — Friday, August 29 — Chancellor Ryan convened his deans, vice chancellors and department heads to discuss evacuation of the students. It was a very different meeting from the one three years earlier. That meeting was attended by only a handful of people, most of whom were joking about yet another false alarm. This time, the meeting was well attended, and all of us knew first hand the potential of a major hurricane. We listened intently as Ryan outlined the situation.

He went around the table, asking each of us what preparations we had made, specifically about the welfare of our students. As with most of the respondents, athletics was better prepared for a disaster than we had been three years before. I had written and distributed an emergency plan to all coaches, staff, student-athletes and their parents detailing how we would handle the next threat. Coaches of our teams that were competing in the fall had made arrangements to take their teams intact to a safe location. Our remaining student-athletes again relied on the buddy system whereby out-of-town students would match up with locals and evacuate with their families.

Ryan said the hurricane was expected to reach landfall on Monday or Tuesday, and we would plan to resume classes the following Thursday, September 4.

Predictably, Jean and her sisters already had mobilized with a plan for the family. Gary and Martha Solomon owned a condominium at Perdido Key on the Florida panhandle, and the families would evacuate to the beach. The storm was tracking to the west, and none of the maps predicted landfall any further east than Gulfport, Mississippi, so the Florida panhandle appeared safe. Layne and C.C. were excited they would be out of school for a few bonus days, and that we were taking our hurricane-tested beagle, Elmo, who was then six. It would be another "evacu-cation."

Despite the kids' glee, Gustav was a major threat that rekindled all the bad memories of Katrina. We took precautions that we had not taken before, such as moving furniture and other keepsakes to the second floor of our house. We also drove both cars when we left for Florida the following day.

Gustav still was tracking right at New Orleans when New Orleans Mayor Ray Nagin declared that Gustav was "the storm of the century … the mother of all storms" as he imposed a mandatory evacuation and a dusk-to-dawn curfew. Nagin received much criticism for his response during Katrina, and he was determined to go overboard this time. His warning, whether exaggerated or calculated, achieved its intent. Most residents left the city to escape another potential disaster, and FEMA estimated that only 10,000 people remained in the city on September 1.

Meanwhile, we were enjoying the break with our families. My brother-in-law Schaffer Mickal and I took our sons to play golf a couple of days while the rest of the family hung out at the beach. I made some phone calls to my coaches and staff members to assure they had reached their destinations and that we would have no repeats of the Jeremie Davis/Wayne Williams imbroglio.

Fortunately for us, Gustav tracked further west, and New Orleans sustained only minor wind damage and several days of power outages. We were back in our house by the following Friday, and our student-athletes began to return for the start of classes on Monday.

A collective sigh of relief could be heard through much of the land, although Baton Rouge wasn't spared. The town that had taken in so many Katrina refugees experienced major damages with wind and power outages, but no major flooding.

When we returned to work, the reopening of Lakefront Arena was our next big event. As Bill Carr told us repeatedly in our strategic planning sessions, "you only get one opportunity to open a new building." We had been positioned well, with Barranco heading up the sales and promotions and prodding our new ticket sales manager, Kevin Breen. However, with Barranco gone, we began to feel his departure more and more as the basketball season approached.

North Carolina State was coming in for the grand reopening of the Arena, and it was a natural draw. Monte Towe, our former head coach, was returning to Lakefront Arena for the first time since he left, and the Wolfpack were stinging from our upset victory at their place a year ago. We had an attractive home schedule with archrivals Tulane and Ole Miss coming in. It would be the first basketball in our arena in three years in a virtually new building. All the stars appeared aligned.

Alas, we again were the victims of our own limitations. Our minimal budget still contained no funds for advertising, which is essential for an event's success. It doesn't matter if you have a better mousetrap or a compelling sporting event, people will not come if you don't keep reminding them of it. My long-time friend, Bob Leffler, who owns a successful sports advertising business in Baltimore, agreed to come in at his own expense and conduct a "beg-a-thon" for free air time on the local radio and TV stations. We used that and other outlets at our disposal, promoting through our website, word of mouth and events such as a Select-a-Seat promotion.

Barranco's departure left behind other residue. I had told Breen, the ticket manager that he would report to me after Barranco left. But with other responsibilities tugging at me, I could not give Breen the supervision he needed. When Barranco left in August, Breen had sold around 370 season tickets. He did not sell many after that.

According to Breen, Barranco implied that if he ever left the department, Breen would be in line to succeed him. That alleged suggestion never reached me, and no promises ever were made to Breen. But after Barranco left, sales virtually stopped, and

Breen soon resigned. The ever-present hiring freeze prevented us from immediately filling the position.

With no advertising out to remind people that Lakefront Arena was back and with nobody actively selling tickets, failure was predictable. We reopened Lakefront Arena against North Carolina State with only 1,300 of the 9,000 seats sold. We had lost the "Wow Factor," our one chance to dazzle our fans and set a higher standard for revenue growth.

Fans who did come to the games found other reasons not to be dazzled, most caused by the interminable renovation delays that continued to push back anticipated deadlines. For example, the new state-of-the-art LED video board we had ordered was lost in the logjam between FEMA and the state office of Facility Planning & Control. With no money to rent a comparable board, we were forced to borrow two small scoreboards that looked as though they were last used in a high school gym. Compounding the problem was the game horn, attached to one of the signs, that sounded more like a security door buzzer than one used in a major arena.

It was a deflating night, since we also had scheduled a ceremony to honor a new naming partner. Former player Gabe Corchiani and his business partner, John Georges, gave us a generous donation of $1 million for the naming rights to the Corchiani Court. I was disappointed that so few fans were on hand to help us thank them.

Not surprisingly, our other potential home draws in the first three weeks of the season, Tulane and Ole Miss, drew less than 1,100 fans each. With all the problems we had endured and the frustrations to get the arena opened, we had just confirmed to our fans that this was the same old UNO athletics that they tolerated more than loved. It was a major setback in our efforts to rebuild our revenue base.

But the turnout begged the bigger questions. Was this sized crowd all we could expect to attract at home basketball games? Had UNO basketball fallen to such depths that nobody cared? Did the return of the Hornets after Katrina and the city's unwavering devotion to the Saints suck out all the interest in town? Would other priorities such as rebuilding or relocation continue to limit the discretionary dollar? Entire sections of our city continued to rebuild from Katrina, and many people still were fighting with insurance companies or with "The Road Home" debacle that resulted in Governor Kathleen Blanco's decision not to run for a second term.

I knew through my conversations with Tulane AD Rick Dickson that the Green Wave were not doing much better at attracting fans. Their basketball crowds were no larger than ours, and they had trouble putting five-digit crowds into the Louisiana Superdome for football games. Published reports have put Tulane's annual athletic losses at as much as $7 million. However, survival of their program was not an issue because Tulane President Scott Cowen never wavered in his estimation of the program's value to the entire university.

New Orleanians are not devoid of entertainment options. The 50-some parades that comprise Mardi Gras occupy weeks of the pre-Lenten period, capped by Fat Tuesday, considered the Greatest Free Show on Earth. Other events such as the Jazz & Heritage Festival and the French Quarter Festival combine with others to make New Orleans a big event city with plenty of free and moderately priced events available to its residents.

That makes life difficult for those of us promoting smaller events for a price.

CHAPTER
25

Jean was doing her best to keep my frustrations at the office from invading our home. She had gone back to work for the Hornets after they returned to New Orleans in the summer of 2007. The team had played the entire 2005-06 season and most of the 2006-07 season in Oklahoma City while the New Orleans Arena was being repaired. The Hornets returned to New Orleans for six games during the 2006-07 season, and we accidentally ran into owner George Shinn and his wife Denise at one of them.

"When are you coming back to work?" Shinn asked Jean, who was politely non-committal. But Shinn was serious. He called me a few days later, asking if I thought she would come back and what did I think about it? I told him I would be happy to negotiate on his behalf, and I would even waive my 50% spousal agent fee.

Returning to work gave Jean a renewed sense of purpose. She was too active to be a stay-at-home mom, and returning to the Hornets was good for her. George and Denise were genuinely good people who admired Jean's work ethic and knew she shared their values. The job gave her a useful diversion from the post-Katrina routine of grocery shopping, picking up the kids at school, working on insurance matters for our home and her destroyed store, and the ongoing home renovation activity.

After she went back to work, we made a point of sitting together every evening with a cocktail to "wind down." Returning to the Hornets gave Jean a distinct advantage over me because she spent every day in a culture that promoted teamwork, motivation and performance. That is hardly the atmosphere I left behind each day at my office, but she tried to boost me up by purposely relating pieces of her day.

If I would whine about one issue or another at UNO, she would counter with something positive the Hornets were doing in the community. We would go back and forth, with time out to fix dinner for Layne and C.C., and we would go back to our "winding down."

I looked forward to our evenings, and they were therapeutic for us both. But after a while, our practice began to raise another concern. Had other New Orleans couples or individuals adopted the same coping mechanism after Katrina? The high incidence of post traumatic stress disorder in New Orleans had been studied and verified, and it was natural for victims to seek a remedy.

As Thanksgiving neared, I had come to the conclusion that our "winding down" meant I was drinking too much. I know that's a bold statement in a town where alcohol consumption is glorified as a by-product of our most cherished institutions. I do not believe my drinking was a cry for help or desperation or depression. After all, drinking isn't a 180-degree proposition, where you are either a teetotaler or a drunk. The great preponderance of those who drink, as the ads say, drink responsibly, and I'd like to think that's the way I've always approached alcohol.

But when you know yourself better than anybody else, you know when things have changed, and I remember the moment I realized I was drinking too much. It was Thanksgiving Day, 2008.

My kids always considered Thanksgiving Day as the pace car for the Christmas holidays; the flag is up, and they're off! This year, Thanksgiving Day became a day for New Orleans to celebrate the endurance and resilience we all had shown the previous three years and for better days ahead. Jean and I looked forward to our annual Thanksgiving tradition — the Turkey Day five-mile race at Tad Gormley Stadium in City Park.

We are regular participants, she to enjoy the unique fellowship of our fellow runners and the cool, crisp fall temperatures, and me to once again try and outrun my age. Just having entered my seventh decade was scaring the hell out of me, which is part of this story. I didn't bat an eye at 30. I was focused on a surefire career of writing books while spending my day job writing sports stories for a large East Coast newspaper. I blew past 40, having gone into professional sports and hobnobbing with people you read about. By 50, I had discovered New Orleans and a loving woman who would keep me and our toddlers in my adopted city forever.

The one constant during all these phases was running. Running has been a passion since June 1, 1971, when I received the "Greetings" letter from my government informing me to report to basic training in three weeks. It was that day that His Flabbiness, who had topped out at 225 pounds in high school, figured he'd best get in shape, and I've been running ever since.

The past decade or so, however, my running evolved from an obsession to exceed my previous best time to an exercise at mid-life survival. Running has mitigated a lifetime of red meat and heredity that mandated cholesterol medicine since 2000. I try to eat a good diet, with the exception of a fairly well controlled addiction to bananas and peanut butter. Most importantly, I have relied on running to keep the stress monster in the closet. My stress antidote has always been a therapeutic 6:30 A.M. wakeup run, which has been instrumental in helping me survive our recent troubles, and that leads us back to my Turkey Day 2008 revelation.

Until then I never just *ran* races, I *raced* races. Leading up to a race, I would train hard, running long, slow distance one day and sprinting shorter intervals the next. If I were a little heavier than I should be, which was most of the time, I would make an effort to drop the pounds I needed to get into race shape. Every pound costs precious seconds in a race. Grapefruit for lunch, vegetables for dinner and no booze for however long it took. And I intended to do the same while training for the 2008 Turkey Day Race.

But that year I just couldn't do the abstinence part.

Since Katrina overturned our lives, alcohol had evolved from a pleasant diversion to a downright necessary ingredient to cope with our circumstances. I'm not talking about 3-day benders or Bloody Marys for breakfast; I'm talking about having a few drinks at the end of another frustrating day.

I've got to admit the best part of my day the past few bewildering years was when Jean and I got home and would "wind down," as we so soberly termed it. She usually had two or three glasses of wine, while my Kentucky heritage demanded a stout Maker's Mark or two. It was very civilized. We sat together most every evening, exchanged our stories about the day, discussed our children, identified our issues and tried to find solutions if any existed. Mainly, we gave each other a transfusion of support so we both could head back into the teeth of the gale the next day.

The Ghost of Carrie Nation is out there somewhere crying from the mist: "You can drink water," but a bottle of Dasani never gave me the comfort I derived from a stiff Makers Mark on the rocks.

Race day was perfect with cool temperatures and a slight breeze and brief drizzle. However, once I began to run, I could feel the effects immediately. My first mile was a decent 7:15, but in the second mile other runners began passing me. Somewhere along the third mile, as I was making the turn down Roosevelt Mall, I could see the lead runners make the victorious turn into Tad Gormley Stadium while I had nearly two miles to go. I felt like I had a beach ball under my shirt, and I don't think I passed anybody the last three miles.

I finished the 5-miler in a respectable 38:22, but well below my goal, and that's what triggered the guilt. If I only had gone on the wagon for the past month, I could have lost the weight and probably reached my goal. Maybe some discipline would have helped me drop another few pounds and maybe given me a better finishing time. I was a journalism major, but I can do simple math and multiply number of drinks times number of nights times number of months and extrapolate that into a couple of lost minutes.

Jean and I had discussed it, but she told me not to spend any time worrying about it. She would rather have a husband who can cope with his demons than a 60-year-old cadaver who can run five miles in 35 minutes.

We did not give up our "winding down," but maybe with everything we've experienced, that's okay. I may never run another race averaging 7-minute miles, but maybe I should be thankful that Jean and I know our demons by name and can keep them at the gate.

Adding to my frustration was the unresolved issue with my own contract, more than 16 months after the initial term had expired. I had mixed feelings about how long I wanted to continue pushing the boulder up the hill, especially after the ill feelings that came out of the 2008-09 budget debate. But I reasoned a contract would at least give me the security to go out on my own terms, if I so chose to do so. My coaches had been more concerned about it than I, because their jobs depended largely upon my status. A new athletic director carries a new broom, and my longevity in the job was in their best interests.

I also felt an extreme loyalty to them. I had hired all seven current head coaches, plus every staff member except Mike Bujol. I felt an obligation to them.

I abandoned the reminders to Ryan and took the liberty of preparing a new contract for myself. I did not ask for more money, but I did ask for the same four-year term as contained in my initial contract. I sent the contract to him in September.

More than two months passed and Ryan did not respond. In late November, we met on another subject, and after the meeting I asked him if he had looked at it. Ryan responded as if he did not know what I was talking about, so I told him I would send him another copy. This time, he quickly approved it and notified me to come in and sign it.

On December 1, 2008, I signed a new contract with an expiration date of June 30, 2012. The end date was seven months short of my 65th birthday, when I had planned to cash in my NFL pension. I figured if I could work up to that time, it would provide financial security, especially with two children not yet in high school.

Still, 2012 seemed a long way off.

CHAPTER
26

If the internal demons weren't vexing enough, a fierce external one emerged to further imperil our program. Throughout the summer and fall, the nation's economy continued to slide toward the abyss. Economic growth was stagnant and many financial institutions were left holding assets that were worth less than the outstanding mortgages. Governmental statistics showed that the U.S. economy had been in recession for a year and doomsayers were predicting another Great Depression around the corner.

The national crisis would trickle down to the state level with a decline in oil prices. The price of oil had fallen from a high of $147 a barrel to less than $40, sharply reducing the anticipated taxes upon which the state's budget was based. A story in the October 29 *Times-Picayune* reported that state budget projections were based on an average oil price of $72.17 per barrel. Every $1 per barrel deviation in oil prices from the official forecast means about $12.5 million to the state budget.

Compounding the problem was a string of actions by the 2008 Legislature that would eat into the 2009-10 anticipated revenue. Chief among them was a $359 million repeal of a "temporary" sales tax on food and residential utilities while another $70 million in discretionary spending authority would be taken up by various other tax dedications and mandated spending increases. That meant the price of oil would have to be nearly $100 to make up for the budget impact of the tax cuts.

The first indication of trouble came with rumors that the failing economy would prompt Governor Bobby Jindal to propose massive budget cuts throughout state government. The threat of budget cuts in Louisiana puts every state department on notice, but it especially tightens the sphincters of those in higher education and health care. Under a constitutional amendment passed during the Edwin Edwards administration, the only two areas of state government not constitutionally protected from wholesale budget cuts are higher education and health care.

Consequently, when state budgets are cut, higher education and health care are the first to feel it.

The rumor was soon confirmed when Jindal's chief budget adviser warned her cabinet colleagues to prepare for a 30 percent cut in discretionary spending in 2009-10 year and suggested that reductions could begin much sooner. Commissioner of Administration Angele Davis said the state faced a projected shortfall of $1.3 billion in the 2009-10 fiscal year, which would have to be taken out of the $4.4 billion general fund revenue that was not protected from cuts by state statute or by the state Constitution.

The story confirmed that health care and higher education programs would be particularly vulnerable, since they are the largest state expenditures that are unprotected. According to a detailed budget analysis by the LSU System, those two areas could expect to absorb 63 percent of any cut.

The first tangible effect of the crisis was a mid-year budget cut on all state agencies. It was the first time since 2002 the state had been forced to make mid-year budget cuts, but this cut of $341 million would be the largest in history. Furthermore, the state's Revenue Estimating Conference projected that the 2009-10 budget shortfall would exceed $2 billion.

The trickle down effect to UNO meant an immediate budget cut of more than $5 million. Chancellor Ryan was determined to minimize the effect on the academic mission of the university, so he made a difficult decision. He took the $1.5 million he had pledged for renovations of the Privateer Park baseball stadium and applied it to the shortfall. Ryan told me he did not have any alternative, because he was going to do everything he could do to avoid cutting any more academic programs.

After Ryan gave me the bad news, I had to deliver it to Tom Walter, our baseball coach. Walter handled the news much better than I did, but it was another in a series of disappointments and broken promises. Walter's teams had held their own with LSU and Tulane in the local recruiting wars, but without an improved stadium, UNO would fall further behind. Tulane had just opened a new $11 million stadium, and LSU was working on college baseball's new Taj Mahal, a $36 million edifice that seated 9,000 fans. We were finding it difficult to keep up in the Sun Belt as rivals such as Middle Tennessee, South Alabama and Troy had opened new baseball stadiums recently.

Sadly, if not for a bureaucratic glitch, the money already would have been approved and dedicated to the project. The state office of Facility Planning and Control had advanced the proposed renovation as far as its architectural selection committee. But the item was inexplicably missing from the agenda at the committee's November meeting. That meant the proposal had to wait until the next monthly meeting, on December 18. By that time, the mid-year budget cuts had been announced, and all such projects were shelved.

Timing is everything.

The mid-year cuts included a hiring freeze, which compounded our problems. Our inability to hire more help compelled both Lauri Mondschein, our assistant AD for compliance, and Angela Dolese, our chief academic officer, to submit their resignations, both effective January 15, 2009. They had been in their current positions less than a year, further exacerbating the instability that created inconsistencies in our compliance and academic support responsibilities.

In the space of four months, I now had lost my top two revenue generators, in ticket and sponsorship sales, and now our compliance officer and the chief academic officer. Losing those positions at the same time is like a baseball team having its pitcher, catcher, shortstop and center fielder taken off the field and not being allowed to replace any of them.

Arguably, the chief academics officer and the compliance officer are the two most important positions in an athletic department. An athletic department's primary mission is to educate, and the chief academic officer is responsible for making it happen. Assuring that the student-athlete is making sufficient academic progress and is on pace to graduate consists of myriad duties. The individual works with advisors in the individual colleges to pick the right classes for each student and then monitors their progress. The bulk of the academic officer's time is spent with the at-risk student-athlete, who requires special attention such as study halls and tutors.

Compliance is essential to assure that all NCAA and conference rules are being interpreted and applied accurately. Specifically, the compliance officer meets regularly with the coaches to make sure they all know the rules. Most rules violations in college athletics are committed by coaches who either do not know the rules or take liberties with them. NCAA sanctions for rules violations tarnish a program's credibility, which can create a negative ripple effect in recruiting and fan support.

Tim Ryan allowed us to make a special request for an exemption to the hiring freeze for the chief academic officer. Eventually, we were able to hire a new ticket manager, but not before losing our entire selling season for basketball tickets. We never received approval to hire a compliance officer, although Wright Waters loaned us a junior member of his Sun Belt Conference staff to handle our compliance duties.

We were holding the department together with bubble gum and bailing twine, but we were still breathing.

CHAPTER
27

Over the difficult years, one voice of comfort was my long-time friend, Mike Casey. We met at age eight when Mike's family moved into the neighborhood, and we remained fast friends through grade school, high school and college.

The public Mike Casey was special to many who did not know him as I did. He was leading scorer of a Shelby County High School team that was ranked No. 1 in a basketball mad state two years in a row and were state champions in 1966. The same year, Casey was named Kentucky's prestigious Mr. Basketball and signed with the University of Kentucky. Casey was the heart of Adolph Rupp's last great team and had been pictured on the cover of *Sports Illustrated*. When he graduated, he was the 6th highest scorer in the school's storied history.

We had gone our separate ways out of college. Mike played basketball overseas for a few years before returning to Kentucky to go into business. We talked frequently on the phone, and when I would return to Kentucky to visit family, we always found time for a round of golf or a beer. After Katrina, Mike was one of the first who tracked me down to make sure we were safe.

I learned the severity of Mike's illness in early January. He had suffered a viral infection of his heart a decade earlier, and over the years the condition worsened. He was undergoing extensive treatment at Vanderbilt University Hospital in Nashville while awaiting a heart transplant.

I wanted to see him, and conveniently our men's and women's basketball teams were to play a double-header at Western Kentucky University in Bowling Green on January 17. I took the opportunity to support my teams and visit my old friend on the same trip. I would drive up to the games on Saturday, and then drive to Nashville and spend some time with Mike on Sunday.

On the drive up, I thought a lot about our boyhood adventures. I remember the day my father told me another boy had moved into our Clark Station neighborhood, so I took my Hutch glove and ball and asked the new kid if he wanted to play catch. I distinctly recall that the first ball I threw at Mike went over his head, but he stretched and reached back and retrieved it with such grace that I said to myself, "We're going to have some fun." For the next three or four years we were inseparable.

We went to church camp together, and I wrote home that our team won a basketball game 72 to 6 and Mike and I combined for 64 of the points. Since it was a church camp, honesty compelled me to admit that Mike had scored 51 of those points.

As we grew out of our childhood and his basketball skills developed, Mike belonged more to the public. We saw each other frequently at UK, more so because I was a freshman sportswriter for the *Kentucky Kernel* student newspaper than because I was his friend. When I applied for the *Kernel* job, I told the sports editor I attended Shelby County High with Mike Casey and Bill Busey, another Wildcat recruit. It was natural that my first assignment as a freshman sportswriter was to interview Rupp about his fabulous freshman team that also included Dan Issel and Mike Pratt.

I was terrified that I was going to interview the legendary Rupp. I had grown up listening to Cawood Ledford's calls of the great Kentucky teams of the Fifties and early Sixties on WHAS in Louisville. I would keep score of every game and then listen to Rupp's post game radio show in which he told Cawood how his coaching genius usually saved the day, despite his players who seldom listened to his wisdom. If Rupp claimed he never used a zone defense, you could bet that the "transitional stratified hyperbolic paraboloid" he employed to beat an unsuspecting opponent looked very similar and achieved the same purpose. In an era before the saturation of sports through ESPN, Fox Sports and the Internet, sports celebrities came through the radio, and Rupp was the biggest of them all to a young Kentucky listener.

I was admitted to his office, and I first noticed a picture of a polled Hereford, a breed of beef cattle which Rupp raised. I tried to start the conversation by complimenting him on what a fine animal that was, but he got right to the point and asked me what was on my mind. I stammered that I was doing a story on the freshman team and that I had gone to Shelby County, and … "I don't want any stories written about those Shelby County boys," he interrupted. "Their heads are big enough as it is."

I don't know whether it was the puddle under my chair or the tears welling up in my eyes that made Rupp smile, but he knew he'd gone a bit too far and said, "I'm just kidding. You write whatever you want about them." Rupp proved a willing source for me that year and the next, probably because he loved to tweak the full time beat writers of the Louisville *Courier-Journal* and Lexington *Herald-Leader* by giving scoops to the school paper.

The years went by and Mike and I talked less frequently, but I saw him at our 25th year high school reunion in 1991, and the time apart disappeared. I called a year later to tell him I was going to take a marriage mulligan and would he come down to New Orleans and stand in my wedding, which he did.

I was happy that the best part of my future would get to meet and spend time with one of the best parts of my past.

Mike was lying in bed, his 6-foot-4 frame drawn and withered, and his face looking gray and tired. His right leg was black from a staph infection he had contracted. He said matter-of-factly that he had been taken off the heart transplant list, at least until the infection healed.

My visit seemed to comfort him as our conversation took us away from our miseries and back to the past that binds old friends. We laughed about our "bike hikes" through the hayfields of Shelby County and about the time I bet Mike a nickel he wouldn't kneel down and lick an almost dried cow pie, which he did. He reminded me of a basketball game when he had a raging case of diarrhea, and a trainer went into the stands asking if anybody had a bottle of Pepto-Bismol and my mother miraculously reached into her purse and produced a bottle that she carried because my little brother was suffering the same ailment.

The hour or so passed quickly, and Mike was getting tired, so I hugged him and told him I loved him.

I remember driving back to New Orleans, thanking God for my health and praying that Mike would survive. But the infection would not go away, and Mike's heart gave out a few weeks later.

I have many wonderful memories of my best friend. But none were better than those final moments in the hospital. Two 60-year-old men embracing, one facing death and the other one thinking he had problems.

CHAPTER
28

I f Katrina was a test of faith, the budget crisis of 2009 was the final exam. The
  university and our program were still in a wounded state when Governor Jindal
  proposed in early March a 2009-10 state budget that would cut higher education
across Louisiana by $219 million.

Jindal's proposal was criticized because of his perceived desire to be seen as a cost-
cutting governor who would be a prime candidate for President in 2012. Jindal responded that the budget crisis was so severe that drastic measures must be taken, and he was
constitutionally restricted on what he could cut. Health care and higher education were
the most vulnerable areas of the state budget, which Baton Rouge political commenta-
tor J.R. Ball called a "decades-long wrong."

UNO's share of the cut would total $15 million. In his computations to achieve
that number, Ryan included the entire $1.4 million in general fund support to the Ath-
letic department. About $900,000 of that support was in tuition costs of our student-
athletes, while the remaining money included salaries of academic support personnel,
spirit groups and maintenance costs of the baseball facility, expenses laid off to other
departments per the Carr Report's recommendations.

That decision left the athletics department in a precarious, and unique position. The
elimination of institutional support would make UNO the only Division I athletic program in America, other than those with prominent self-supporting football programs,
that received zero support from its university.

The other Division I institutions in Louisiana supported athletic programs that
included football, college athletics' most expensive sport to maintain. The University
of Louisiana in Lafayette and the University of Louisiana in Monroe, both in-state Sun
Belt Conference rivals, received about half of their budgets from non-student fee university support. UL-Monroe's enrollment in 2009 was just 8,400, 30% less than UNO's.
Louisiana Tech, with an enrollment comparable to UNO of just over 11,000, supported
a Division I football program in the higher profile Western Athletic Conference (WAC).

That begged the obvious question: if other institutions in our state had found ways
to support more expensive athletics programs, why couldn't UNO support a *non-football*
program? The answer was that Ryan had inherited a precarious "manage by enrollment"
system, in Bill Carr's words. If enrollment was high, more revenue would come to the
athletic department because more students were paying a student athletic fee. If enrollment was down, revenue would drop proportionately, as revealed in the aftermath of
Hurricane Katrina.

But Ryan had resisted recommendations to change the system, and now, as he had at the mid-year cuts, he insisted that to support athletics would sacrifice academic programs. Others in his administration argued that a successful athletics program enhanced a university's overall reputation and, therefore, its core academic mission. But those voices gradually had been weeded out to the point that Ryan's inner circle had become his personal Greek chorus that applauded his every decision.

Not only was the university eliminating $1.4 million in support, but Ryan declared that the university no longer would absorb the annual athletics deficit. Athletics would spend about $5.6 million, including tuition costs, in the 2008-09 fiscal year. About $2 million of that would be covered by student fees and another $1.2 million would be covered by self-generated revenue such as ticket sales and sponsorships. Even with the general fund support, the deficit for 2008-09 was expected to run close to $1 million. Without it, we would be $2.4 million short.

The deficit bugaboo was not new. After I became athletic director in 2003, I learned I had inherited a $3 million deficit; however, by careful planning and the diligence of my business manager, Mike Dauenhauer, we had cut the deficit to $750,000 the summer that Katrina struck.

The ensuing freefall in revenue coupled with the rising costs of supporting an athletics program had ballooned the athletics deficit to nearly $6 million. Ryan said he was under intense scrutiny by the LSU System office and could not allow it to grow any more.

It continued to chafe that the entire deficit issue was purely a spreadsheet exercise. We were the only athletic department in the state whose annual deficit was accumulated and which was required to pay it back. But pay it back to whom? The university did not borrow money to pay off the annual shortfall in athletics or any other department. Any department's shortfall is covered by the university on an annual basis. Other athletic departments could not support themselves without institutional support. The conundrum was that UNO never had provided adequate institutional support to athletics in the first place.

The administration argued it could not provide such support because athletics was an auxiliary enterprise, like the bookstore and food service. As such, athletics was expected to make a profit, no matter how unrealistic the prospect. Because of the annual shortfalls, athletics' annual deficit was exceeding the profits from the other auxiliaries, and the net number was approaching zero. With no surplus left in the auxiliary reserve, there soon would be no money to cover athletics' debt, and that is where tolerance ended.

The deficit issue was another example of UNO's uneasy relationship with the LSU Board of Supervisors and the LSU System office. The clock began ticking on the UNO athletics deficit in 2001 with the board resolution that increased the student athletic fee but required that part of the proceeds go to an annual debt service payment. When the department's annual debt after Katrina far exceeded the $250,000 annual repayment, the LSU System office began to badger CFO Robison about the growing deficit. Robison began to push the issue with Ryan.

At some point, it would have been prudent to take the issue back before the board and negotiate a more realistic solution. Such a proposal should have included increased institutional support as recommended in the Carr Report, transferring certain expenses to the university's general fund that would help eliminate the annual deficit. However, Ryan was reluctant to take issues before the system office or the board because the reception usually was less than cordial. The financial health of the athletic department obviously was not a battle he wished to fight when comparatively more important battles were looming.

Deficits are a product of two factors: (1) Overspending or (2) lack of revenue. We kept our spending lean, but we had no control over most expenses because of conference and NCAA obligations. We still had to travel with transportation prices rising. We had to pay our coaches competitive salaries, although our pay ranked in the lower quartile of the conference. We still had to pay game officials the same as everyone else, and we still needed personnel to execute the events.

We did not have the revenue to create revenue generating initiatives such as ticket sales drives or to hire additional personnel to increase sponsorship sales or solicit donations. Without the general fund support, we were faced with again cutting back sports simply to survive.

Since Katrina, I had felt that every day I had to pull a rabbit out of a hat just for our program to make it to the next day. Now, I couldn't even do that. The governor had stolen the hat.

I met with Ryan, who was insistent that our only option was to ask the students for an increase in the student athletic fee. It still rankled with me that the other Division I programs in the state, all with football, supported their athletic programs with little to no student fees. However, Ryan insisted on shifting the responsibility to the students; if they wanted an athletics program, then let them vote for it. It was out of his hands. An increase in the student fee was an option we had discussed several times over the years. It also had been recommended in the Carr Report, although the report criticized the "manage by enrollment" funding model.

Despite Ryan's insistence on pursuing the vote, he was not optimistic it would be approved. Our students were faced with a tuition increase the following year, and students would be reluctant to vote themselves another fee increase during tough economic times. But it was the only alternative he left us.

We discussed the parameters of the vote, particularly how much of an increase we should request. The current fee was $100 per semester for a full time student taking 12 or more hours. That amounted to $8.33 per credit hour. My calculations showed we could make up the $1.4 million in lost general fund support with a per hour increase of $6, which would produce a total of $3.5 million.

However, Elizabeth Lowry, Ryan's chief assistant who had risen rapidly in his inner circle, recommended that we seek to *double* the fee. After all, she argued, anything short of doubling the fee would not provide us with the revenue we needed to also cut into the deficit. Doubling the fee to $200 per semester was an extremely aggressive request of the typical cash strapped UNO commuter student. Asking for any increase would be a challenge, but could we sell a doubling of the athletic fee?

I went back and recalculated and scaled back the increase to $8, which would equal $16.33 per credit hour. While providing sufficient revenue, it was not exactly a doubling of the fee, which could be a perceptual advantage. In any case, we would pull out all the stops to sell it.

The best case scenario would solve our major problem for the immediate future. The new fee would mean an additional $1.5 million in revenue to the department, which, in addition to the $2 million from the current fee and the $1.2 million in ticket sales, sponsorships and other revenue, would mean about $4.7 million in total revenue. If any of the institutional support were restored from the proposed cuts, even the $900,000 tuition component which was more of a pass through than an actual expense, it should make us whole for the 2009-10 fiscal year.

After our plans for the student vote became public, we were asked by many supporters if a vote was a requirement or if Ryan had the authority to propose a fee increase without a student vote. When I asked a member of the staff at the LSU System office, the individual told me a vote was not required if the chancellor recommended it. However, a member of the LSU Board of Supervisors backed Ryan's position. He said that under "PM 29," a presidential memo signed in 2006, the Board would not approve any measure that did not include support from the students. The most graphic measure of that support would be an affirmative vote in a student referendum.

A positive vote would be difficult enough, but Ryan implemented a voting procedure that I believed ignored accountability and invited abuse. The vote would be conducted over the Internet and spread over three days, procedures that I believed empowered the cowards. A handful of students opposing the vote could conceivably collect student ID numbers of their friends, access the online platform and cast "No" votes one after another. The American democratic process is an open vote, and I argued why should UNO's process be any different?

I proposed a conventional method with a number of polling places set up around campus that individuals would be required to visit in order to cast their vote. It was the way every election in America is conducted, and it provided one-person, one-vote accountability.

But Ryan disagreed, saying he needed to assure that all students had access, and an e-mail vote was the most accommodating form of access.

Having lost that battle, I asked Ryan if he would voice his support of the increase, but he refused. He said the chancellor must maintain neutrality on such contentious issues. I failed to see how this issue was any different from his current support of a tuition increase, but he would not relent.

This was not a time to play Woodrow Wilson, I thought. However, unless the opposition sank the *Lusitania* and pushed public opinion to our side, we were stuck with his neutrality.

I drafted a bill to increase the athletic fee that would be taken up in a student government meeting. The SG president, Justin Cottrell, opposed the idea of another fee increase, and proposed some amendments to my original bill. I was invited to an SG hearing where I could state my case. After debate, the student government senators would vote on which version of the bill they would send to the student body.

My proposal tied the fee to the total number of credit hours the student took per semester, without limitation. Cottrell's first amendment capped the fee at 12 hours, consistent with existing practice. I obtained figures from the university that showed about 12% of all credit hours taken were more than 12 hours per semester. Cottrell's amendment meant we would lose 12% of my projected revenue, or about $480,000. That was a huge chunk, which could mean the difference between break even or a deficit.

His second amendment required that at least 10% of the student body — or about 1,200 students — vote in order for the election to be official. Although I objected to it on the grounds that a no-show would be a "No" vote, that amendment did not concern me greatly. I felt our student-athletes could deliver 1,000 votes on their own.

I lost on both issues, as the senators voted to send the referendum, as amended, to the students. I was hoping my losing streak would end with the actual vote.

With a three-week campaign ahead of us, we mobilized all of our assets. I had spoken with Rick Villarreal, the athletic director at North Texas, who had recently pushed through a fee increase to build a new football stadium. Rick shared some of his research on student fees around the country, and he gave me some ideas on tactics. Other research on campus polling revealed that telephones, mailings and even e-mail were not considered effective for a college audience. If you wanted students to get a message, you had to utilize the new technology, which meant YouTube, Facebook, Twitter and texting.

Fortunately, the new technology was inexpensive, and we planned accordingly. We created a Facebook account that would carry daily updates of our activities and why the fee increase was important. I wrote scripts for three 60-second promotional spots on YouTube that a group of students agreed to produce and that our student-athletes could forward to their friends.

I asked our coaches to recommend three or four of their student-athlete leaders who would be out front leading the campaign, with our direction. All of our teams were represented, but the men's and women's swimming teams took a special interest. They campaigned daily at the University Center dining areas and at special events such as the traditional spring crawfish boil.

Our proposal also contained a provision that the first $50,000 of the proceeds be set aside to support a club football team. The team had enjoyed instant popularity after it was organized the previous fall. The university's Director of Admissions, Andy Benoit, was the team's head coach and had done a commendable job getting his kids into the community to promote his team and sell tickets. They raised about $80,000 in their first year to buy uniforms and to pay for one road trip and one home game. It was a lesson for our students on how to get out and promote something you believed in.

Benoit welcomed our interest at helping his cause, and we added about 50 experienced salesmen to our current sales roster of student-athletes.

The Privateer Athletic Foundation, our fund-raising organization, paid for "Vote Yes" stickers that we handed out liberally. The YouTube videos received much positive response and compared favorably to a single opposition video that showed a student at a blackboard trying to figure out why our department needed more money.

Our student-athletes attended Student Government meetings and rallies on the "Vote Yes" campaign. Our international students, which comprised most of our men's and women's tennis and our men's golf teams, rallied their fellow internationals. Other student groups such as the Tau Kappa Epsilon and Lambda Chi Alpha fraternities came to our rallies and handed out stickers.

I was feeling extremely optimistic, especially since no organized opposition had surfaced. Student Government sponsored one forum at which only three or four students voiced their opposition to the plan compared to three dozen student-athletes and civilians who spoke in favor.

Still, during the forums and letters to the *Driftwood* student newspaper, we saw ripples of a subtle anti-athletics feeling on campus. Cottrell, the Student Government president, wrote a factually challenged piece that appeared in the semester's final issue, which left me no opportunity for a rebuttal. Others weighed in both pro and con. We knew some faculty members and many staff members were critical of our program simply because they perceived that a dollar going to athletics was a dollar that did not go to their department.

What we did not see was organized opposition. We saw no banners or pickets carrying signs against the increase. The dissent was subtle, but revealed in comments at public meetings: "Why should we support athletics since nobody goes to the games?" "Athletics should work harder to sell more tickets." "Athletics should sell more sponsorships and raise money on their own." "Tuition is going up in the fall, so why should I add another fee increase to my burden?"

157

Five days before the vote, I received an e-mail from Ryan which I believed changed his previous position on the intent of the student vote. We had discussed a student vote for several years, but the budgetary threat to remove our institutional support now made it necessary. But Ryan sent a "clarification" stating if the vote passed, and the legislature restored some of the cuts, he would not ask the Board of Supervisors to implement the fee because "it would be dishonest."

That argument might have been acceptable to me if the institutional support of our program had been adequate, but it was far short of that. I fired back an immediate response reminding him that we had been discussing a fee increase since he became chancellor. An increase also was an element of our strategic plan. Without that additional revenue, we had no chance to start adding back sports to restore our full Division I status.

I also cautioned him that his stance put us in a position of hoping the cuts were as bad they could be, so we would have the fee increase implemented, and then hope the economy improves in the future so we can get some General Fund support back. Where is the logic in that? I characterized the fee increase as our one chance to climb out of the hole, to operate without a deficit and a chance to restore our Division I standards.

I suggested that a more logical approach would be to implement the fee and if the cuts aren't as severe, then restore only enough of the general fund support to assure that we break even then devote the rest to another entity that was cut. "Otherwise," I wrote, "this department will never be anymore than it is right now, which is unfair to our student-athletes, our coaches and to our alumni and students who care about athletics."

I did not receive a response to my e-mail.

The vote was to begin at 12:01 A.M. on April 28 and last until midnight on April 30. We had a final meeting on Monday, April 27, at which I asked our student-athletes how many votes they thought they could deliver. The tally was close to 1,000. On the first day of the voting, the local TV cameras were on campus interviewing students and me. Bill Capo, a veteran WWL-TV reporter, told me he had talked to 15 students and only one said they voted against the fee increase. Similar informal polls were conducted, and all appeared positive. I was feeling even more confident.

The day the voting ended, I sent an e-mail to our student leadership group and others, thanking them for their efforts and inviting them to a meeting of all staff, coaches, students and supporters on Friday at the Human Performance Center.

I was ready for a victory celebration, and I wanted to share it with all the people who had worked so hard on it. I had told our students at our last meeting that they had experienced a great example of the democratic process. They embraced an issue, and they sought to persuade others to help them enact it. I was proud of them, and I was proud of our effort.

My cell phone rang at 8:03 A.M. Friday morning. I had just finished showering from a brisk three-mile run, and I felt upbeat. The Caller I.D. showed the caller as "Tim (Pvt.) Ryan." That was the first time he had called me from his private office line. I chuckled at the suggestion of the movie *Saving Private Ryan,* and I answered.

"Jim, this is Tim," he said.

"Tim, how are you?" expecting him to give me the good news.

"Not so good," he replied. "The vote failed by 1,418 to 1,250."

I was stunned. I sat down and all I could say was that I couldn't believe it.

"Actually, it was closer than I thought it would be," he said, which is not what I needed to hear. The day that had started out so well had truly become Black Friday.

CHAPTER
29

I told Jean the vote failed, and she reacted as I had, like it was a death in the family. "We're done," I told her. "We've got no chance now."

I went to my desk and wrote an e-mail to our staff, coaches and the Student Leadership Group, informing them that the vote had failed. I toed the party line, saying that our next option was to lobby hard in the Legislature to reduce the governor's proposed cuts to higher education, in which case our support from the university would be restored.

I also encouraged everybody: "Don't you give up now, because I'm not!"

I was lying through my teeth, because at that moment I did not see any hope for us. We were "deader than Kelsey's nuts," as my old boss Jim Finks used to say. The rollercoaster that we had been riding for nearly four years was plummeting hard on a downward rail.

I had no emotion left, but I forced myself to dress and drive to the office. It was less than a 10-minute trip, but it seemed like an eternity. I tried to come up with some idea, some magical potion, some elixir that would cure us from this terrible malady we had battled. I could see nothing but a repeat of 2006 when we had to tell our coaches and student-athletes that we were cutting their sports and changing their lives forever. Except this time, I would be presiding over the death of an entire program.

I searched desperately for a villain to blame. Ryan was the object of my ire, but he did not create the situation. Was Governor Jindal the culprit? Was it the drop in oil prices that reduced the state's revenue? Was it the general economic malaise that had spread over the country? Could I have done more to get out and raise money or to try and put us in a better position to endure these storms? Was it the entire UNO community who didn't support athletics in the first place? Was it the people who complained about a losing basketball team but who would not come to see the best baseball team in the conference? How could we have prevented this from happening?

I never had experienced such a feeling of helplessness and utter lack of hope. I felt like the Monopoly player who landed on Boardwalk with a hotel. It cost me most of my property, but I went around the board a few times untouched, and I kept playing. Just when I'd started to build back, I landed on Boardwalk again. The rent was more than I had left, and I was wiped out. Game over.

Two stops on Boardwalk — the first one Katrina and the second the 2009 budget disaster — would kill Privateer athletics.

I arrived at the office and was besieged with e-mails and telephone calls from supporters who were angry at the result. Most of the rage was directed at Ryan. One caller complained that Ryan either could have told the students he was recommending the increase because it was the best thing for the university or, if he insisted on a vote, he could have voiced his support of the referendum. "One took big nuts, and the other took heart, and he showed neither," the caller complained.

Rob Broussard, my assistant AD for media relations, asked how he wanted me to handle our public acknowledgement. I told him I had scheduled a 2 P.M. meeting with our students and staff to celebrate our expected victory, but now we would turn it into a public wake. I also sent Ryan an e-mail inviting him to join me at the press conference.

Ryan soon issued the following statement to all students, confirming what we already knew: "The only hope we have to preserve UNO athletics as a Division I program is in the hands of the Louisiana Legislature. If the proposed budget cuts are not reduced, we will have no alternative but to eliminate the general fund support for athletics. The program cannot survive without this support."

Over the next few hours, coaches and staff were asking questions and wanting to know if they still had jobs. I told them I would meet with staff and coaches after the 2 P.M. press conference. I also sent an e-mail to Betty Dauenhauer, Mike's wife and assistant director of Human Resources. I wanted to know what my benefits would be if I should choose to retire in the next few months.

I had the same questions as everyone else, and I didn't have any answers. I had calls of support from Wright Waters and some of the other athletic directors at conference schools. College athletics is a small fraternity, and every athletic director experiences the same problems in different degrees. When one experiences a tragedy or difficult time, they all believe in the words of John Bradford, the 16th century English reformer who was quoted as saying, "There but for the grace of God, go I."

We convened the press conference at 2 P.M. sharp, on the floor of the Human Performance Center, the 40-year-old gym that had survived Katrina. I took the podium and expressed my disappointment for the result of the vote and my gratitude to the students who believed in our program and supported us, especially our student-athletes who worked so hard on our behalf. I also called it "sad" that an athletic tradition could be terminated by a few student votes.

Ryan took the podium and told the crowd "the game is not over," and placed emphasis on the university's efforts in the legislature to combat the cuts to higher education. He appeared more statesmanlike than partisan, which generated one spontaneous display of irritation.

It came from Ron Maestri, who came to UNO in 1970 as assistant baseball and basketball coach, took his baseball team to the College World Series in 1984 and served as athletic director until 1999. I noticed him edging closer to the podium with a grave expression on his face. Ryan paused as Maestri came closer, and all eyes and cameras turned. Maestri stopped five feet short of the podium and looked Ryan in the eye.

"What upsets me," Maestri said loudly, fighting back tears, "is that I don't hear anybody in this community talking about the University of New Orleans." His forefinger thrusting, emphasizing every point, he continued: "I don't hear the business community. I don't hear the legislature. I don't hear the Board of Supervisors. I hear nobody talking about the University of New Orleans, and it upsets me."

"It upsets me, too," Ryan said softly as Maestri walked to the back of the auditorium amid applause from the spectators and students.

Maestri's outburst, fueled by 30 years of his own fights with the administration and the state over budgets, was the tipping point. The nightly news on each channel reported the failed vote, but every one featured video of Maestri's outrage. The news suddenly became not that UNO had failed but that nobody seemed to care except an angry former athletic director and coach. The organization that Maestri bounced on his knee and watched grow into maturity would be allowed to grow into old age if he had anything to do about it.

And, it appeared that he did.

That night and through the next morning, I began to receive calls and e-mails from people wanting to help. One call I did not expect was from George Shinn, owner of the New Orleans Hornets. I should not have been surprised since Jean was his executive assistant, and I had known George socially since the team came to New Orleans in 2002. Shinn offered to chair a committee of business leaders who would seek to raise the money we needed. He also said the Hornets would extend any business, marketing or promotional advice that we needed to help us sell tickets and generate more excitement.

The situation was swinging back toward a positive direction, 180 degrees from the day before.

Immediately following the press conference, I had met with my staff and coaches and told them that I was not optimistic about our future. At that time, our only hope for rescue would be for the legislature to modify the governor's proposed cuts, and that did not seem likely. I told them the possibility existed that Ryan would pull the plug on the department on July 1, the beginning of the new fiscal year.

I told the head coaches that their contracts would be honored in any case but that any assistant coaches who had other opportunities might wish to explore them. I also approved a suggestion from our interim compliance officer that we prepare a statement that would allow our student-athletes to contact other institutions in the event the program was terminated.

Nothing Ryan said during the one-on-one sessions that followed the press conference suggested any hope we could survive. His comments were directed more at the situation facing the entire university and less about athletics specifically, but his failure to express hope for the department was interpreted by many as indifference.

Saturday night, I sent Ryan an update on the day's events, telling him that an outpouring of support for our program had given me great encouragement. However, I asked him pointedly to refrain from his neutral stance. I told him I would appreciate a show of support for any efforts to help UNO athletics get through this crisis. I cautioned him that student-athletes, parents and coaches continued to ask why he was against us. So-called neutrality is not a neutral position.

I did not know if he would listen to my advice, but if the public finally was outraged about our situation he could use it to exercise his leadership. I've always heard if you see a parade passing by, you might as well get in front of it.

I followed up the e-mail to Ryan with one to my head coaches and to Mike Sapera, president of the Privateer Athletic Foundation. I listed names of the people who had called to express a willingness to help, including Shinn. If our coaches and staff knew that some influential people were stepping up to help, it would offset the dark mood that prevailed on Friday.

But my enthusiasm overrode my good public relations sense. When I named names in the note, my only intention was to give our people some hope. I did not want it to become a press release, which it did once I sent it and some of the recipients forwarded it on. It became a major news story the following day.

I met on Monday morning with Shinn, Hugh Weber, president of the Hornets, and Harold Kaufman, their vice president of media relations. Shinn already had received calls from the press on his involvement, and he almost pushed his sword back into the scabbard before it was barely out.

He told the press he would do anything he could to help New Orleans, and that included helping UNO. Privately, he was disappointed that the message was becoming diluted. I agreed to clamp down on the leaks and that any information distributed on the effort would come from Kaufman.

We discussed goals and strategies, potential members of a task force and some likely donors. We decided to assemble a committee to meet on May 15, which was a little less than two weeks away. I did not like wasting another two weeks, but the legislature would be in session until the last week of June, and our fiscal year deadline was July 1.

On Tuesday morning, I sent an e-mail to my staff instructing them to make no further comments on Shinn's role or on the effort to enlist the business community. I told them I did not mind sharing information so long as I knew it would be kept confidential. Meaning, I was no longer sharing anything with anybody.

Shinn agreed to hold a press conference at UNO on Wednesday, May 6. He would have preferred a later date, when we had met and had more details about our plan. But I felt it was important for him to speak while our students were still on campus. It was the last week of final exams, and most students would be heading home for the summer in another day or two. Some already had expressed an interest in transferring, and I wanted to allay their fears as best we could.

I invited Ryan to the press conference, but he declined the invitation at first because of a meeting in Baton Rouge. Rob Broussard coordinated a press release with Kaufman of the Hornets that went out about 4 P.M. on Tuesday. After 6 P.M., Ryan sent me an e-mail that he had gotten his meeting changed and would be at the press conference.

I learned later that Malcolm Ehrhardt, a former UNO student government president whose public relations and marketing firm worked for the Hornets, convinced Ryan to attend. Ehrhardt correctly believed that for Ryan not to appear would reinforce the perception that had lingered since the student vote, that Ryan did not care if athletics survived, and would, in fact, prefer that athletics be eliminated.

That perception was not supported by the hard evidence. Ryan was a season ticket holder at baseball and basketball games, where he had first row seats at floor level, and he considered himself a knowledgeable fan. He also had found funds for the baseball field resurfacing after Katrina as well as other initiatives that required unscheduled funding. If Ryan had any intention of eliminating athletics, his perfect opportunity would have been during the university downsizing after Katrina.

But his decisions after Katrina haunted him. Under the justification of financial exigency, 26 tenured faculty members were terminated, a rare occurrence in academe. Some disgruntled faculty members had not hesitated to remind him of the offense ever since. I do not believe Ryan wanted athletics eliminated, but I believe he began to go out of his way *not* to show athletics any undue favoritism.

A strong perception existed that Ryan's boss, LSU System President John Lombardi, was prodding Ryan to devalue the athletics program at UNO. That would be consistent with other sentiments expressed privately by LSU System officials that Ryan's insistence on UNO as a premier "urban research institution" was misguided. One official even suggested in an e-mail that UNO "can't afford the luxury" of its graduate school and that its undergraduate programs should serve as a feeder for LSU's graduate programs in Baton Rouge. It was no secret that Ryan did not trust Lombardi and on many occasions indiscriminately expressed concern about "losing my job" over these and other issues.

Whether pressure from above encouraged Ryan to remain neutral on the student fee vote or not, his reluctance to state a position was widely interpreted as opposition to the vote. He did not help himself with an oft-repeated comment that "athletics is not essential to the academic mission of the university." One former student government president chastised Ryan in a much distributed e-mail, saying he could have taken a bold position but, instead, "decided to hide behind the student vote."

Ryan's performance at the press conference with George Shinn did little to dispel the negative perception.

CHAPTER
30

George Shinn is an accomplished public speaker. He has written books on positive thinking and self motivation, and is an individual powered by a strong moral mainspring. At his press conference at UNO's Homer Hitt Alumni Center, he talked without notes, was folksy and glib and had the full attention of the student-athletes. He made them promise they would not transfer during this trying period and that they would give him and the department a chance to come up with a solution. It was an uplifting moment, with the student-athletes nodding their heads, clapping at his comments and agreeing that they would give us a chance to fix things. When Shinn finished, I nearly expected one or more students to shout "Hallelujah!"

Then Ryan took the podium. He looked uncomfortable, stiff and read from a prepared statement. He focused his comments on the plight of higher education in Louisiana and said this was not an issue faced only by athletics but by the entire university. He seldom looked up from his text as he read. He did not elicit any enthusiasm from the students.

In his one-on-one comments to the cameras afterward, Ryan threw a soggy blanket over Shinn's comments, saying there were no guarantees that sufficient money could be raised to save athletics. He also repeated his earlier comment that athletics was not essential to the academic mission.

Ryan's comments fed the perception that if athletics was going to pull itself out of the water, the chancellor would not be the one to throw it the rope. Subsequent phone calls and e-mails to the department were unanimous that if Ryan were against athletics, he should just say so. "This is not a time for indecisive talk," one e-mailer said. "When guys like Shinn step up and attempt to help only to find that their efforts are fruitless just *hurts* us all."

Ryan could have eliminated these problems by having an experienced media relations person on staff. It was another example of Ryan's reluctance to surround himself with strong people who could give him sound advice that would help avoid stumbles. His executive staff was loyal, but inexperienced in the tasks he assigned them. And they seldom disagreed with the boss. "He has surrounded himself with a retinue of personal cheerleaders," one former colleague said. When Ryan spoke, their heads nodded so fast you could make butter if you poured cream in their ears.

That night, I was at Maestri Field watching our baseball team play Tulane when Shinn called me to express his deep disappointment at Ryan's comments. "Is he with us or not, because if he's not, I'm not going to put my good name on the line."

Shinn said he wanted to write a letter to Ryan saying he was disappointed in his public comments and to ask him if he was on board. He even suggested leaking the letter to the press. I did not believe embarrassing Ryan publicly would be beneficial to our task in general or to me personally. Shinn got involved because of his relationship with Jean and me, and Ryan knew that. If Shinn suddenly backed out, fingering Ryan as the reason, I would be caught squarely in the middle.

After discussing the situation with team president Hugh Weber and Malcolm Ehrhardt, Shinn decided to continue his efforts in spite of Ryan's lukewarm reception.

My relationship with my boss was clearly deteriorating. In several e-mails, Ryan accused me of being defiant and suggested I did not support him. His feeling was fueled by two well intended, but ill-advised efforts of some coaches and boosters.

Several weeks earlier, one of our boosters had expressed his frustration to state senator David Heitmeier, who represented the 7th District comprising the West Bank suburbs of Algiers, Gretna and Terrytown. Heitmeier offered to help, and he invited representatives of the program to Baton Rouge to explain the issues. I accompanied Tom Walter, PAF president Mike Sapera and basketball coach Joe Pasternack to the meeting, which I believed was a good opportunity to educate and enlist a powerful supporter.

However, in my political naïveté, I did not realize the meeting was a violation of policy. Unbeknownst to me, the LSU Board of Supervisors has a rule stating that any LSU System employee who wishes to discuss official business with a member of the state legislature must get the permission of the System president. Ryan learned about the meeting second hand and, understandably, was not happy about it. I met with him and explained our intentions, and he seemed satisfied.

He was not so understanding, however, when he learned of a second meeting, one that took place without my knowledge. Walter and Pasternack sought the advice of Robert Bruno, a member of the Louisiana Board of Regents, the state's highest governing board for education. Bruno's son was a baseball prospect whom Walter had recruited, and Bruno was a partner with Walter confidante Rob Couhig in the development of the University Tennis Center.

Walter and Pasternack solicited Bruno's thoughts of our unsettled situation, and he also offered to help. Bruno contacted Dr. John Lombardi, president of the LSU System and Ryan's boss, about meeting with the UNO coaches to learn about our situation. Lombardi contacted Ryan, who, understandably, was furious at this obvious breach of protocol.

The contacts with Heitmeier and Bruno, no matter how innocent the intentions, supported Ryan's suspicion that the peasants were in open revolt and trying to overthrow the king. He sent an angry e-mail to the coaches with a copy to me chastising them for wanting to meet with his boss without talking to him first. He said he was "getting tired of the words and actions of all three of you to the effect that 'I am the enemy'." He also took a singular shot at me for my constant chiding of him for being "noncommittal on whether we are going to be here or not."

Ryan's e-mail also stated he had "been waiting for some ideas from the Athletic department for some time." I wasn't sure what new ideas he expected since he never responded to most of the ideas and suggestions I had given him the previous three years. He ended the note by demanding our presence in his office at 8 A.M. the following morning.

Joe's and Tom's actions put me in a precarious position. I called them both to find out what they were thinking. After hearing the apparent sincerity of both, I replied to Ryan's e-mail. I defended Tom and Joe as two coaches who love the university and would do anything they could to help us succeed. I told Ryan that none of us questioned his efforts on behalf of the university or his personal support of athletics, but I said I wasn't the only one who chafed at his public posture of neutrality. That perception was shared by parents, boosters and others, including George Shinn. I told him candidly that Shinn was very concerned about his ability to raise money without Ryan's support.

Ryan was less confrontational in person at our meeting the next morning than he had been in his e-mail. The coaches apologized for their zeal and told Ryan they were merely trying to help. Ryan assured us he was working daily with legislators to mitigate the proposed cuts to higher education. However, he said he was not optimistic that the cuts would be reduced. He said he wanted to save athletics, although it would be "a very different athletic department."

That comment sent up a red flag. Assuming the "very different" athletic department he envisioned would not be one that enjoyed a sudden infusion of financial support, my fears grew even greater. Sure enough, Ryan instructed me to prepare a budget in which we would spend no more than $3.2 million, which was the sum of anticipated revenue from the student fee plus our self-generated income. He followed up later that day with an e-mail outlining what he had told us in the meeting. He also added a final paragraph that I found curious at best and troubling at worst.

"It will take a fighter and a hard manager to make the tough decisions on what to cut to pull athletics through in these circumstances," he wrote. "If you do not feel that you can, or that you want to continue to lead UNO athletics under these circumstances, it is important that we discuss this immediately."

Was this a not-so-subtle invitation for me to resign? Did he no longer believe I could effectively lead UNO athletics? Or, was he taking me at my word when I told him several times before that you can't strip a Division I program down to the gunwale and expect it to survive as a viable representative of the university? During the budget crisis of the previous year, I told him in jest that I had written three letters of resignation but had torn up two of them. Was he suggesting I give him the final letter?

I am not paranoid by nature, but I had suspicions for some time that Ryan was trying to build a case against me for insubordination or malfeasance. His chief aide, Elizabeth Lowry, had asked Pasternack about my budgeting skills, obviously trying to extract some inside information that would support Ryan's contention we were profligate spenders. He also began copying our university counsel on e-mails to me in which he questioned a decision or criticized something we had done.

I always told Jean that resignation was an attractive alternative to dying with my boots on. Many times, I feared that the frustration of the job would begin to affect my health. But the downside of resigning was abandoning my staff, my coaches and the student-athletes. I had been asked before why I stayed on amid all the frustrations. My pat response was a rule I learned as a contracts negotiator in the NFL: the man with the iron ass wins!

But I believe the actual reason breaks down somewhere between 98% loyalty to the people who I brought here and 2% stubbornness. The man with the iron ass wins only if it's a fair fight, and this wasn't a fair fight.

I responded to Ryan that I appreciated his concern, but I would have the $3.2 million budget to him by June 5.

CHAPTER
31

I was working on Ryan's challenge to give him a budget that equaled our previous year's revenue when Adam Stowe, our director of fund-raising, stuck his head in my office.

"Did you know a Logan Wickliffe Cary?" he asked.

I thought a minute and didn't recall the name, but then I said it aloud and the middle name popped out.

"Oh, yeah, Wick Cary," I responded. "Nice old guy. I used to talk to him at baseball and basketball games."

I could picture Wick, who was tall and white haired and walked a little bent over, typical for a man in his Seventies. He always wore a blue Chicago Cubs jacket, a style of cowboy hat worn by Texas Rangers and he carried a scorebook to chart individual performances at our baseball and basketball games. He always sat by himself.

"He died a few days ago," Adam said.

I told Adam I had not heard the news but what a shame. Another good guy lost to the world when there were so many others whom I would gladly offer up in his place.

Adam said one of our former vendors, Walley Borries, called him with the news. Borries also told Adam that Wick had left his entire estate to his first loves — the athletic departments at the University of Oklahoma, LSU, Tulane and UNO.

I was more intrigued than surprised to hear that news. I knew Wick was a friend of former AD Ron Maestri and that Kathleen Gross, our former fund-raiser, had talked to Wick at every game. He had told her he graduated from Oklahoma and still had season tickets to Oklahoma football games. And we knew from others he was a regular at Tulane baseball games and that he attended LSU events.

But to think we were considered a close enough part of his family that we'd be in his will was a bit hard to believe. I asked Adam for Walley's number so I could call and get some details. Walley operated a novelty business, and we bought what in our business are called "trash and trinkets" from him. His wife was a Tulane supporter and had worked in their development office, so we always kidded Walley about "sleeping with the enemy."

Adam gave me the number, and I reached Walley in Birmingham, where he and his wife had moved after Katrina.

I had not spoken to Walley for some time, but after some pleasantries I asked him what he knew about Wick Cary. He said he did not know Wick personally, but his friend Alden Hagardorn, a New Orleans stockbroker and Tulane grad, was a very close friend of Wick. He said Hagardorn told him Wick was a lifelong bachelor, had no children and no brothers or sisters, and so he had nobody to leave his money to. Walley said Hagardorn told him that Oklahoma would get half his estate, and LSU, Tulane and UNO would share the other half.

I asked him how much are we talking about?

"Sit down," Walley said. "We're talking about $120 million! If my math is right, UNO's share would be $20 million. Would that solve your financial problems?"

Lord, I thought, would it! If it were true.

Walley gave me Alden Hagardorn's phone number, and we finally hooked up. Hagardorn said he handled some of Wick's investments, "but he never left me a nickel, and don't think I didn't encourage him to do so," he joked.

He said Wick lived in the same apartment at 2833 St. Charles Avenue he bought when he moved to New Orleans as a young petroleum engineer in 1960. Hagardorn said Wick rented another apartment in the same building, just to house his collection of scorebooks and sports memorabilia. He said Wick had a regular routine of eating breakfast at the Pontchartrain Hotel every morning, lunch at Joey K's on Magazine Street and dinner at the Milan Inn or St. Charles Tavern when he wasn't at a ballgame.

Hagardorn also confirmed the information that Walley had told me. "Wick always told me that his heirs were OU, LSU, Tulane and UNO, while he reminded me that I wasn't going to get a penny of it. He was a unique man, and he told that story to others, so there's got to be some truth in it."

Hagardorn said Wick had told him he owned 400 acres of oil producing land in Oklahoma and a strip shopping mall that provided the income he lived on. "The way he lived, he probably banked most of that money, too," he said.

Hagardorn pointed me to an obituary that had run on May 17 and 18 in *The Oklahoman* of Oklahoma City, which provided further details about this man we had befriended but knew so little about. He was born on April 23, 1930, in Oklahoma City and went to Yale University where he earned a mechanical engineering degree in 1952. He attended the University of Oklahoma and obtained a masters degree in geophysics in 1954 and went to work for Amoco in offshore and other oil ventures. He moved around until 1960 when Amoco sent him to New Orleans. He had no relatives but stayed active in several upscale social clubs. The obituary confirmed that "first and foremost Wick was a dedicated sports fan. In his pocket he always kept the current schedule for OU, Tulane, LSU, UNO and the New Orleans Saints."

Hagardorn said he had called the funeral home to see who was making arrangements and was told a gentleman named Jack Thomson from "Parriere, Mississippi." Mr. Thomson was an attorney and friend of Wick's who also was executor of the estate. Hagardorn gave me a telephone number with a "601" prefix, which confirmed the Mississippi location.

I told Hagardorn that I obviously wanted to get some more information, but it was an awkward situation for me. The amounts being floated around would save our department, not only for this year, but could enable us to implement some revenue producing initiatives that could ensure our financial stability for years.

It's like the old adage: "If you give a man a fish, you feed him for a day. If you teach him to fish, you feed him for the rest of his life." We were asking George Shinn to give us a fish, but a Wick Cary endowment could feed us for the rest of our lives.

I told Hagardorn I did not want to appear that I was dancing on Wick's grave by calling Mr. Thomson so soon. He understood and offered to make a call on behalf of our interests as well as Tulane's.

On Friday, May 29, I was meeting with several of my staff when my cell phone vibrated, and the caller ID identified it as Hagardorn.

"I finally talked to Mr. Thomson," he reported, "and he confirmed what we have heard, that the athletic departments of the four schools, quote, 'will be taken care of,' unquote. He said these things do not happen overnight and since Wick had property that must be disposed of, he would not venture to say how long the process would take."

That word was comforting, but I only had about 30 days to show Ryan that we were in line for a windfall that could forestall the dismantling of our program. If I went into his office claiming our poverty stricken department was going to inherit millions of dollars, without proof, he would probably duct tape my mouth shut and give me a road map to my next assignment, presumably far from UNO.

Hagardorn suggested I write to Mr. Thomson, introducing myself as the point person for UNO athletics and request a meeting. That was a good idea, but Hagardorn did not have an address. "Parriere" was a mystery. Neither of us had heard of a town by that name, and nothing turned up on "MapQuest," although a Google query asked, "Did you mean 'Carriere'?"

I have an extended family connection with an attorney who practices in New Orleans but lives in Mississippi, not far from the Carriere-Picayune area, so I called him. Henry "Tut" Kenny is my brother-in-law's brother-in-law (my wife's sister's husband's sister's husband, if you're keeping score). He had never heard of Mr. Thomson, but he did have a friend who practiced law in Pearl River County and would call.

A day later, Tut called to say that his friend did not know a Jack Thomson who practiced law in the area. I had not given Tut enough information on our first call, because then I asked if Wick Cary were a resident of New Orleans at his death would the will be filed in Orleans parish? His response suggested I made a good decision not going into the law, because he said he could find out immediately if anything had been filed in the 12 days since Wick's death.

It wasn't 15 minutes later that Tut called to tell me the estate had been registered in Orleans Parish and that he knew the attorney whose signature was on the record.

"He's a great old guy who doesn't usually handle these things, but it makes sense that he probably is a friend of Jack Thomson and was asked to do the filing."

Tut called back again to tell me he'd hit pay dirt. The will did, indeed, specify a significant contribution to the "UNO Foundation." There was no mention of athletics anywhere in the original will, although a two-page addendum included a paragraph that specified Wick's season football tickets to Oklahoma would go to his cousin, Jack Smith. The will contained a long list of bequests to individuals, most from $20,000 to $50,000, many of whom obviously were neighbors in Wick's building.

The most enticing part of the document was that the division of assets, after a long list of smaller bequests, would be split thusly:

To the University of Oklahoma Foundation, a 1/3 share.
To the University of New Orleans Foundation, a 1/3 share.
To the Administrators of the Tulane Educational Trust, a 1/6 share.
To the LSU Foundation, a 1/6 share.

So instead of sharing 1/3 of one half share, or 1/6 of the total, UNO would receive 1/3 of the total, or a full share with the University of Oklahoma. Apparently, those late spring afternoons on the bleachers at Privateer Park and at basketball games in Lakefront Arena had given Wick pleasure and the joy of being part of the UNO family.

I tried not to get too far ahead of myself, and I stopped for a moment to consider this apparent godsend. It must have been the skepticism I'd built up in my 11 years as a working journalist, but this all appeared too good to be true. This is what happens in Frank Capra movies, not in real life!

The poor widow and her starving children kicked out of their house because she can't pay the mortgage! The evil banker twirling his mustache as she and her bedraggled brood are turned out into the raging blizzard. But wait! A mysterious stranger in a white hat riding toward us on a golden Palomino, throwing a bag of money at the banker's feet! "Be gone, malicious cur!" our hero shouts to the banker, who picks up the bag and slinks away, foiled because the money would never replace the satisfaction of exiling another deadbeat to their fate. "Oh, thank you, kind sir," says the widow, as the mysterious stranger rides away into the night.

It was nice to lean back, close my eyes and dream about Wick Cary in his white Texas Ranger hat riding in on his golden Palomino to save our program. But reality quickly interrupted my brief reverie. We had other crises to deal with.

Our widely known situation was creating problems for our coaches, particularly in men's basketball. Joe Pasternack had reveled all year in the fact that he had signed a point guard in November whom he said could be the equal of Bo McCalebb. Carl Blair from Houston, Texas, would be the poster boy of the Pasternack era.

The problem was that all the published reports of the past month, specifically Black Friday and our decision to allow our student-athletes explore other options, prompted

Blair's parents to request a release from the binding National Letter of Intent. I refused the request, based on the fact that if we did not enforce the NLI with Blair, we could not enforce it with the unborn. The document would be worthless if we established a precedent of releasing student-athletes. The next basketball player whom our coaches identified and signed during the early period could bolt after a stellar senior season attracted the likes of Kentucky, Duke or North Carolina.

Pasternack cajoled, wheedled and sweet-talked Blair's parents, but to no effect. The family went public, and a story in the *Times-Picayune* painted our department as unyielding, unrealistic and oppressive for not allowing the young man his freedom of choice. The next couple of days, we received messages that we were the bullies and the bad guys. "Shame on you," said an e-mail writer, for affecting this kid's future.

The Hornets PR people, who already had begun working to improve our image, were appalled that we would allow such a story to appear in the first place. We came off like tyrants, forcing a poor unsophisticated student to play where he did not choose. From the PR perspective, style was more important than substance. Damn the precedent if it affected the perception.

We dug in our heels on the issue, with support from Sun Belt Commissioner Wright Waters, who agreed we needed to protect our program first. Carl Blair had made the choice to attend UNO, and despite the public protestations of our situation, we were alive and well and planned on an athletic season in 2009-10.

We fought the PR battle for a week, and then on May 28 I made the decision to release Blair and cut our losses. Of course, the damage was already done.

An even greater impact on our program was looming with baseball. Tom Walter told me he had been invited by Wake Forest to interview for the head coaching job. Student-athletes come and go but to lose my best and most successful coach was more than I wanted to take.

Walter's news was eased somewhat later the same day when Tut Kenny called to inform me that Wick Cary's executor was willing to release the first portion of the bequest. I met with Walter and told him the Wick Cary story. I assured him that our first use of the funds would be to make the long promised renovations to our ballpark.

"Would that make a difference in your decision to leave?" I asked. He said it would make "a huge difference." Tom has been disappointed before. He signed his contract extension in June 2008, based largely on Ryan's assurance that the renovation would be done within the next year. Then, on the brink of execution, the funds were diverted into the mid-year budget cuts.

Time was against us. Walter had to make a decision before we could get confirmation of the amount or the delivery of the Cary gift, and he agreed to a contract with Wake Forest. I immediately named associate head coach Bruce Peddie as interim head coach, a seemingly logical decision which would spark yet another confrontation.

CHAPTER
32

Despite all the frustrations and challenges, I always have been able to count on one outlet that would allow me to cope. I've been running since June 1, 1971, when I received my induction notice into the U.S. Army. Chubby and soft, I thought it was a good time to get in shape for basic training. After three weeks, I had worked up to two miles, and the physical part of basic training was a breeze. My modest start evolved into a culture that included daily runs, high mileage and five marathons, including a personal record of 2:58.28 in the 1984 Long Island Marathon.

Over the next three decades, running was my crutch. Whether I was living in Baltimore, New York, Buffalo, Chicago or New Orleans, I would bundle up or strip down according to the weather and get out early to start the day. Physically, it was an obvious benefit, but its more powerful effect was mental, giving me the satisfaction that I started every day ahead of the other guy.

A ruptured L-4 disc in 1989 ended my marathon career, but I recovered enough to resume running, albeit at a greatly reduced mileage level. After age 60, a three-mile morning run became the norm. I'd take out Elmo a couple of days a week, but most days it was just me, my challenges and my God. My daily run always has included a devotional, mostly asking for the good health of my family and my own personal strength.

My devotional took on new importance after Katrina, when I included the plea: "God, please let something good happen today." We had been beaten down by the constant frustrations, and we were desperate for anything positive. It could be progress on facility renovations, a team on a roll or a positive grade point average report at the end of a semester. We'd take anything, and if the only way to produce it was Divine Intervention, so be it.

I must admit I was a lukewarm Christian for much of my life, maybe because of the old reporter's irreverence. I believe in God and I was brought up to believe that Jesus Christ is the Son of God. But I also subscribed to Pascal's Wager. Philosopher Blaise Pascal determined that there is no downside to believing in God. If you believe, and there is a God and heaven, you've gained eternal life. If you believe, and there is no God, you haven't lost anything. But if you don't believe in God, and there is a God and heaven, you're screwed.

I recite this devotional during my morning run:

"Father, bless our little ones — Layne and Charles Connor — that they may grow to be tall and true and straight and good. Bless my beloved (older daughter) Lindsay and (her husband) Andrew and bless my beloved wife Jean. Bless Jerry and Laura and (their daughter) Jessica and (her husband) Matt and baby Kate.

"Bless Nanny G (Jean's mother) and may her physical health and strength equal her immaculate moral and spiritual health and strength. Bless Gary and Martha and (sons) Gary, Jr., Sam and Conway. Bless Schaffer and Tricia and (daughter) Kendall and (son) Shay. Bless Saint and Gloria and (daughter) Jordan, and (Jordan's father) Rick and (his wife) Jennifer and Saint's and Jennifer's children.

"Father, bless me that I am ever mindful of 1st Peter 5:7: 'Casting all your cares upon Him, for He careth for you,' and Proverbs 3:5-6: 'Trust in the Lord with all thy heart and lean not into your own understanding. In all ways acknowledge Him, and He will direct thy paths.

"Father, help me to be a better husband, father, brother, friend and manager. Help me to make the right decisions to help our program survive, and may something good happen this day.

"Father, let me value the past but not dwell in it; let me embrace the present and let me prepare for the future."

"Father, I pray now that you will help me to achieve the inner peace I so desperately seek, and may I have the strength to reject those who threaten that inner peace.

"Chart my course. Map my future.

"In Christ's name I pray, Amen."

I figure that prayer covers the important things for me. I pray for the good health of my children and my and Jean's families. I pray that I will trust in God and draw strength from Him during the frustrating days I experience. I pray that I will be a better person to my family and those around me and that I won't sit there and wish I had never left the NFL.

And I pray for the inner peace that will allow me to get through the day.

I have told Jean that my devotional also works for Catholics. After all, working at UNO has bolstered my chances of getting to heaven since I have spent ample time in purgatory.

As instructed by the chancellor, I created a budget for 2009-10 that would limit spending to no more than $3.2 million. The budget would require the immediate suspension of five more non-revenue sports in addition to the termination of some essential staff members. It would be a disaster for our department, if executed.

To Ryan's credit, he told me to go back and redo the proposal with the restoration of the tuition portion of scholarships for our student-athletes. That amounted to about $900,000 of the original $1.4 million, which Ryan considered a "pass through" since it was, in effect, money we paid to ourselves. The hard costs for scholarships, such as room and board and books, would remain a liability of the department.

That certainly helped because it would at least allow all of our sports to continue operating. That was a huge consideration because we were nearing the end of the initial NCAA sports sponsorship waiver. I feared that suspending sports again would affect any possibility of receiving an extension of the initial waiver, which we almost certainly would need.

A $4.1 million budget that allowed the sports to compete still would require significant cuts in staff. We had spent $5.6 million in 2008-09, and the new number would cripple us. We had a minimal staff anyway and to cut it significantly would severely hamper our ability to operate.

The new budget would require us to terminate the assistant business manager and the administrative assistant, leaving our business office a one-man operation. We would eliminate the fund-raising position, which would stifle efforts to increase revenue. We would eliminate the equipment manager, strength coach and field maintenance positions, requiring assistant coaches to perform those duties for their teams. We would terminate the assistant sports information position, which would create another one-man operation. We also would eliminate our academics assistant, leaving the academic fate of 140 athletes in the hands of our assistant AD for academic services.

If the budget were executed, we would be left with a skeleton staff for now and no hope to meet the NCAA waiver within the initial five-year period. We were hanging on for now, but for how much longer?

CHAPTER
33

It was obvious that Wick Cary's gift was our last best hope to preserve even the shell of a Division I program. George Shinn was finding it difficult to obtain pledges as the economic downturn was affecting even those who normally would be receptive to donations. But Shinn's efforts were stymied further after word of the gift leaked to the press and Alden Hagardorn was identified as a friend of Cary who had inside knowledge of his financial empire. In one interview, Hagardorn declared the estate was worth $150 million.

I did not like to see such conjecture being leaked, but whatever the actual amount, we needed to assure that the money would go to athletics, as Wick intended. Although Wick's will did not specifically name "athletics" as the beneficiary, it did at least name the UNO Foundation. Legally, the chancellor did not control the foundation, but he did exercise considerable influence over the decisions of their board. Fortunately, Gary Solomon was a board member, and I was confident he would protect our interests if a flap arose.

I met with Pat Gibbs, president of the UNO Foundation, on June 10, before the news became public, to inform him of the gift. I also wanted Gibbs's advice on how we could make sure the money would be used in accordance with the donor's intentions. Gibbs was a veteran administrator, having served as university CFO before spending time in the LSU System office. He was respected and had a good sense of how things worked. I believed it was essential to get Gibbs on board, because I feared Ryan would be tempted to apply the money against our paper "deficit."

I laid out a wish list of my uses for the gift that I wanted to bounce off Gibbs, just to have him aware of what my intentions would be for the money. It was difficult trying not to spend the money before we received it, but I was energized at the prospect that finally we might be able to achieve financial stability.

My plan would devote more than $1 million to add back the five sports needed to regain our Division I status, $1 million for a beach volleyball center on Lake Pontchartrain that would accommodate a new intercollegiate sport and serve as a recreational destination for students and $5 million for the oft-delayed renovation to our baseball field.

However, Gibbs and I agreed that the first dollar spent must address the department's cumulative deficit, which was a hot button issue with Ryan and CFO Robison. It grated on me that earmarking an estimated $6 million for a paper deficit was like paying a ransom. Ryan could make political hay by reporting to the LSU System that he had eliminated the deficit, then use the cash to bolster another part of the university. At this point, however, the offer appeared to be the cost of doing business, so long as he would leave the rest of the money to benefit the department.

After meeting with Gibbs, I met with Ryan to give him the news. As Gibbs suggested, I told Ryan I wanted to inform him of a development that would take one big problem off his plate. I told him the story of Wick Cary, that I had seen the will and, after a list of specific bequests, it contained the split that would give UNO one-third of remaining proceeds. He asked if the bequest mentioned any specific sports, such as women's basketball, and I told him the legatees of each institution were their foundations.

I told him we had additional documentation that specified Wick's intention was the athletics program. Alden Hagardorn sent me a letter that recounted his many discussions in which Wick told him he wanted his legacy to support the athletic programs at the specific institutions. In addition, Jack Thomson sent a handwritten note to Gibbs verifying that UNO would be a legatee of the estate and that Mr. Cary's intention was to benefit the athletic program.

Ryan suggested I get university counsel, Patricia Adams, involved because lawyers were high on his list of people he distrusted. He suggested that an estate that size would have lawyers circling, and we needed to get ours into the flight pattern. Ryan appeared moderately pleased at the developments, suggesting that the funds could go into an endowment that would spin off annual interest to help support the program.

The meeting went pleasantly, but when I left I had an uneasy feeling. Either the news of a possible lifeline for athletics had disappointed him, or that his brain already was working on ideas to separate us from the money. I was hoping it was neither and that my paranoia was merely asserting its ever increasing presence.

I wanted to get the news to Gary Solomon, so we met the following day in Gary's office at Crescent Bank & Trust. As I related the story, Gary's eyes grew wide in disbelief and he said, "You know, you hear about these things happening all the time. There are people out there who have the money, but unless somebody touches them, as you all apparently did with Wick, they will leave it to somebody else."

I repeated to Gary what I had told Gibbs, that I only wanted the athletic program to be able to compete and to enjoy stability for years to come. I told Gary what he already knew, that it takes money to make money. We needed to establish a ticket sales operation, but we never had the seed money. We needed to hire more sponsorship sales people, but we never had the resources. UNO's first response is that "we can't afford it." They were too provincial to ever think they could not afford *not* to invest in revenue producing operations.

Gary assured me that the four most influential people on the Foundation board, including himself, would make sure that athletics was protected. Dr. Al Merlin was a patron of basketball coach Joe Pasternack and had helped us in the past. Tom Kitchen was my backyard neighbor before Katrina and had served as a member of the athletic foundation board. I did not know Mike Flick well, but Gary said that when it first appeared that athletics might be dropped, Mike had suggested that the UNO Foundation look into propping up the department.

"You are the only one who could have done this," Gary told me. "It was smart going to Pat Gibbs first, because Pat knows how things at the university *should* operate but also how they, unfortunately, *do* operate. I'll call Pat and let him know that the board members are excited about this gift and will support athletics."

I felt a lot better after talking with my influential brother-in-law.

Despite news of the Wick Cary gift and the possibility that we might have a means to stability, Ryan continued to make our lives difficult. First, he directed that all scholarship recipients, whether academic or athletic, would be housed in Pontchartrain Hall instead of Privateer Place. Pontchartrain Hall was a traditional dormitory with small rooms and no kitchens. Privateer Place was an apartment complex that included kitchens, a community area and a pool. Privateer Place was a huge recruiting benefit for our coaches, because it was one of the few advantages we had over other colleges.

The problem was that Privateer Place was not owned by the university. It was created by former Chancellor O'Brien in which a third party built the apartment complex and the university would receive annual royalties. It did not turn out the way the university had hoped, because the annual royalties were far less than had been predicted. In 2008, the university finished construction of Pontchartrain Hall, which was solely owned by the university. Therefore, all rent paid by students went directly into the university's coffers.

It was strictly a financial transaction, which I understood, although it would cost our department more money. We had negotiated a bulk rate with Privateer Place that was a significant savings over what other students paid and was lower than we would be charged by Pontchartrain Hall. Ryan was convinced we overspent at will, but when we showed him evidence that we were trying to save our department money, it apparently did not matter because the higher cost now would go directly to the university.

Our coaches and student-athletes were angry about the move for other reasons. A lease to Pontchartrain Hall required participation in a meal plan that at first analysis suggested we would be paying far more money for fewer meals. We still had other questions that were not resolved when I was presented with a letter to our student-athletes about the new policy.

The director of financial aid created the letter which had her name and my name at the bottom. I had a natural objection about attaching my name to anything about which I had no knowledge or no participation in creating. I sent a note to the director of financial aid, requesting that my name be removed from her note.

She apparently notified Ryan immediately, and he sent off a terse e-mail to me that stated simply: "Do you want to be part of the team or not?" Here was another suggestion that he would prefer an athletic director who was more obedient, like the rest of his senior staff.

The practical answer was that I did not want to be on his team of sycophants, "yes" men and small thinkers, but I was committed to hanging in for my coaches and the student-athletes. It was ironic that I was being portrayed as a traitor when my primary concern was the welfare of our student-athletes and coaches.

The second irritant was Ryan's directive that the department would no longer pay for coaches' cell phone usage. The issue was a financial one in Ryan's mind, but a compliance and recruiting issue in mine. The department had paid for coaches' cell phone usage primarily because it was an essential recruiting tool. It was common practice for coaches and recruits to text one another frequently, because it was convenient and the communication of preference for young people.

I considered company provided cell phones just as essential for compliance reasons. Coaches are permitted contact with potential student-athletes at certain times, which can be verified through phone records. If the department had no ability to monitor this contact, we would be setting ourselves up for a major NCAA violation. If the NCAA would spot check us on compliance, we would have no legal way of compelling our coaches to turn over their private telephone records.

Ryan, however, saw it as strictly a financial decision, and he prohibited the department from paying for the phones. I argued that we could raise the funds and take it out of our Privateer Athletic Foundation, but he countered that to do so would reduce our ability to raise funds for other needs. It would be a financial blow to our coaches. I wasn't so worried about the head coaches, but the coaches making $40,000 with families couldn't afford a $100 monthly cell phone bill.

All my appeals were denied. As of July 1, 2009, the university no longer would pay for coaches' cell phones. It appeared that Ryan was now making all the decisions on how to run the athletics department.

The head coaches asked me to schedule a meeting with Ryan in hopes of changing his mind, at least on the dormitory issue. I did so reluctantly, because I knew Ryan had gone too far out on the limb to give in. The meeting started with a lecture from Ryan and progressed downhill after he told the coaches that the only reason our athletes preferred an on campus apartment complex to the university dormitory was "so they can have their boyfriends over and smoke dope."

Ryan continued to make other curious comments, particularly one that the athletics department must operate like the university, "lean and mean," always able to do more with less. He suggested that our "lean and mean" athletic department consider such cost cutting devices as virtual swim meets where two schools swim in their own home pools and compare times over the phone to declare a winner. That declaration understandably inflamed our swimmers and their parents.

Parents of other current student-athletes as well as those of several prospective recruits called our coaches asking what Ryan meant by "lean and mean." Excess is best when you are talking with 18-year-olds and their parents who have several choices among suitors. With the chancellor continuing to make such comments, they asked, what kind of an athletic department were we going to have in the future? That was the $64,000 question nobody could answer.

Coincidentally, former Governor Kathleen Blanco provided one answer with comments she made while encouraging Governor Jindal to restore the funding to higher education. "You can't do more with less," Blanco said. "You do less with less."

Another mini-crisis soon erupted over my naming Bruce Peddie as interim baseball coach. I received a contentious e-mail from Ryan, who said he was at the Legislature lobbying on the university's behalf when he was "grabbed by several legislators." They were angry at a story in the *Times-Picayune* quoting me as saying we would not have a national search for a new head baseball coach. He said we needed to talk about it.

After Tom Walter resigned to take the head coaching job at Wake Forest, I named Peddie, our associate head coach as interim head coach. In the story announcing my decision, I said I was comfortable with Peddie and that he had been a successful head coach in Division III. To open up a coaching search at this time would create yet another disruption in our program at a time when we did not need any more. I had not taken the "interim" tag off Peddie, but I did make it clear that I thought he was the man for the job. The reporter made it sound a bit stronger, and that sentiment was supported by a headline that said: "UNO picks Peddie to run baseball program."

Ryan always told me he didn't hire or fire coaches; he hired or fired athletic directors. But his e-mail suggested that he not only wanted to micromanage things like our student housing and cell phones, he wanted to hire the new baseball coach.

I learned later that Ryan's inquisitor was New Orleans legislator Cedric Richmond, a member of the Legislative Black Caucus. Richmond asked Ryan why a black coach such as Southern University's Roger Cador was not being considered. Ryan was still battling the budget cuts in the legislature and did not want to offend any bloc, especially an influential group such as the Black Caucus. He was vulnerable, because he had no strong black presence in his administration. The only black vice chancellor he inherited had resigned two years earlier.

Ryan instructed me to conduct a search. I wrote out an ad for a head baseball coach and instructed our administrative assistant to place it in the online version of NCAA *News*. Ola Adegboye came to my office and informed me that the ad would cost $200, and Financial Services would not approve the expense.

Unbelievable!

I could have called Ryan and asked him to pay for it, but I was done. I gave Ola my personal American Express card and told him to charge it to that. I knew I would never get reimbursed.

CHAPTER
34

J eremie Davis was released on probation from the Claiborne Parish Detention Center on July 17, 2009. Since his incarceration in February 2008, his every thought and action was directed toward reviving his basketball career. He sidestepped trouble inside, spent his one hour of recreational time daily shooting baskets, and he stood in line hour after hour to use the phone whenever he thought of somebody else to call who might help him when he got out.

In order to achieve that goal, he knew he had to make one change if his life would ever be anything more than it was. He could not stay in Arcadia, in the same environment that had turned him from a basketball star into a convict.

Davis knew he could not do it alone. He needed an angel, like the Navy helicopter after Katrina, to swoop down and pluck him from his cesspit of despair. He had only been out of prison for a couple weeks and was sitting at his mother's house watching television when the angel called.

The seraph came in the person of Brian Ellis, a young basketball coach at Delta State University in Cleveland, Mississippi, who was looking for players. Ellis was no stranger to college basketball at the level seldom seen on ESPN or CBS Saturday. He had played at Okaloosa Walton Community College in Florida before transferring to Enterprise Ozark Community College in Alabama, and finally to the University of West Florida in Pensacola, where he obtained his undergraduate degree.

Delta State was a second chance institution for some good basketball players who, for whatever reason, did not make it after spending a year or more at places like Ole Miss, Nebraska or Alabama-Birmingham. All but three of nearly 20 players on Delta State's summer roster had previous college experience.

Brian Ellis did not care what they had done before they came to Delta State, so long as they could play basketball and were kids with good character. Jeremie Davis did not seem to fit the latter requirement when Ellis first heard about him from Turmaine Rice, a former DSU player who had played against Davis in high school. Rice told the coach that at 6-foot-6 and 190 pounds Davis was "long," could play the "2" or "3" positions — shooting guard or small forward — was a good kid and could drop rainbows from the sky. But he had gotten into some trouble.

Ellis began investigating. He talked to Davis's high school coach Oswald Townsend and learned that Davis was a sweet shooter who never caused a problem on the court. He talked to Sheriff John Ballance of Bienville Parish, who told him the kid had a tough upbringing, and he ran with a bad crowd. He talked to Davis's probation officer Carson Cowart who told him that Davis's only chance at survival was to get out of Arcadia and get into a structured environment. He talked to Davis's smother Barbara who pleaded that her son could straighten his life out if given another chance.

But all that was just information gathering for Ellis. He had to sell his boss, Head Coach Jason Conner, whose policies on discipline prohibited earrings and got tougher from there. Conner was accustomed to second chance kids, but had little experience with "last chance" kids such as Davis. College basketball is full of players who have court talent but come with baggage, and Conner had learned over the years how to putty over those holes in character, academic deficiencies or environment. If you support them with discipline, purpose and tough love when required, they have a chance to succeed. Conner never before had been asked to save an ex-con, but he was intrigued with Davis's story, and he agreed to let Ellis bring his new find to Cleveland for a recruiting visit.

In early August, Davis visited Cleveland, a blue collar town in the Mississippi Delta known as the birthplace of the Blues. The legendary Howlin' Wolf played in Cleveland both on the streets and in the Coconut Grove and Harlem Inn nightclubs, and the "Father of the Blues," W. C. Handy, wrote that he was enlightened to the value of the Delta's native music in Cleveland when he witnessed a local trio being showered with coins.

It was ironic that Davis's rehabilitation might start in Cleveland, which was flooded during the 1927 Mississippi River flood. The fact that Cleveland was 13 miles from the river underlines the devastation imposed by the nation's greatest natural disaster before Katrina.

Ellis took Davis on a tour of the DSU campus and they met with Conner and Athletic Director Jeremy McClain, a 32-year-old former DSU pitcher who had played minor league ball for five years. All greeted Davis warmly and convinced him he would get the support necessary to succeed.

But the deal almost died after Davis was arrested again when he returned to Arcadia. He had violated his probation by leaving the state of Louisiana. Ellis immediately contacted Cowart, the probation officer, to explain their role in the violation and found a sympathetic ear. Cowart knew the chances of Davis succeeding would be greatly enhanced if he were as far away from Arcadia as possible. He agreed if the coaches would take responsibility; they could work out Davis's probation under an interstate compact that allows one state to enforce the probation imposed by another state.

Conner and AD McClain agreed if Davis was willing to follow the rules, work hard on the court and even harder off it, then DSU would offer him a second chance, contingent on one final condition. Conner had given out almost all the financial aid he was allowed for scholarships and could only offer Davis what amounted to less than half a scholarship. If Davis wanted to come, he would have to pay more than half the required tuition, room and board and fees himself, which totaled about $8,000. Davis readily agreed. He did not know at the time where he would get it, but eventually brother Antoine stepped in to guarantee a student loan that bridged the gap.

Ellis took Davis through the admissions process and started selecting classes for him when his newest recruit gave him unexpected instructions. He wanted no classes in badminton, underwater Monopoly or any other subject designed merely to keep him eligible. He wanted classes that would help him earn a degree in business. Against Ellis's better judgment, he enrolled Davis in five business classes.

Davis reported to Cleveland, Mississippi, in mid-August, 2009, to start school and begin working out with the team. It was apparent from the start that Davis was rusty and his court skills would need polishing. Classes also provided a readjustment since Davis hadn't cracked a book since he left UNO more than three years earlier.

But he displayed a positive attitude and a willingness to work hard, both on his study habits and on the court. Davis *wanted* to do well for coaches Ellis and Conner and the others who had gone out of their way to help him. More importantly, he *had* to do well for himself.

So more than three years after his last basketball game, a 20-point effort in UNO's Sun Belt Conference tournament loss to Western Kentucky, Jeremie Davis would be suiting up again.

He had his second chance. What he did with it would be up to him. But he was motivated by one certainty. He had spent 515 days in the Claiborne Parish Detention Center, many of those nights kept awake by the clinging sweat, voracious mosquitoes and the lingering regret of blowing an opportunity that few ever receive. That would not happen again.

Especially since this was his last chance.

CHAPTER
35

W ick Cary's will included four IRA's and other retirement vehicles that would be immediately available to the legatees. Jack Thomson, the executor, informed Gibbs's staff at the Foundation that our initial share would be $680,000.

Finally, it appeared that something good was happening. The $680,000 could bolster our budget for 2009-10, which would allow me to save a handful of staff members who otherwise would be terminated. It also would provide seed money to establish a proactive ticket selling apparatus that would provide much needed revenue. I had met with Matt DiFebo, who was fast becoming the collegiate ticket sales guru, to establish such an initiative at UNO. DiFebo was an assistant AD at Central Florida who had set up the same sales structure at South Alabama, which had produced positive results. It takes money to make money, and now we could implement a huge vehicle to help drive us out of our financial hole.

My plan required Ryan's blessing, but I did not see how he could object. The ticket sales initiative would help us achieve the major goal he had set forth for us, specifically that we needed to be self-sustaining.

I met with Ryan and laid out my plan to utilize about $200,000 of the money to hire staff, buy computers and software and provide money for an advertising campaign. The remainder would go toward our 2009-10 budget to mitigate staff cuts. However, he had another idea.

He told me he had decided to take the entire amount and put it against our deficit for the 2008-09 fiscal year.

I sat there with my mouth open, not believing what I had heard. I told him we were so close to wiping out the entire deficit with the remainder of the Cary gift, why couldn't we use the initial portion toward generating revenue and assuring stability of our staff? He countered by repeating that the LSU System was pressuring him on finances, particularly on the growing athletics' deficit. He needed that money to help save his job. Ryan again was displaying an inexplicable resistance to basic sales principles. ROI — return on investment — means more people selling equals more sales. No people selling means no sales. Period, full stop! I could not understand how he could resist a principle taught in every college of business in America, including the one he headed up for many years.

I was disappointed yet again, but I wasn't surprised. The rollercoaster was headed back down the hill. Every time we would get a rare piece of good news, something negative would pop up to slap us right back into the toilet.

Ryan's decision limited our options for survival to either George Shinn's ability to raise money, or Jack Thomson's assurance that we would get another distribution of liquidated assets within the 2009-10 fiscal year. Our staff had been meeting with Hugh Weber of the Hornets to help us rebrand ourselves so we could mend fences with some of our constituents and generate interest in our program. It was a good exercise, and our staff and coaches participated with enthusiasm. The desired outcome would be an increase in ticket sales and fund-raising over the next year and beyond. But there were no guarantees. We were talking about long term benefits and indefinite revenue. Ryan said he could no longer give us any consideration on faith that he needed to see a guaranteed dollar amount.

The pressure now was on Shinn's group to give us a bridge until we saw any of the Wick Cary gift. Shinn's group was meeting again on July 21. Although final budgets were due on July 1, Ryan gave me until the meeting date to come up with additional money. If no pledge was apparent, the bare bones budget I had submitted to him would go into effect and staff positions would be eliminated.

More bad news soon arrived that in one sense took us right back to Black Friday. Pat Gibbs, the UNO Foundation president, called to say that Jack Thomson had provided him with an estimate of the total proceeds we could expect from the Wick Cary estate. Gibbs said Thomson estimated the total residual interest of the estate would be between $25 million and $27 million. I asked Gibbs if he meant that was to be our share or the total? He said that was the total estimate, and we would get one-third of the final number.

Our actual share would be between $8 and $9 million and not the $40 million or $50 million that Alden Hagardorn had suggested. I thought I was being conservative when I did most of my wish list estimates for the future on a $90 million estate and a $30 million share. I would hear later from Jack Thomson that Hagardorn was well intentioned but did not have as much knowledge of Wick Cary's estate as he portrayed. Whatever his motivation, his exaggeration of the amount of Wick's estate would have major repercussions.

The executor's confirmation that the estate would be far short of our expectations only increased my fear that athletics never would be able to put a penny of the money to good use. With Ryan already expressing an intention to use the first $680,000 to reduce the 2008-09 athletics deficit, my suspicion grew that he would use whatever amount we did receive to pay off the total deficit.

Gibbs's news stripped my last shred of hope that we would be able to save our department. We would have no Cary distribution that could bail us out for the 2009-10 fiscal year. There would be no money to launch a ticket sales initiative. There would be no additional money to add back sports to regain our Division I standing. There would be no money to finally renovate the baseball stadium. There would be no money to fund an endowment that could stabilize us into the future.

And with word out of the governor's office that next year's higher education budget might be cut yet again we would be facing this same dilemma again next year. It was not a battle I wanted to fight again.

The last glimmer of hope remaining would be the meeting with Shinn's group on July 21. But with our pot of gold now shrunken to a teacup, any slim hope about restoring sports and with it our full Division I status, had just died a disappointing death.

CHAPTER
36

Shinn met with Ryan on July 20, the day before the task force meeting. The Hornets owner had made his fortune through a chain of small business schools, and he offered Ryan one of his foundations. Buck Lattimore had recently resigned his position with state government in North Carolina and, at 65, was looking for another challenge. Lattimore was a career sales specialist whom Shinn credited with helping build his business school empire.

Shinn offered to pay Lattimore to analyze UNO's efforts to recruit students and promote itself. Before the meeting with Ryan, Shinn and Lattimore took a walk around the campus. Lattimore was shocked at the dreary surroundings and especially at the disheveled appearance of the personnel in Admissions. "How can these people sell the university if they can't take care of themselves?" he asked. Lattimore said if given a chance, he would change things quickly.

Ryan told Shinn he would accept the offer. The Hornets' owner was encouraged, and characterized it publicly as simply one New Orleans business with expertise in a critical area helping another that needed such expertise.

After that meeting, Shinn called and said he needed to see me. I was only a few blocks away, attending the summer meeting of the Sun Belt Conference athletic directors in the conference office. I left the meeting early to meet with Shinn.

Shinn and Hugh Weber gave me details of their meeting with Ryan, which included a tidbit of information that was no surprise. Ryan saw me as an impediment. Weber said Ryan did not specifically mention me by name, but unflattering comments from Ryan and his assistant, Elizabeth Lowry, made it obvious.

Shinn told me if his efforts were going to be successful I needed to meet with Ryan and mend fences. I readily agreed to do so, but I also told Shinn and Weber if Ryan really thought I was an impediment then I would not hesitate to resign. Weber said, "I don't think you being a martyr and falling on your sword is what we need here."

I told them I already had put in a request to Ryan's secretary for a meeting Friday, July 24, on the 2009-10 budget, and I would take that opportunity to offer an olive branch. But I told them it would be difficult if I went into that meeting without some assurance from Shinn's group that they would prop us up until we received some of the Cary gift.

Shinn's intention was to ask the group to do that, and he even said he might ask me to leave the meeting when he made the ask. I would leave any room of people who were discussing ways to help our program.

On July 21, Shinn opened the meeting of his UNO Task Force by discussing his meeting with Ryan of the previous day. He characterized it as positive and said Ryan appeared genuinely interested in having the Hornets' help, particularly the involvement of Buck Lattimore.

Shinn also said his efforts to ask people for money had been stymied by the news of our Wick Cary windfall. Gabe Corchiani, the former UNO point guard responsible for a $1 million gift to the men's basketball program, interrupted Shinn. Corchiani said the critical issue was what the committee could do now to prevent UNO athletics from having to terminate coaches and staff by Friday.

I had told the group that without an additional $700,000, I would be forced to terminate 10 coaches and staff members in order to cut to Ryan's mandated number. Those cuts would make it virtually impossible for us to execute any of the initiatives that Weber and the Hornets' marketing people had been working on because we would have no staff left to do it.

After Corchiani threw the gasoline onto the table, attorney David Sherman, a former UNO Student Government president, ignited it. He gave the group the "secret" news that Ryan had diverted the first $680,000 of the Cary gift to mitigate the deficit for 2008-09. I was surprised Sherman mentioned it, because I had not shared that news with many people. However, I had told Pasternack about Ryan's intention, and he evidently had passed it on to Sherman.

Shinn was livid at the news. He directed Jean, who was taking notes, to get Ryan on the phone immediately. He turned and asked the group, "How in the hell can we raise money when he's got money the department needs, and he's not helping?"

Malcolm Ehrhardt, the public relations executive and UNO graduate, was stunned at the news. The group began questioning me on the details, and I told them I had gone to Ryan with a proposal to invest some of that money into revenue initiatives and put the remainder into the 2009-10 budget, but Ryan said he was leaning toward putting all the money against the 2008-09 athletics deficit.

Shinn was determined to face Ryan down on the issue. He wanted to ask him if the news was true, and, if so, how did he expect his group to raise any money when it became public that the university was using the money to pay off a paper debt to itself? Shinn met with Ryan the next day.

He asked Ryan about the first installment of the Cary gift, and Shinn said that Ryan confirmed the amount and that he intended to apply it to the deficit. Ryan told Shinn he felt obligated to reduce the debt primarily because of the mandate he has from the State of Louisiana. Shinn told him if the money is being used for something other than what it was intended, and the public found out about it, it would be virtually impossible for Shinn's group to raise any money.

Ryan relented somewhat, telling Shinn he would meet with CFO Linda Robison and figure out how much of the $680,000 he could apply toward the athletics program.

Shinn encouraged him to devote it all to athletics now as a bridge so we could start the rebranding and revenue initiatives with necessary staff intact. "When the bigger money comes in," Shinn said, "then you can apply it to the deficit." Ryan was noncommittal, but said he would call Shinn later that day after meeting with the financial officer.

Ryan had not called by Thursday morning, so Shinn sent him an e-mail around Noon stating: "Maybe I misunderstood, but I thought you were going to call me back after you talked to your CFO?" Ryan responded a short time later that he did not have the information yet but would call him when he did.

I predicted to Shinn that Ryan would not give him an answer before my scheduled meeting with him on Friday morning. That meant my department would be decimated.

Gary Solomon called me Thursday afternoon to say "a little bird told me" about Ryan's diverting of the money. He said he would call Ryan and get involved if I wanted him to. He said that a chancellor diverting foundation funds for uses other than their stated purpose was just the offense that got the previous chancellor, Greg O'Brien, fired. I reminded Gary that Ryan could argue that it *was* going to athletics since the money ostensibly would be put against the athletics deficit.

"I'm just very disappointed in Tim," he said. "He has the opportunity to give the program a chance, and he's not taking it. And he won't get back to Shinn, either, before you need the money."

Our predictions soon came true.

Ryan had not responded to Shinn before my Friday morning meeting. That left me in the unenviable position of having to present a budget that would force me to terminate 10 staff members and coaches.

I first presented to Ryan the results of the search committee's interviews of head baseball coaching candidates. I had interviewed a handful of candidates, including Roger Cador at Southern, but to me Bruce Peddie, our current associate head coach, was the clear choice. I had hoped to make the announcement that afternoon. Ryan told me "the Board" needed to approve the selection before it was made public. This was another new twist. We had been allowed to announce new head coaches in the past, so long as we attached the line "subject to LSU Board of Supervisors' approval." That approval always was perfunctory to be handled at the next monthly meeting, but it never had impeded the process.

Ryan, however, felt he was under such scrutiny by the LSU System that he did not want to provide them with any more ammunition. He asked me to write a letter outlining the process and our recommendation and to send it to him. He said he would send it to LSU System president John Lombardi and request a quick decision so we could move forward.

After discussing a couple of housekeeping issues, I brought up our budget situation. I told him I knew he and Shinn had been talking about diverting some of the Wick

Cary gift back to athletics. In hopes that he had reconsidered putting all the money toward the 2008-09 deficit, I had prepared two budgets. The first would utilize less than half of the Cary gift, $300,000, and the second included none of it.

He told me once again that he had looked at it and had discussed it with Linda Robison. It still appeared as though he would need to put the entire amount toward the deficit. He then made another disingenuous statement when he said he believed that Shinn was using the issue as a way to "get out of" his commitment to help us. I told him he was wrong, that during my conversations Shinn only expressed a sincere desire to help us.

I told Ryan if his mind was made up on devoting the entire Cary installment to the deficit, then I would send him the lesser budget that would require the terminations. I cautioned him when word got out that we were terminating people, he could expect a firestorm. He said he knew that and would be ready for it.

I also told him that when he looked at the budget he would note that the line item for athletic director's salary would reflect a number less than my annual salary. The reason was that I would pick a date in the fall and announce my retirement from the university. He could use the savings to preserve two staff positions that otherwise would have to be eliminated.

His expression did not change. I could not tell if the news surprised him or if he felt he had just been handed a trip to Disney World. I told him I did not know where we had gotten off track with our relationship, but that it was clear he had no confidence in me. He looked at me as I talked, slightly nodding when I'd make a point but not showing any emotion.

When I finished talking, he responded that he felt some of our coaches continued to undermine him, that we needed everybody on the same team and that the budget needed to be managed better. He did not mention me, but it was obvious that the offenses he mentioned were laid at my feet.

I did not feel there was anything more to say. I rose to leave, and he offered his hand and said simply "Good luck."

It was as if none of the past had mattered. No Katrina, no post-storm planning in the Baton Rouge bunker, no NCAA baseball tournaments, no Sunday morning golf, no efforts to keep the university's most visible asset afloat. No appreciation for services rendered. No consideration for time served. It was a farewell that one might give to the yard boy who had told you he was going to California to get a job picking lettuce. Good luck to you, and now I have to find somebody else to cut the grass.

I went back to my office and tried not to let my employees see any emotion. My meeting had not gone well, and my face usually betrayed my feelings. I made it to my office without seeing any staff members, and I shut the door. I first wrote the letter recommending Bruce Peddie as the new head baseball coach, and e-mailed it to Ryan. Then I called my two senior assistants into my office.

Mike Bujol, the associate AD, and Ola Adegboye, the assistant AD for business operations, heard my description of the meeting and Ryan's insistence on the lesser budget. I gave them my suggestion on who should stay and who should go, they gave me their thoughts, and we agreed on who should be terminated.

I did not tell them about my "retirement," the savings of which provided the money to save two other positions.

After they left the office, I sent an e-mail to George Shinn informing him that, despite what Ryan had told Shinn, Ryan told me it was unlikely he would free any of the money from the Cary gift for use by athletics in the 2009-10 budget. I told him Ryan asked me to submit the bare bones budget, which would include the termination of 10 employees. I also told Shinn that the budget would include my "retirement."

That message prompted a flurry of e-mails and telephone calls over the next few hours from Shinn and Malcolm Ehrhardt urging me not to resign. They both advised I should refuse to execute the terminations and make Ryan fire me. My contract did not expire until June 30, 2012, and to walk away from that was not good financial sense. I informed them that my contract was specific in identifying one of the hanging offenses as "insubordination." If I refused to execute his order, he could fire me with cause. If I "retired," then I would be eligible for partly funded medical and dental benefits. That's a big deal to a 60-something without a job.

I also told them I was tired of fighting. I was tired of going to work every day with a knot in my stomach. I was tired of a suffocating bureaucracy, which funneled every major decision into the black hole of the chancellor's office. I was tired of telling my coaches that our expectations to educate our students and to win games are the same as those of our Sun Belt rivals whose budgets are up to five times our own.

I was at the point where Samuel Johnson, the Eighteenth Century British essayist and novelist, found himself. A prolific writer his entire life, Johnson was silent in his later years prompting his friends to ask why he had stopped writing. Johnson's response, as recorded by his faithful biographer, James Boswell: "I am not obliged to do any more. No man is obliged to do as much as he can do. A man is to have part of his life to himself."

Maybe it was time for me to stop doing any more and to finally have part of my life to myself.

I was tired of watching hope die time and time again.

CHAPTER
37

Other communications were going on at the time between Shinn, Ehrhardt and Gary Solomon. As a member of the UNO Foundation board, Gary had insisted all along that Ryan needed to get the board's blessing to divert any part of the Cary gift toward the budget deficit. Gary was ready to go to war on the subject, and he wrote an e-mail to Ryan and the committee, which expressed his concern that the Foundation Board was not aware of any of the actions being taken.

Gary said that since the named legatee of the Cary gift was the UNO Foundation, any disposition of the funds should be discussed and approved at the board level. He reminded the board that despite the fact he is my brother-in-law, our communication on the issue had been professional and, in fact, "Mr. Shinn has told me more than Jim Miller has."

Gary's memo confirmed that Shinn was willing to raise money for the university, not just for athletics, but also to help with recruitment and retention of students. However, Gary said Shinn had made it clear to him that if the Wick Cary gift is not used to benefit the athletic department, he would not offer any support financially and/or personally to the university.

The e-mail apparently convinced Ryan he had unleashed a firestorm. Ryan immediately sent an e-mail to Shinn which appeared to backtrack on his decision to put all the money against the deficit. In fact, he told Shinn he was working on a solution that could allow athletics to use a portion of the Cary money. However, he did not communicate that to me, which meant my standing orders still were to terminate staff.

I submitted the budget by e-mail to Ryan about 4 P.M. Friday, and then I drove home. At least I could give the unlucky employees a final weekend of peace before I was forced to lop off their heads.

I was trying to reconcile to myself that my tenure at UNO was done. I did not feel good about leaving the university, especially when it needed all the help and leadership it could get. On the other hand, if we did not have a chance to succeed, then I did not want to hang around just to pick up a paycheck. As therapy, I wrote a press release announcing my retirement. I hoped it would remain in my laptop, as had my previous letter of resignation, hidden forever to all but my bad memories.

The battle, however, was not yet over. Ryan's message to Shinn sparked a lively exchange of e-mails and telephone calls over the weekend. Gary called Ryan Saturday to review the facts and the possible repercussions of a further cut in athletics' personnel. When the news got out that we had terminated employees, questions would arise about the effectiveness of Shinn's involvement. Shinn's ability to raise money had been drastically altered by the news of Wick Cary's gift. The reported number of $150 million had Shinn's targeted donors asking why they should donate anything if UNO athletics was set to receive around $50 million?

But Shinn was not about to look like he had failed. With the Hornets' strong public relations machine behind him, he was prepared to say he offered to help the university, even by funding a specialist in growing enrollment. But when he asked Ryan to reciprocate and help athletics get over this rough patch, Ryan refused. The chancellor would look like the villain.

Gary wanted to prevent that from happening for many reasons, not the least of which was his 33-year relationship with Ryan. In a telephone conversation with Gary Saturday, Ryan confirmed his message to Shinn and told Gary he would revisit his decision on diverting the Wick Cary money to the deficit. He also said he would work on a long term plan to provide athletics stability.

Gary then asked him if he would use the remaining Cary gift — now estimated at $8 million or so — to eliminate the deficit? Ryan said he would consider a plan that would allow a gradual payback over a longer period that would allow athletics to use most of the money as it was intended by Wick.

Ryan did not, however, tell Gary of another meeting that took place in his office on Saturday afternoon.

In a conference call Sunday, Gary told Shinn, Hugh Weber and me that Ryan had cracked the door open to a resolution. Gary asked how much we needed to avoid the cuts. I responded that half of the first Cary installment, or $340,000, would enable us to retain four of the employees to be cut, including the three individuals who would be responsible for executing the promotion and marketing strategies that Weber had devised.

Shinn was adamant that we ask for all of it back, but Gary correctly sensed that Ryan politically had to put some of the money toward the deficit, and a split would be a reasonable compromise. Gary agreed to call Ryan to see if he would agree to the 50-50 split before I had to announce anything on Monday.

Once again, hope had peeked around the corner and winked.

Ryan told Gary he would meet with me Monday with a resolution. We had scheduled a ribbon cutting Monday morning for the grand reopening of our restored aquatic center. It was a happy occasion and one more small step back from Katrina. Ryan was pleasant, and I was optimistic when he told me to come by his office at 4 P.M.

He was in a good mood when I walked in, and I apologized for the time he had spent on the phone with "my agent," Gary. He said they spent a lot of time talking, and he had a resolution to our situation.

He told me he would put $400,000 back into the budget, whether it came from the

Cary money or whether he borrowed it from the Foundation to be paid back when the bulk of the gift arrived. That certainly was good news for the department, because it meant that all of the staff cuts contemplated in the bare bones budget now would be saved.

That was good, I told him, because I wanted to be here to see it through.

"Well, I think there's been too much water under the bridge for that," he said, looking around the room, over my shoulder and anywhere but in my eyes. The words cut through me like a laser.

I think there's been too much water under the bridge for that.

Ryan reminded me that my budget of Friday suggested I would retire in the fall. I interrupted and said that offer was tied to the bare bones budget he had requested and would allow the department to save two more staff members who otherwise would be terminated. For him to tell me now he did not want me around, when I expressed a desire to stick it out, was tantamount to firing me and would make him liable for the remainder of my contract.

That apparently had not occurred to him, because he acknowledged that he was more concerned "what Shinn will do" when I'm out of the picture. Shinn's initial decision was made out of friendship with Jean and me, and it would be logical he would step away. But Shinn had told me he wanted to help the university, despite the chancellor's reluctance.

Ryan reiterated his comment of Friday that "Shinn is looking for a way out anyway. The Cary money was just an excuse."

I told him he was wrong, that I believed Shinn was sincere. That prompted Ryan to infer that I was gullible and that Shinn convinced me because that's how he made his fortune, in motivational speaking and convincing people of things they might not ordinarily believe.

"He's nothing but a snake oil salesman," Ryan said.

I did not believe Ryan could disappoint me any more than he already had until that moment. I did not bring up the issue of being liable for the rest of my contract. It didn't matter any more. I told him if he'd pay me until the end of the year, I would walk away. He agreed. I already felt the weight being lifted from my shoulders.

Ryan informed me he already had started on the transition. I learned later that Ryan met with my associate AD Mike Bujol on Saturday and Bujol and Ola Adegboye again Monday morning. Bujol was to become the interim AD until the end of the fiscal year. As for me, Ryan said he would like to put me on administrative leave, which meant I would not be required to perform any official duties until my time was up, but he could not. Again, Ryan made reference to his tormentors at the LSU System Office who would find out and surely use that against him. He told me he was assigning me to his development office, and I could help the university raise money until my retirement date.

My final hope to resurrect the athletic department lay lifeless on the floor of the chancellor's office. I told Ryan to have his development people call me, and I left. The call never came.

CHAPTER
38

Ileft Ryan's office and drove out Lakeshore Drive. I parked in a lot used by swimmers and picnickers and walked over to sit on the levee wall, looking out at the gentle ripples of the lake. The university's technology complex nearby occupied the spot where the Pontchartrain Beach amusement park gave joy to so many over the years. I had wanted to use the Wick Cary gift to build a beach volleyball center to add the newest sport approved by the NCAA. It would be a destination for students, to play volleyball and drink a beer while watching the sunset. That would not happen now.

I thought about alternatives. I could change my mind and refuse to retire, trying to force Ryan into a more favorable contract settlement than paying me for five more months when my contract extended nearly three more years. That was the advice of those who had not sat in my chair and endured the daily frustrations. But resistance carried risks of its own, primarily health ones. Nearly 62 years old at the time, I had been blessed with good health. How much longer would that last with the daily drip, drip of mental anguish hitting my forehead, frustrating my efforts and eroding my will? As I had told Jean more than once, they were not going to carry me out of here feet first.

Our program had endured Katrina, persevered during the lost years of turmoil, survived the failed student vote and been pushed to the brink of extinction. Then we were lifted up by renewed hope from George Shinn and Wick Cary, only to see it die once again. I thought about our nearly completed Athletic Administration Building, which I would never see. I was counting on that building to lift attitudes and give our department a platform for positive change. But I guess Moses never got to the promised land, either.

I wondered if someone else with a different set of skills and a different supporting cast could have endured the hard times and completed the job? Can a man change the culture before the culture changes the man? Obviously, I could not change a provincial mindset that treated the athletic department the same as every other unit on campus, despite its more visible assets. No matter what I had done to nurture, train and love this jackass of an athletic department, it would never run in the Kentucky Derby.

But UNO's failure to support its athletics was more than that. The incestuous culture of resistance that ruled the university was not going to change so long as those who contributed to its choking evolution were still in power. A road map to a new day was handed to Ryan in the Carr Report, but not one of the recommendations was adopted permanently.

I have belabored the fact that the university ignores the principles of ROI — return on investment — in operating its own expense driven business. George Shinn told me at one of our first meetings that our solution was simple. First, you take the number of seats in your arena and calculate how much money you make with a sellout. Then you calculate how much money you would have to spend to achieve that and take it out of the profit. I stopped him right there. The UNO approach, I explained, is "here is what you can spend, and good luck to you!"

This hoary financial struggle that bedeviled Ron Maestri was hammered into impossibility by Hurricane Katrina.

Maestri tolerated it for so long and told me I would not beat it. Wright Waters warned me about it and suggested I would never change it. They were right. I was wrong.

I got back in my car and drove west down Lakeshore Drive, looking out onto the expanse of Lake Pontchartrain. A sailboat with a blue sail bobbed in the wake of a jet skier about 100 yards offshore. Two old fishermen were sitting in metal yard chairs on the seawall, hoping to snag a speckled trout or just "sittin' on the dock o' the bay, wastin' time," as Otis Redding sang. Bikers were taking advantage of another sunny day along the lake, zipping past me in their yellow and red spandex suits and matching helmets. They all were oblivious to the guy in the black car whose latest stop in life would be revealed in the morning newspaper.

As I drove, I recalled reading that life consists of a number of silos, each representing an important aspect of our lives. We have the freedom to fill them however we choose. Some we fill with happiness and satisfaction, and some we fill with regret and discontent. Over the phases of our lives we will enjoy elements of each. You might start out with a job you like, move on to a job you like less and wind up with a job you endure until retirement. Sometimes you marry a spouse with whom you grow apart and then you find and marry your life's partner. You might live in places you don't particularly like, and then in retirement you choose where you wish to spend your remaining days.

Since we have a lifetime to fill our silos, the best we can hope for is to have as many as possible filled to our satisfaction as we enter the final phase. Jean has fulfilled the marriage silo for me at the right time of my life, as I round third and head for home. My work silo was more fulfilling when I was younger, and the frustrations of being a college athletic director at a low support institution was not the way I wanted to end a career. The quality of life silo is a work in progress.

I was thinking far too philosophically for a late afternoon drive along the lake. I turned left onto Marconi Avenue and drove down past the "bird" streets, Snipe, Warbler, Wren and Hawk. I beat a yellow light at Robert E. Lee Boulevard and kept going past the lagoon and Equest Farm stables where Layne learned to love horses. I turned right onto Filmore and drove the six blocks to Vicksburg Street. I turned left into the alley between the houses and parked in my garage.

Elmo jumped up on me when I emerged from the garage, and got a good ruffling of his floppy ears. I opened the back door with my key and saw C.C. sitting at the kitchen counter with an opened book and a puzzled expression. He was struggling with one of his summer reading assignments, and school was only two weeks away.

"Dad, can you help me with this?" he said.

It was good to be in a place where my help was welcomed, and where I could make a difference. I should have thought of this sooner.

CHAPTER
39

Jeremie Davis's escape from his Hydra of Katrina, rejection, drugs and prison began with promise. Starting the 2009-10 basketball season at Delta State as the first or second substitution, he eventually started 11 games and averaged 11.2 points in 21 minutes as the Statesmen went 19-8.He also was the team's leading long-range threat, hitting his three-point shots at a commendable 39.3% clip and ranked fourth in the Gulf South Conference with a 81.7% free throw percentage.

Head Coach Jason Conner was pleased with Davis's progress and contribution. "We've had people through here who just didn't fit, but JD fits," Conner said midway through the season. "He's a good person who was in a bad situation. He's still got a little con in him, but even that is getting better."

The gap between Davis's present and his past appeared to be widening for other reasons. A week before Christmas, four of Davis's former Arcadia High School teammates were convicted of cocaine distribution and sentenced to 10 years in a federal prison. Officers believe the cartel, based 18 miles east of Arcadia in Ruston, was responsible for distributing cocaine across most of north Louisiana and even into southern Arkansas. Law enforcement officers called it the most well organized and complex drug operation they had ever seen. The investigation resulted in 27 federal indictments and 10 guilty pleas, including that of Trent Sampson, who had enlisted Davis as a drug seller three years earlier.

After Davis scored 17 points in his last game, a 93 to 89 loss to North Alabama in the conference tournament, assistant coach Ellis began investigating the possibility of another year of eligibility for Davis. The NCAA had been receptive to other Katrina-related requests, and Ellis intended to apply for a waiver. However, Davis's habitual inattention to his studies had taken its toll. He did not make sufficient academic progress to remain eligible.

Davis was finished at Delta State, but the year back on the court had restored his credibility as a basketball player. In July, he moved to Houston where he worked out with current and former NBA players, including the tight fraternity of former Louisiana basketball stars. Current NBA players Von Wafer (Houston Rockets) and Paul Millsap (Utah Jazz), as well as others such as Marcus Fizer (ex-Chicago Bulls playing in Israel), Antonio Hudson (ex-LSU playing in Poland) and Bernard King (ex-Texas A&M playing in Cyprus) all told him he could make it, if not in the NBA then with the myriad international leagues that cover the globe.

Davis received encouragement from his former Privateer teammate Bo McCalebb who went from UNO to successful seasons in Turkey and then Macedonia. In June, 2010, McCalebb signed a $4 million, three-year contract with Montepaschi Siena of the Italian League. Davis hired an agent who began making inquiries. Several international teams showed initial interest, but on further investigation they learned about Davis's criminal record. He could not leave the country during his probationary period.

Another door closed, the creeping vines of depression began to wrap around Davis. Why did everything he tried seem to fail? Maybe basketball wasn't his destiny. He still had his music, and he began to write more songs about a boy whose aim was good but who could not find the right target.

Basketball was still in Davis's blood, and he participated in numerous tryouts with minor league teams in the Midwest. After a workout with the Tulsa 66ers of the NBA Developmental League, Davis stopped in Dallas to visit some friends and family. It was his 25th birthday, a festive night, and for a short time he escaped the hovering clouds that blocked the warming rays of hope. Unfortunately, roiling thunderheads returned the following morning, darker and more sinister than ever. A friend woke up Jeremie with an urgent message. His oldest brother, Antoine, had dropped dead of a heart attack at age 28. The brother who had dropped out of school to help support his younger brothers. The brother who tried to provide good advice and support when times were hard. The brother who had stepped up to help Jeremie pay his tuition at Delta State. The brother who was always encouraging Jeremie to follow his dream.

And now he was gone.

It was enough to make most people throw up their hands, yield their will to the fates and never again flirt with hope. But what would it do to a young man whose path always contained another pothole or an unscheduled detour? Would he bow his back, as Coach Townsend had told him at Arcadia High, or would he give up and slip back down the rabbit hole of drug abuse and dead ends? Jeremie Davis might have provided the answer in a letter, informing a friend of his brother's death.

"Losing Antoine hurts so much, because he believed in me," Jeremie wrote. "Whether it was music or sports, he always knew if I stopped making mistakes and put my mind to it I could do whatever I wanted. I am going to continue to write music, and I am working on an album that will tell the story of a good kid who was the victim of bad circumstances. Throughout the gunshots of my childhood, the horror of Katrina, my incarceration and other obstacles life has thrown at me, I still stand with dreams and aspirations to be successful."

CHAPTER
40

Three months after my departure from the University of New Orleans, interim athletic director Mike Bujol informed the department's administrative assistant he needed some time to himself and he was taking a four-day weekend. The next Monday, Bujol followed up with an e-mail to all staff, informing them not to expect him back in the office for another week. The volleyball season was past its midpoint, golf and tennis were in their fall schedules and men's and women's basketball practice had begun. It was not a time for the boss to take a vacation.

Speculation began to swirl that Bujol, who had inherited oversight of the program, had succumbed to the demands of the job. Bujol's actions after taking over the program left little doubt among the coaches that he had become Ryan's pawn. He communicated Ryan's instructions to the coaches, apparently without objection. If a coach questioned a directive, Bujol would respond, "That's what the chancellor wants, and he's the boss." To quell the hearsay, Bujol put out the word that the reason for his absence was "kidney stones and stress."

The reality was that Bujol and Ryan had met and mutually agreed that Bujol would step aside. It was not clear whether Bujol had resigned or whether Ryan had fired him. According to Bujol, he had met with Ryan and told him his inability to hire staff or make normal administrative decisions without the chancellor's approval made his position untenable. If Ryan insisted on making all the decisions for the department, he did not need an athletic director. Once Bujol brought the frustrations home and began yelling at his wife, two children and the dog, he knew it was time to quit.

After 27 years in the department, most of them as the No. 2 man to three athletic directors, Bujol had reached his lifetime dream. But in three months, he had discovered firsthand what his predecessor knew. Ryan's apparent plan was to strip the department of any resources to the point he could justify its termination as a Division I program.

Others suggest that Bujol oversold his abilities after he assumed the position. He promised Ryan an uptick in ticket sales and sponsorship dollars, but when Ryan asked for an accounting the results were far short of expectations.

After Bujol's departure became known in early November, Ryan called a meeting of his executive committee of vice chancellors and deans to discuss the athletics program. Ryan confirmed Bujol's departure and said his alternatives were either to try and hire a new athletic director to maintain the current program, to drop down to Division III, which did not allow athletics scholarships, or to terminate the program altogether.

The news could not have come at a worse time for the head coaches. November 11 was the "early signing period" for prospects to sign the binding National Letter of Intent signifying their college choices. Coaches attempt to sign the bulk of their recruits during the early period to secure their roster and to forestall the panic that often typifies the spring recruiting period. However, when the national letters of intent went to the university's Financial Aid office for sign off before being mailed to the recruits, athletics business manager Ola Adegboye was told Ryan would not approve new scholarships for athletics.

The coaches were panicked, interpreting that directive as a sign that Ryan intended to pull the plug at the end of the 2009-10 academic year.

Basketball coaches Joe Pasternack and Amy Champion and baseball coach Bruce Peddie, whose sports were most affected, requested a meeting with Ryan to get some answers. They wanted to remind Ryan that a prohibition of early signings would lead to speculation that the program was going to be terminated. Such word could prompt a stampede of transfers after the fall semester. If that happened, the coaches feared, their squads would be so decimated they would not have enough athletes left to execute their schedules of competition in the spring.

Word that the interim athletic director had resigned would be interpreted similarly. The department was floundering without leadership, and rival recruiters would use that to their advantage. Even if Ryan lifted the signing day prohibition, the only recruits UNO's coaches could sign would be those who nobody else had recruited or who were isolated from cell phones, social networking sites or the Internet. In other words, they would sign nobody!

In his meeting with the head coaches, Ryan shifted the blame elsewhere. He said the looming state budget cut for the 2010-11 fiscal year was further threatening the university's academic mission. He told the coaches he went out on a limb to provide the $900,000 or so "pass through" funding for student-athlete tuition in the current budget, a fact he said was not known to the faculty. He said that if the faculty found out about it, they would demand his resignation. He told the coaches he could not make the same commitment in the next budget, and suggested strongly he would be forced to terminate the program or seek a drop to Division III.

In short, he was setting the stage for a decision he already had made.

Ryan's meeting with the coaches was leaked to an Internet blogger, which prompted another firestorm. Ryan sent a message to the head coaches to come back to his office immediately, and he proceeded to chastise them for their disrespect and their defiance. In a profanity-laced tirade, Ryan proclaimed he was working hard to preserve the program, but he could not do it if they continued to defy him. They did not appreciate the things he had done to save the program when a lot of people around the university wanted it eliminated. He had sacrificed for athletics, and he could not understand how they could be so selfish that they did not appreciate his efforts.

The coaches returned to their offices and called the student-athletes who had committed to UNO and were expecting to sign the national letter. One highly rated basketball player had to cancel a school assembly and press conference to announce his signing with UNO. The coaches told the recruits the university had frozen scholarships and prohibited early signings for now. But, they said, your verbal commitment is valid so hang in there, have a good senior year, and we'll get it done in the spring.

They knew they were lying, but they had no choice but to keep hope alive one final time.

Unfortunately, their hope would be short-lived. The following day, Ryan put out a press release, stating that UNO was "considering" moving its athletic program from Division I to Division III. He had not informed the coaches or any of the student-athletes of his intentions or that the release was coming. The announcement came on the first day of the national signing period for Division I athletics.

The list of schools that have dropped down from Division I is short and with little athletic distinction. Birmingham Southern is the most recent school to drop from Division I to Division III in 2006. The list also includes Brooklyn College in 1998, Utica in 1988, NYU in 1984 and Catholic University in 1981. Centenary in Shreveport is scheduled to complete the moving process in 2012.

But none of them abandoned Division I after experiencing recent success in the NCAA's highest division. That makes the UNO story unique and serves as a cautionary tale for the great majority of institutions that support an athletic program. Less than two dozen NCAA athletic programs across all classifications are self-supporting, all nourished by the golden goose of big time football. The remaining programs, including the 320 or so in Division I, need strong institutional support to survive.

Universities with limited resources have made the commitment to maintain a healthy athletic program. None have yet faced a cataclysmic disruption to that fragile balance the likes of which befell UNO. Other than the cash rich football powers, every other athletic program in America is vulnerable. The disruption that prompted the administration to devalue Division I athletics at the University of New Orleans can happen to any other program that is dependent upon university support.

A few weeks later, on December 11, Ryan formalized his intention by presenting a proposal to the LSU Board of Supervisors to withdraw from the Sun Belt Conference. He told the board that the university no longer could afford a Division I program, and his only recourse to maintain any kind of athletics program would be a non-scholarship Division III program.

Speaking in favor of the proposal were several university administrators and faculty members who worked for Ryan. They talked about how the financial drain of Division I athletics took resources away from the academic mission and about how a Division III football team could be an incubator for more admissions. Arguing the latter point was director of admissions Andy Benoit, who doubled as coach of the university's nascent club football team.

Among the handful speaking against the proposal were former AD Ron Maestri, PAF President Mike Sapera and former student-athlete and benefactor Gabe Corchiani. All cited the rich history of UNO Athletics and the current administration's refusal to accept advice such as the Carr Report that could have led the program out of its financial lethargy.

After little debate, the Board voted 11 to 1 to authorize Ryan to petition the Sun Belt Conference and NCAA for a withdrawal from the conference.

Speaking outside the board's chambers, Maestri told the waiting cameras if UNO followed through with the withdrawal from Division I he was "finished," and UNO could take his name off Maestri Field, the baseball complex that he helped build and his teams helped memorialize. Sapera said he would inform the alumni office to take his name off their rolls. Corchiani, who had paid two of the ten installments that comprised his $1 million gift, told friends that Ryan's move voided his deal and that he had given his last nickel to UNO.

On January 20, 2010, UNO gave notice to the Sun Belt Conference that it was withdrawing its membership, effective July 1. A charter member of the Sun Belt, UNO's decision was a sad counterpoint to the uplifting story of the New Orleans Saints. Three weeks after the notice, the Saints won Super Bowl XLIV amid widespread praise for showing strength and resilience for enduring a tragedy and prevailing. The Saints proved the underdog can overcome disruption and succeed when it has the resources to do so. The same tragedy devastated the UNO athletics program, but it was denied the resources to recover.

During this time, Ryan was conducting a search for a new athletic director who would implement his Division III plan. Applicants were screened and a short list of five names was assembled. However, after two candidates turned down the job, Ryan called a surprised Amy Champion, the women's basketball coach, and persuaded her to take the job on April 16.

Having his own AD in place, however, did not end the athletics instability for Ryan. The NCAA Division III Management Council approved UNO's application on July 20, but long-time supporters of the program continued to work behind the scenes, hoping they could somehow preserve UNO's Division I status.

Their efforts took on new life after an unexpected development two months later.

CHAPTER
41

Chancellor Timothy P. Ryan was called into the office of his boss, LSU System president Dr. John Lombardi, on September 16, 2010, and was relieved of his duties. A press release issued by the LSU System said Ryan "resigned," but the combative Ryan refused to go out gracefully. After he returned from Baton Rouge, he told a sympathetic crowd of employees and students he was fired because of his poor relationship with Lombardi and his staff.

"I was fired because I wouldn't play the game with the system staff," Ryan said, claiming the LSU System was not responsive even to simple requests for building repairs. Ryan suggested that he alone stood in the way of Lombardi's eventual plan to make UNO a "feeder school" for the Baton Rouge campus, thereby forfeiting the autonomy the institution achieved when it changed its name from LSUNO in the early 1970s.

During a visit to the UNO campus the following day, Lombardi responded to Ryan's charge saying: "Anyone who believes that is deaf, dumb or blind."

Ryan also took a parting shot at UNO's athletic boosters.

"Athletic supporters are quite often fanatics," he said. "All they see is athletics, all that's important to them is athletics, and we made a decision (Division III) that I would make again and again."

Less than three weeks after Ryan was fired, the decision he defended so vigorously was quickly sabotaged by his final hire. Interim AD Champion determined that scheduling for the athletic teams would be difficult with so few Division III programs in the region. A graduate of Division II Delta State, Champion launched a campaign to abandon plans to enter Division III and apply for membership in Division II. With its 10-sport minimum and fewer scholarship demands, Division II could fit within the economic restrictions imposed by CFO Linda Robison and blessed by interim Chancellor Joe King. On March 4, 2011, the LSU Board of Supervisors approved UNO's latest request to leave Division I and apply for membership in the Division II Gulf South Athletic Conference.

However, a few weeks later, a pair of heavyweights entered the controversy. New Orleans Mayor Mitch Landrieu and City Council President Arnie Fielkow wrote to King, asking that UNO table its decision to leave Division I, at least until a new chancellor was hired.

"Given that the NCAA Katrina Waiver does not expire until after 2011-12 academic year, we believe it would be prudent to hold off on the NCAA Division II application at this time," they wrote. "This action would also provide all parties with an opportunity to properly assess whether, with appropriate action, continuation of Division I status can be successful."

A note from the two highest ranking elected officials in New Orleans would be expected to elicit a courtesy response, but it was not to be. According to Fielkow, no response came from the office of King, the interim chancellor, nor anyone else in the UNO administration. However, another movement was afoot that would continue to give hope to the Division I advocates.

On July 12, Governor Bobby Jindal signed a law that transferred UNO out from under the LSU System and into the University of Louisiana system. The move was one pushed by Ryan before his departure in the belief that UNO never would be given its proper respect nor have the ability to grow in the LSU System. Louisiana has four different higher education systems: LSU, UL, Southern and the Community and Technical College system. In the UL System, UNO would be governed by the same board that oversees eight institutions, all of which participate in NCAA Division I athletics.

"UNO now has the opportunity to stretch its legs and show what it can do," said House Speaker and bill co-sponsor, State Representative Jim Tucker, R-Algiers, a UNO graduate.

"We are unlocking that potential that we've had on this campus for all these years," said state Senator Conrad Appel, R-Metairie, another co-sponsor of the legislation. In the 2011 regular legislative session, Senator Appel also coauthored non-binding Senate Continuing Resolution 68 that recommended UNO suspend the reclassification to Division II process until a new president was selected.

Division I advocates immediately saw hope in both the shift to the UL System and in the political chatter that recommended reconsideration of the Division II reclassification. In the UL System, UNO would appear to be a perfect fit for the Southland Conference, whose members include Southeastern Louisiana University in Hammond, Nicholls State University in Houma, Northwest Louisiana in Natchitoches and McNeese in Lake Charles. Dr. Stephen Hulbert, president at Nicholls, publicly promoted UNO's possible addition to the Southland Conference.

However, a Division I restoration could not be executed from the outside. Political resolutions, system shifts or letters from the mayor and city council were useless if the university administration did not respond. The existing administration's silence on the matter prompted D-I advocates to request that any plans to reclassify the program be tabled until a new president were aboard. Their reasoning: Why saddle a new leader with a significant aspect of the university that might conflict with his or her vision?

The D-I advocates received support at the next UNO Foundation board meeting in the form of a recommendation to give the new president the final word on athletics' future. Present at the meeting was interim provost Dr. Lou Paradise, who had occupied the same position from 1995 to 2003 under Ryan's predecessor, Greg O'Brien. During his years as provost, Paradise was known as an advocate for athletics but fully cognizant of its budgetary restraints. After discussions with the UL System, Paradise convened a meeting that included King on the wisdom of postponing any decision on the athletic program's future until the new president was selected.

On Halloween, UNO released a statement headlined: "New UNO President Will Have Input on Future of Athletics." The story quoted King as saying the new president "will have input and be the final decision maker on the direction the athletic department pursues." That sentiment was underlined a few weeks later when the UL System released a 52-page report titled "UNO Institutional Review" that contained 28 recommendations to guide UNO's next leader. The recommendations touched on every area of campus life, including governance, strategic planning, budgeting practices, communications, institutional partnerships and athletics.

The full report, available online at www.ulsystem.edu/UNOReview, put the future of the athletics program squarely on the new president's shoulders when it said: "The new president of UNO will have to decide almost immediately in which NCAA Division the university's teams will compete into the future." The recommendations included the following:

- UNO should take the steps necessary ... to ensure regular and adequate academic counseling and support services for its student-athletes.
- UNO should develop a strategic plan for athletics, which includes fundraising and marketing plans, to support the expense and revenue projections contemplated in the plan.
- UNO should review its staffing to ensure that student-athletes are receiving the assistance they need in such areas as medical support and strength training.

The recommendations were a disheartening reminder that nearly every area cited as a shortcoming once operated at a level the recommendations now aspired to achieve. However, the document was encouraging in one respect. The eight current campuses in the UL System all sponsored programs that compete in some level of Division I, although they vary widely in the amount of local support. If all eight UL System institutions can find the resources to fund Division I programs, could not the means to restore it be found at UNO?

CHAPTER
42

I had not spoken with Tim Ryan since our "water under the bridge" meeting in his office at the end of July 2009. It was remarkable we had not bumped into each other, since our houses are located a few blocks apart in Lakeview, and New Orleans is a small social community. It was just as well, because I did not know what I would say if I ran into him. I was still angry for the decisions he made that affected our program, hundreds of student-athletes, coaches whom I had hired and me.

From time to time, my wife Jean, in her continuing role as my in-house psychologist, advised me to get rid of the anger. She counseled that my experiences at UNO, both good and bad, were over and done and that I should move on. Resentment is a disease and when not treated can only fester and the infection spread. But, like the doctor's suggestion to lose 25 pounds, it was sound advice but tough to follow. If I did let go of my anger it would take more than her soothing words to do it.

Little did I know that an unlikely instigator was about to intervene.

My brother-in-law, Schaffer Mickal, invited me to play in a golf tournament, benefiting his son's school. I never miss the opportunity to play free golf, and I enthusiastically reported to the course at the appointed time for a relaxing afternoon of camaraderie. Tee time was nearing, and Schaffer and I retreated to the clubhouse for a final restroom break when I, almost literally, bumped into Tim Ryan. We shook hands guardedly and made small talk about the Stonebridge golf course, which, coincidentally, was where our regular Sunday group played in more pleasant times. Schaffer went ahead to the restroom, and I turned to do the same when Ryan stopped me.

"I need to talk to you," he said, looking down almost sheepishly. I expected him to say something about the book I was writing about the decline of the athletics program, the existence of which was widely known. Instead, he surprised me.

"I owe you an apology," he said firmly. I immediately responded that he didn't owe me anything, but he held up his hand and continued.

"When we were having our problems, I thought you were the reason," he said. "But you weren't. Everything you told me was right. Nobody could run a program on the support you were getting. I wanted you to know that I was wrong and you were right, and I apologize."

Ryan added that we had been friends before UNO and he hoped we would continue to be friends, "since we're both retired now." I repeated that he did not have to apologize, but I told him I appreciated his comments.

My immediate reaction was one of déjà vu. After owner Tom Benson had fired me at the Saints, he also had come to an epiphany and apologized months later in a similar bump-in at a League meeting. What was it about me that made my superiors want to throw me overboard and then have a change of heart after the body is washed up on shore?

Ryan's foursome that day was behind mine, and we saw each other several more times, commenting on shots, playing conditions or other minutiae a thousand miles from UNO.

After the round I went home and told Jean about bumping into Ryan and about his apology. She had a tear in her eye, and she hugged me.

"You know, I think you and Tim shared a lot of the same feelings at what happened," she said looking up, her chocolate brown eyes boring into my soul. "Don't forget that he and Louise lost their house, too. They were going through the same things we were with rebuilding and with their daughters. While you were trying to save your program, he was trying to save a university. You both did some good things, and you both made mistakes. Now maybe you both can appreciate what the other went through and move on."

I held her, torn between giving up my well-crafted resentment or, once again, taking her advice. Jean's view of any situation was filtered through her heart, while mine was sometimes clouded by emotion or hubris.

As I held her, I couldn't help but thinking if my six-plus years at UNO had been worth it. Leaving the NFL when I still believed I had something to contribute. Taking a job that people in the know told me was Mission Impossible. Trying to put a positive spin on what surely was one of the most difficult jobs any athletics administrator ever had to endure.

The difficult times during my years as athletic director would be easier to reconcile if I thought any good had come out of it. Had I been a positive influence on those around me or merely a placeholder? Did I really do what I had set out to do, which was to make a difference, or was the only difference made within me?

I have no regrets about trying to bring a sense of professionalism to UNO athletics. I had spent a career striving to excel at whatever position I held, but I found myself in an environment where an aggressive pursuit of excellence was considered an impediment. Preserve the status quo or suffer the consequences appeared to be the secret to longevity at UNO. My refusal to accept conventional practice or to slog around daily in the bureaucratic bog was viewed as rebellious. It was unlike any other job environment I experienced in a career that was nearing its 40th year.

I believe my resilience and resolve to endure was appreciated. Mike Sapera, president of the Privateer Athletic Foundation, may have gone a bit overboard when he sent me a note that said: "Nobody else could have done this with the grace and dignity that you put forth. You were the right man at the right time."

A similar note came from Bob Leffler, an old friend from Baltimore who operates the largest collegiate marketing firm in the country. Leffler wrote:

"The example you set is far more meaningful than the daily headlong, tireless push. What cannot be missed is that your efforts and those of your coaches saved the name of the university. In your selfless quest, you transcended the modern 'plastic scoreboard' of achievement. You are an exception to the modern driven contest liver/achiever rule because you have Old World ethos running through your veins! You have truly won life's game."

I appreciated sentiments like that, but maybe I endured for this long simply because my tolerance and pain threshold were higher than others. Or maybe it was simply because I truly cared about what I was doing.

To the latter point, the greatest tribute I ever received in my professional life occurred early in my first year as the Baltimore Colts beat writer for *The Evening Sun*. The late 1970s still featured cities with more than one daily newspaper, and competition was intense. *The Evening Sun* went head-to-head with the stately *Sun*, its sister publication, and Hearst's lively *News-American*. The *News-American* beat writer, Richard Kucner, was a Louisiana native, tall and slim and aloof to strangers. He would look down at you, literally, out of the corners of squinted eyes, feeding the perception that he liked few people and trusted even fewer. More importantly, he was an aggressive reporter who was rarely beaten on a story. In my first month on the beat, I scooped Kucner on a couple of minor stories, which got his attention.

The season had not even started when we were alone in the team's press workroom, and he said to me, "Miller, I want you to know something." I looked at him curiously, not knowing what was to come. "You're going to be a pain in my ass this year." I chuckled and I asked him how did he come to that conclusion after we'd only known each other a few weeks.

Kucner raised his chin and looked down at me. "Because you give a shit."

And I did. I cared then about pursuing stories, and I cared later about trying to restore a wounded program to stability. I would like to be remembered as one who shepherded the department through its most difficult time in history because I cared about my coaches, my staff and the students.

I regret that I left the job unfinished. I am nagged by the fact that mere endurance does not translate into the conventional definition of success. After all, I did not save the program. At best, I merely prolonged the inevitable. But, as Bob Leffler suggested, maybe personal success in this case should be measured in the attempt itself. The effort is more important than the result. I tried my best, and, in doing so I gave hope to all around me. Without my prodding, persuasion and perseverance, this thing might have crashed sooner.

Maybe my tenure *was* a success simply because I went out every day intending to slay the dragon, despite being armed only with the equivalent of a toothpick and a match. It was more important that I fought the beast to a draw most days than the fact I was consumed in the end. I have a greater appreciation for the Buffalo Bills and Minnesota Vikings for their combined 0-8 record in the Super Bowl. *They were there, and that counts for something!*

So many times, I had the feeling that I was just spinning my wheels, but never once did I consider bailing out when things went bad, like others did. Sometimes to quit is merely to stop an unwinnable fight so you can regroup. Many have claimed it, but Demosthenes said it first: "The man who runs away may fight again." I came to the conclusion that it depends on how you define "quit." If a wife leaves an abusive spouse, did she quit? If you stop banging your head against a brick wall because the wall doesn't break, did you quit?

You don't quit until all hope to succeed is taken away.

And that might be the saddest part of the story. Every time things looked darkest, my coaches and staff looked to me for the hope I tried to provide. They looked for answers and too often they received only commiseration. I was another guy in the foxhole who was going through the same battles they were who only could empathize and offer encouragement. These good people who hoped and fought with me will move on and be stronger for it, and that is what is important. The legacy of UNO athletics will be its people and its student-athletes.

The kids always were my most important consideration. My greatest frustration was the fact that I could not give them the experience that other Division I student-athletes enjoyed. It was excruciating to constantly feel as though we had to apologize because our resources and facilities were inferior to the teams we expected our student-athletes to beat.

But I saw signs time and again that our students appreciated our efforts. I saw it in their eyes after the press conference announcing that the student vote to raise the athletics fee had failed. I went over to a crowd of about 40 of our student-athletes, some with tears sliding down their cheeks. I told them how much I appreciated their efforts. One of the men swimmers, whose name I did not even know, said back to me, "No, Mr. Miller, it's we who appreciate what you've tried to do for us."

They learned something through our resilience and our willingness to fight for them, and that will help them on their life's journeys.

I received another confirmation a few weeks after my last meeting in Ryan's office. I was at home working in my upstairs office when I heard a car door shut outside. With Jean at work and my car in the garage, our house appeared as if nobody was home. I looked out and saw Jaci Bayley, a senior volleyball player who was graduating that summer, walking back toward a car. On the porch sat a decorative gift bag she had left. I came out onto the porch and Jaci's father, Don, and mother, Delia, got out of the car.

Jaci was a freshman when Katrina struck, and her team's season was suspended.

Since then, she had been through three head coaches and all our other tribulations, but she persevered without complaint and eventually became team captain. That summer, she was awarded her masters degree in business administration.

You can't help but have your favorites, and Jaci was one of mine. She was bright, a team leader and she always had a smile on her face. Her parents would come in from California several times a year to see games, and I had come to know them in a warm, yet casual, way. It was a good feeling knowing these parents trusted you to take care of their little girl.

We chatted on my front lawn for 20 minutes and talked about our neighborhood's restoration, the university's ongoing struggles, Jaci's prospects of playing overseas and my plans. Don Bayley had a camera, and he took pictures of me with Jaci and her mom. Don and Delia told me how much they appreciated what I had done and tried to do. I told them that having young ladies and men with the character of their daughter made the battle worth fighting.

We hugged, and I wished them all well as they drove away. I picked up the bag off the porch and went back inside the house. In the bag was a bottle of red wine and a card from Jaci:

"Mr. Miller, Many thanks for everything you've done for me. I will keep you in my thoughts and I'm happy that you'll finally have time to get to things that you enjoy doing. As I keep saying, you are the best! The student-athletes and parents are sad to see you go because they know how hard you worked and how much you went through. UNO will miss you."

As I stood there holding Jean, I thought about Jaci's note and about how much I missed not only the students but all the people who gave an athletic director's job meaning and purpose. My time at UNO was a memory, good for some and maybe not so good for others. The opportunity now existed for new leadership, someone who cares fervently to come in and make a difference. May God bless the new AD and lead that person to success.

I gave Jean a big squeeze as a sliver of late afternoon sunlight smiled through the back window.

AFTERWORD

O n December 9, 2011, the University of Louisiana System announced that Dr. Peter J. Fos, program director for health policy and systems management at LSU Health Sciences Center, had agreed to become UNO's new president. Fos, 62, graduated from UNO in 1972, became a dentist and practiced for 10 years in Metairie before switching to the life of an academic.

Fos said his priorities for UNO would be to increase enrollment, raise academic standards and improve the university's "branding," or the reputation widely shared by parents, students and potential applicants. The latter suggested the new president would be receptive to utilizing a university's most cost-effective marketing, promotions and branding tool to achieve the national recognition that UNO enjoyed with a Division I athletic program.

Full restoration of the Division I program could not come on the wishes of a few, however. Fos must have a conviction that a university is in part a creature of the company it keeps. Will UNO be competing for students with Tulane, LSU, Mississippi, Alabama, North Carolina State, Southern Mississippi, UL-Lafayette or other institutions it traditionally faced on the athletic fields? Or will it be competing with institutions that are not among the more than 800 currently accredited by the Southern Association for Colleges and Schools? Many such schools were included in the 2010-12 athletic schedules.

That is a logical question in a sports-mad state and in a system in which the other institutions, all members of NCAA Division I, would argue affirmatively.

A pparently, Dr. Peter Fos agreed. True to the University of Louisiana System's review that challenged the new president "to decide almost immediately in which NCAA Division the university's teams will compete," Fos made the decision and rather quickly. On March 7, 2012, barely three months into his presidency, Fos assembled members of the athletics department and informed them he would provide sufficient institutional funding to restore a Division I program at the University of New Orleans.

At a press conference the following day, Fos confirmed the decision, citing reasons that sounded eerily familiar.

"It is simply not about winning games or winning conference championships," Fos said to an enthusiastic assembly of boosters, faculty, staff and others. "This decision is about the university fully recovering from the effects of Hurricane Katrina and the economic downturn. The decision is about the University of New Orleans's future, which I feel is very bright. The decision is about working to improve enrollment, which in part is influenced by a viable successful athletic program."

Fos acknowledged that the university stopped transferring funds to the athletic budget in 2009, but he said "we will begin transferring funds at a level at which UNO athletics will be competitive and successful." Fos said the amount to be transferred would equal about 2% of the university's $124 million budget, but he was quick to point out that "not one penny" would come from academics. Fos said increases in enrollment that come in part from having a successful athletic program will cover the funds needed.

"My goal in five years is to be the premier university in the University of Louisiana system in all aspects, including athletics," he said, turning to several coaches in the room. "My message to the coaches is to start recruiting Division I student-athletes."

Fos's pledge meant that approximately $2.5 million would be transferred to athletics, an unprecedented amount of institutional support. That amount would supplement roughly $2 million in student fees, about $400,000 per year from the Wick Cary gift, which was placed into an endowment, plus a renewed likelihood of another $1 million from sponsorships and guarantee game proceeds. The total of approximately $5.9 million represents the largest budget ever enjoyed by the department, exceeding the $5.3 million in 2004-05. That was the year before Hurricane Katrina when enrollment was 17,000.

Fos's commitment was fueled by his obvious belief that athletics can play a major role in the university's recovery. Athletics had been ravaged along with every other department and program at UNO, but the university's decision makers rejected its potential to contribute substantially to the recovery.

Fos's investment in the athletics program displayed his belief in the concept of ROI — Return on Investment. His investment in Privateer Athletics demonstrates a conviction that restoring and enhancing institutional support to the program will show a major return through higher enrollment and its accompanying benefits.

More germane to this discussion is the satisfaction that the long NCAA Division I tradition of UNO Privateer Athletics, which was callously tossed aside and left for dead, had been resurrected.